Humanoid Encounters

THE OTHERS AMONGST US

1965-1969

Albert S. Rosales

2nd Ed. 2021 – Saucerian Press

1st published 2016 - Triangulum Publishing.

Copyright © 2016 Albert S. Rosales

ISBN: 979-8549396043
ISBN: 978-1534744868
ISBN 10: 153474486X

All rights reserved. No part of this book may be used or reproduced in any manner whatsoever without permission except in the case of brief quotations embodied in critical articles or reviews.

Designed and edited by Ash Staunton.

Kentucky Lizardman image © Barton Nunnelly.

Introduction

The second half of the 60's was a major turning point in Ufology worldwide; it was indeed the end of innocence, and the beginning of the high-strangeness concept. 1965 ushered in a huge wave in the US that lasted well into 1968. The focus this year was South America, with numerous incredible reports of encounters and contacts.
The year 1966 will be remembered as the year when a bizarre entity made its appearance in a little town called "Point Pleasant" West Virginia. It was a winged oddity that for reasons unknown made that little section of West Virginia his home for almost two years. Along with his appearance there were numerous high strangeness reports in the area, including MIB encounters, UFO sightings, and animal mutilations. Of course its origin has never been determined, and its purpose will remain hidden. A tragic event was to unfold in that little town at the end of the year 1967, that some investigators link it to the enigmatic appearance of the "Mothman." Besides the bizarre encounters in West Virginia, there were scattered reports worldwide of humanoid encounters, mainly in the US, which continued in the throes of an unprecedented UFO wave. Other incidents of note were reported in Australia, and Canada. Suddenly it was no longer just UFOs and little men, but flying humanoids and MIB's galore, disappearances, strange deaths, etc.
These went on into 1967 when an unprecedented "wave" enveloped the US and Canada. Mysterious characters were walking among us; so-called, "Men in Black" reports were frequent and bizarre. A reported abduction of one "Betty Andreasson" in late January opened the gates to a much deeper mystery. The files for 1967 are thick and strange.
1968 continued the mainly ignored worldwide wave of encounters in Canada, Argentina, Spain, France the United States and beyond. Everyone was focused on the Condon report and its implications. 1968 was the year we lost Martin Luther King and Robert Kennedy, the days of rage in Chicago during the Democratic presidential convention. Nixon came to power. The Tet offensive in Vietnam. The students of the Prague revolt. But other events were occurring worldwide. 1968 could possibly

be the most overlooked year as far as UFO and Humanoid high strangeness reports, but it was a strange and important year; something was happening behind the scenes.

There was a decline for 1969, maybe due to the Condon report and the Air Force supposedly terminating their Project Blue Book investigations, but the 70's were approaching and the 'Age of Aquarius' would be not stopped. While violence seemed to dominate the US and other points globally in '69, bizarre events were being reported in Brazil, Canada, England, and other locations. Brazil seemed to have been in a yearlong grip of bizarre humanoid encounters and contacts, in Canada similar events were steady, and in the US strange events also occurred, but remained hidden in the background.

My hope is that this information will be useful for future generations, be it for entertainment or any other purpose, just hopefully useful. Something strange has been happening, perhaps for thousands of years, mostly ignored, covered up, debunked, but it still happens. Every day someone becomes part of the mystery. 'Others' amongst us are reaching out to us, be it from outer space, other dimensions, other realms, etc. Beware, some might not have the best intentions. But I feel this is a necessary process for our species to make that giant leap forward and become the Universal citizens that we were meant to be.

Albert S. Rosales

TYPES OF CE (Close Encounter) CLASSIFICATIONS:

Type A: When an entity or humanoid is seen inside or on top of an object or unidentified aircraft.

Type B: When an entity or humanoid is seen entering or exiting a UFO.

Type C: When an entity or humanoid is seen in the immediate vicinity of a UFO.

Type D: When an entity or humanoid is seen in the same area where UFOs or unknown objects have been reported.

Type E: When an entity or humanoid is seen alone, without related UFO activity.

Type F: When there is a 'psychic' contact between entities or humanoids, but an entity or humanoid is not necessarily seen.

Type G: When there is direct contact or interaction between a witness and a humanoid or entity; either involuntary, as a result of a forced abduction, or as a voluntary contact.

Type H: When there is a report of an alleged crash or forced landing of a UFO with recovery of its occupants, or when an anomalous entity is captured or killed either by a witness or military personnel.

Type X: When the situation is so uncanny that it doesn't fit any of the previous classifications. A new classification, there are several such cases in the files already. I would call these cases, 'extremely high strangeness events.'

1965

Location: Near El Aaiun, Morocco (former Spanish Sahara).
Date: 1965.
Time: Unknown.

Medium and Seer; Carmen Yague, reported encountering a landed disc-shaped object in an area within some sand dunes. Around the craft; she saw several man-like figures wearing white, shimmering outfits. On the chest area; the humanoids had what appeared to be a large H-shaped figure and what something that looked like binary numbers.

According to Yague; the men communicated with her and told her they came from a planet called 'TUFOL.' They allegedly then provided her with three 'curative' stones which she still uses to this day.

HC addendum.
Source: Ignacio Darnaude, *'UMMO File.'*　　　　　　　　　Type: C?

* * * * * * *

Location: Brasilia, Brazil.
Date: 1965.
Time: Unknown.

A man claimed to have been abducted by a crew of Ufonauts and taken to their home planet. The planet was cold, the air was thin and its surface was pitted with craters. He was put through a series of rigorous physical exercises and tests. The personnel stationed there lived in specially equipped quarters. The witness also saw thousands of UFOs. He was told that they were being readied for "a peaceful invasion" of Earth "next year." It was reliably established that the man was on the ground, nothing near the tree. But it's that image of the 'golden boy' with the most intense nastiness in his gaze that will never go away.

The witness uses the term "golden boy," as that is how the family story has evolved; but it was no boy. It was a humanoid, as best as the distance would reveal, but that sense of malice and dread made it impossible to stick around for more details.

HC addendum.
Source: *Phantom & Monsters* blog, August 14, 2015.   Type: E

* * * * * * *

Location: Anaheim, California.
Date: 1965.
Time: Daytime.

A family was vacationing in Disneyland and was in one of the small shops ogling the stuff and deciding whether to buy anything. The wife heard someone say; *"Hello."* She ignored it. *"Hello,"* again and again. She straightened up and looked around; no one except her family, the clerk and a customer being checked out. The voice again; *"I am speaking to you."*

She stood back and whirled around. There was a person who hadn't been there before, very strong facial features, and large pointed ears. She was being contacted telepathically, and was frightening. The man was very tall, and knew that he was scaring her. He told her not to be afraid, that he was 'Velusian,' and he was there on vacation.

Her husband was still blissfully unaware of his wife's state, and was bending over looking in the display cases. "By this time I was terrified because I had never encountered anything like this before and I am trying to get my husband up, you know, to try to explain to him. What am I doing, am I losing my mind? By the time I got him up, he's saying; *"What's wrong?"* and I said, *"This man here,"* and by the time I turned around, the man had vanished. Just vanished."

HC addendum.
Source: Michael D. Swords, *'Grassroots UFOs.'*   Type: E
Comments: Very strange report; an alien in Disneyland!

Location: El Yunque, Puerto Rico.
Date: 1965.
Time: Afternoon.

In an area ripe with reports of UFO sightings and other weird encounters, 8-year old Maria Esther Figueroa had gone camping along with her school friends and several teachers. Maria mysteriously disappeared in the thick jungle and was never heard from again.

Years later, the other girl that had been in the woods with her at the time of her disappearance, came forward and told reporters that she had heard Maria scream, and saw her struggling with two tall men dressed in light blue/gray coveralls, that had apparently grabbed her. The girl also screamed and the men saw her, telling her, in no uncertain terms to leave the area or she would too be taken. The men made a sudden move towards her and she ran away in a panic, apparently blocking the incident from her mind for years to come.

HC addendum.
Source: Jorge Martin, *Evidencia OVNI* #7.   Type: D or G?

* * * * * * *

Location: Near Sydney, New South Wales, Australia.
Date: 1965.
Time: 7:00 p.m.

A woman, visiting near Sydney, watched a strange cloud come toward the base of a cliff in the house where she was staying. The "cloud" then was transformed into a snow-white saucer, from whose edges emerge steam like vapor. The UFO emitted a hum-like sound as it hovered near the cliff and from it emerged a shining ladder, lowered from a hatchway.

A man descended the ladder and shone a strange beam of light into the sea below. Shortly after, the object emitted a brilliant pink flare, which ascended out to sea and the ladder, with the man still on a rung, was retracted into the UFO. The object sped off in the direction of the flare; in the moonlight, the woman could see a long shape farther out in the water toward which the UFO moved; when it reached this floating object, both disappeared in a vivid pink flash.

HC addendum.
Source: Keith Basterfield.   Type: B

Location: Rio Claro, Sao Paolo, Brazil.
Date: 1965.
Time: Night.

Edemilson Mendes heard the frightened shouts of a neighbor. Upon going outside to investigate, he saw two strange figures approaching him on the pavement. He described the figures man-like, but greenish and scaly; reptilian in nature. As they approached he became dizzy and apparently passed out. He woke up two hours later not remembering what had happened.

HC addendum.
Source: GRESUPE, also direct communication from witness.   Type: E

* * * * * * *

Location: Chester, Cheshire, England.
Date: 1965.
Time: Various.

Suzanne Brown claims she was visited numerous times by a 5ft alien with shoulder-length blond hair who wore a skintight membrane suit. Originally the visits which began when she was just 12, were relaxed and even "loving," but by the time the contacts ended, she says she was terrified. According to Suzanne the creature communicated via telepathy. He told her his name was, 'Myriko.' At one point she was taken onboard a spaceship where she met other humans.

A few months later and while home alone, she began experiencing terrible pain from pressure in her lower abdomen. The pressure was crushing and becoming very painful. She then opened her eyes and Myriko confronted her. Telepathically, he told her not to worry; that his people were merely taking what was theirs. She passed out and after waking up, realized that her clothes were soaked with blood and it looked like she had suffered from a miscarriage. Her pregnancy appeared to have been terminated.

Finally Myriko took her onboard a craft and showed her what appeared to be a nursery. There was an infant entity lying in a nearby cot, gray skinned and frail. It was apparently her child. Somehow she knew it was her child. Her final visitation was when she was 39-years old.

HC addendum.
Source: Carl Nagaitis, *Without Consent.*   Type: G

Location: Near Provo, Utah.
Date: 1965.
Time: Night.

A 19-year old semi-literate shipping clerk, reported being taken from his house in a glassy sphere, into a large black object where he met a 6-foot 7-inch tall man; apparently the leader, and a beautiful copper-skinned girl with blond hair and blue eyes, who wore black uniforms with disc-shaped shoulder epaulets and serpents motifs on the pockets. No other information.

HC addendum.
Source: Dr. Frank Salisbury.   Type: G

* * * * * * *

Location: Thermalito, Oroville area, California.
Date: 1965.
Time: Night.

Three women living in a small house in a yet undeveloped area, reported that on several occasions, Noreen, one of the women, was sitting up alone in her living room when strange lights illuminated the entire house. Noreen remembers seeing figures in the windows and also spotting a triangular craft on several occasions hovering above the house.

A second witness, Laurie, remembers seeing a strange elf-like creature coming through a closed window. She also had a strange feeling of being surrounded by "little people" about the house, even though she never actually saw them, but always felt that they were around and under her bed.

HC addendum.
Source: http://www.starbuck.20m.com   Type: D?

Location: Near Callington, South Australia.
Date: 1965.
Time: Night.

A railroad security guard traveling on an interstate freight train, was one night leaning out of the brake van as they went through a clearing, when he saw a "thing" about three foot tall, glowing pink in color with massive ears, piercing dark eyes and arms like a gorilla. He could not believe what he saw as they passed the train siding. He never told a living soul.

HC addendum.
Source: Dominic McNamara AUFORN. Type: E

* * * * * * *

Location: Tarqui, near Cuenca, Ecuador.
Date: 1965.
Time: Night.

A female peasant reported to authorities that at a local 'abandoned house' she was able to see on separate occasions; somebody or 'something' taking refuge or hiding in the old dilapidated structure. According to the witness, Noelia, whoever it was, it always arrived around three in the morning, apparently to sleep. Noelia immediately thought that it could be a thief or 'drug addict' that had begun to frequent the region. Thinking that things might get out of hand, Noelia decided to investigate herself.

She went to the location one night accompanied by several other neighbors or locals, and decided to confront what they were sure was a thief or robber. The abandoned house was located at about 200 meters from hers, in an almost direct line, except for several hills that blocked certain angles of vision. Armed with sticks and knives, they invaded the house, sure they were going to catch someone hiding there but were surprised to find it empty. Looking around for clues, one of the group suddenly noticed a strange odor, which the group could only compare to rotten eggs or sulfur. There was a sudden change of ambience and the group felt that some unseen presence was stalking them. Suddenly something appeared to leave the abandoned house, something that could not be seen, at the same time the strong odor permeated the air.

The group, now afraid, decided to leave the house and as they stepped out of the house they all saw at about 40 meters away a "man" that appeared to be staring intently at them. Apparently the stranger had been observing the group's behavior for quite some time. The man appeared to be wearing a worn gray cloak or hooded outfit, which covered him completely, his face was not visible. His height was about 1.8m. There was a bright full moon that night, thus the visible details. Upon seeing the strange figure the group immediately ran in his direction in an attempt to capture 'him.' At the same time, the stranger did the same, but according to Noelia in a very peculiar manner.

As he ran away, the group noticed that he never seemed to turn around, and seemed to be able to 'run,' remaining in the position facing the astounded crowd of pursuers. He maintained this position the whole time he fled from the group. The stranger seemed to be able to gain distance from the group in great leaps and bounds, and as the group advanced they noticed strange tracks on the sandy terrain on which the strange had fled over. The strange tracks were not normal feet or footwear; the stunned witnesses could only compare them to those of "goat's feet." Alarmed, the group stopped in unison and ended their pursuit. Terrified they watched as the 'man' also stopped and then began to glide away at high speed without touching the ground until he disappeared behind a nearby hill.

HC addendum.
Source: Esteban Coronel, Ecuador.
http://moradaparanormal.blogspot.com/2009/08/tras-las-huellas-del-diablo.html   Type: E
Comments: Translated by Albert S. Rosales.

* * * * * * *

Location: San Miguel, Andes, Argentina.
Date: January, 1965.
Time: Unknown.

It was reported that an object had fallen from the sky at San Rafael, 4 kilometers from San Miguel, and a photograph of it appeared later in *FSR* May/June 1965. The Argentine Air Force subsequently removed the object, whatever it was. Most folk thought it was a satellite of some kind, but a few inhabitants of the area were convinced that it was a UFO and several said they had seen small individuals, near the object, that wore "strange diver's suits" which gave off a greenish phosphorescence.

HC addendum.
Source: Donald Hanlon, *'The Humanoids.'*   Type: H

Location: Near Woodstock, New York.
Date: January, 1965.
Time: 4:00 a.m.

A group of musicians (including Jimi Hendrix) driving back to Manhattan, were stranded in a blizzard and had gotten stuck in a heavy drift that reached the hood of their vehicle. It was bitter cold. Unexpectedly, the road ahead of them suddenly lit up, as a bright phosphorescent object, cone shaped, like a capsule, landed in the snow about 100 feet up ahead. It stood on a tripod landing gear.

Before any of the stunned occupants of the vehicle could move, a door opened on the side of the craft and an entity stepped out. He stood eight-feet tall, his skin was yellowish, and instead of eyes, the creature had slits. His forehead came to a point, and his head ran straight to his chest, leaving the impression that he had no neck. The being proceeded to float to the ground and glided towards the trapped occupants of the van. The snow melted in the wake of the creature. His body seemed to generate tremendous heat, so much so that as it came across a small rise, the snow disappeared around in all directions.

In a matter of what seemed like seconds, the being came over to the right hand side of the van, where Hendrix sat, and looked right through the window. According to other witnesses at the scene the creature seemed to be communicating telepathically with Hendrix. Immediately the interior of their vehicle began to heat up. The heat coming from the being evaporated the snow enough to free their imprisoned van. The being glided behind the van and the snowdrift by now had completely vanished. Turning the ignition, the driver gunned the engine and drove away at high speed. As they looked back, they could see the road filling in with snow again. The object was at the same instant lifting off like a rocket from a launching pad.

HC addendum.
Source: Timothy Beckley, '*UFOs among the Stars.*'   Type: B

* * * * * * *

Location: Brands Flat, Virginia.
Date: January 19, 1965.
Time: 6:15 p.m.

William Blackburn was chopping firewood in preparation for an archery match when he noticed a large conical object in the sky, which he judged to be 240 feet in diameter. While he watched it, a similar but smaller UFO, 60ft wide, with a bubble-like cupola on top, appeared and landed 50ft away. It was made out of metal, polished to a mirror finish.

A pie-like section opened out and three small entities only 3ft tall emerged and floated toward him. They were dressed in close-fitting uniforms of the same high polish as the UFO, and wore shoes with 3 or 4-inch soles. Their skin was of an orange red color, and one had "a long finger on his left hand." Their faces were human-like in appearance.

These beings approached to within 12ft and addressed him in a language that the witness could not understand. When he made no reply, the little men re-entered their vehicle, and both objects then rapidly disappeared. The sighting occurred during a localized wave of reports in the area, and the witness was subsequently asked by an un-named government agency not to discuss his sighting further.

HC addendum.
Source: Richard Hall and Joan Lusby for NICAP.   Type: B

* * * * * * *

Location: Brands Flat, Virginia.
Date: January 26, 1965.
Time: 7:30 p.m.

Steven Houffer, 16, and six friends were driving near Brands Flat on U.S. Highway 250, when they saw what looked like a man walking toward the road from a field. They thought nothing of it until the 'man' sat down and began peering intently at passing cars. It suddenly occurred to Houffer that the stranger might be from one of the UFOs which had regularly been reported in the area during the last few weeks and, with this in mind, he stopped the car and stepped out. When he and his friends approached the being, though, it ran up the hill and quickly vanished over the other side. Two similar 'men' also appeared, fleeing in the same direction. "They left us way behind," Houffer explained to the police, to whom he reported the experience shortly afterward. The creatures he said, wore one-piece, skintight, silvery garments. They were about 3 ½ feet tall, and, in a peculiar sidelight; did not leave any footprints in the muddy field across which they were alleged to have dashed.

The police of course were skeptical, but still interested enough to send 16 reserve officers to the area, along with photographer Charles Weaver. The search failed to produce any evidence for the claim and everyone left except Houffer and Weaver, who stayed to look around further. Shortly thereafter, the two sighted what they described as a "glowing aluminum barn" which they went down to investigate. Weaver was walking inside when suddenly something struck him on the head. The whole left side of his face was blood red and his eyes had a peculiar red glow, according to Houffer. The two turned to run, but Weaver stopped briefly and flashed a picture. In the light thrown off by the exploding flashbulb, a little man standing by the "barn" was visible.

HC addendum.
Source: Local Police and Newspaper source and Jerome Clark, *FSR*.
Type: D?

* * * * * * *

Location: Manresa Beach, California.
Date: January 30, 1965.
Time: 2:00 a.m.

Towards midnight on January 29, George M. Clemins, mayor of Monterey, and several other people reportedly saw a brilliantly illuminated spherical object hovering over Monterey Bay. It appeared to slowly descend out of sight on the other side of the bay. Two hours later a forty five year old TV repairman named Sidney Padrick shut down his ham radio rig and decided to take a stroll before going to sleep. On Manresa Beach directly opposite Monterey, he heard a loud humming noise and saw a strange machine shaped like "two real thick saucers inverted." He was none too happy about this apparition, he admitted, and so he turned and started to run away.

"*Do not be frightened,*" a voice reportedly boomed from the object. "*We are not hostile.*" Mr. Padrick kept running. "*We mean you no harm. You are welcome to come aboard.*" Padrick stopped and considered, feeling slightly bewildered and foolish. A door slid open, he said, and he cautiously approached it. The voice urged him on. He stepped into a small room about six by seven feet, where he was greeted by a medium sized man with very pale skin. He had, Padrick noted, a very sharp nose and chin and unusually long fingers. "His hands were very clean. The fingernails looked as if somebody had just given them a manicure."

Padrick stated that there were several others onboard and they wore two-piece suits with no buttons or zippers that he could see. The bottom section actually included shoes; it looked like boots which continued on up to the waistline without any break around the ankles, just like a child's snowsuit. They had soles and heels similar to ours; he could hear them walking with a "thump-thump" sound on the rubbery like floor. The collar had a very pretty design on it; it came down to a V in the front, and the neckpiece, right around the neck, had a braid of some kind on it, very pretty. It had colors, but he couldn't tell what they were, because they weren't colors that he had ever seen before, they were much more beautiful than ours.

When Padrick's asked the man's name, he was told; *"You may call me Zeeno."* Although the witness didn't know it, the Greek word for stranger (xeno) is pronounced 'zee-no.' Being a technician, Padrick was able to supply a detailed description of the interior of the craft and was nonplussed when Mr. Zeeno showed him a room 'similar to a chapel.' "The color effect in that room was so pretty that I almost fainted when I went in. A mixture of beautiful colors; I can't describe it. There were eight chairs, a stool, and what appeared to be an altar. Zeeno said, *"Would you like to pay your respects to the Supreme Deity?"* I didn't know how to accept it, I'm forty five years old and until that night I had never felt the presence of the Supreme Being, but I did feel Him that night."

After taking a short flight in the object, Padrick claimed he was returned to the beach where he had been picked up. He reported his experience to the Air Force immediately and was later interviewed for three hours by officers from the nearby Hamilton Air Force Base. "They wanted an account of it, word for word," he said in a later telephone interview. "I told them exactly what happened. They were the first to hear it. There were certain details which they asked me not to talk about publicly; but I think in telling it, everything should be disclosed. The Air Force didn't want me to say that Zeeno told him the space people had no money. They did not want me to disclose the type and shape of the craft because they said that would indicate the Air Force was not doing their duty."

HC addendum.
Source: Major Damon B Reeder, Air Force, Sam Vestal and Paul Cerny.
Type: G

Location: Near Chicago, Illinois.
Date: Early February, 1965.
Time: Dawn.

Walking along the shore of Lake Michigan about sunrise, Harvey Keck saw a saucer about 6ft high resting on a 4-legged landing gear. Near it was a 5ft "robot or being, stocky in build and similar to the entity reported by Reeves in Florida;" the being's skin was tanned, eyes set far apart, and he had a pointed chin. His head was encased in a glass-domed helmet.

HC addendum.
Source: Humcat quoting Newspaper source. Type: C

* * * * * * *

Location: Bulach, Switzerland.
Date: February 3, 1965.
Time: 2:00 a.m.

Billy Meier was summoned telepathically to a place on a severely cold morning (also his birthday). The site was on top of an isolated hill. He had barely arrived when he saw, shooting down from the sky, a brilliantly luminous flying object that immediately landed near him on the hard frozen ground. The bright light went out and he could see a matte-silvery disc shaped object, which stood majestically on its three landing spheres and seemed to wait for him. Following a brief telepathic instruction and some gentle urging, he went toward the ship, and was immediately lifted into it through an opening, by some unknown force.

Inside, he only saw one seat, and there was nobody around. He was alone. He sat on the single but very comfortable seat. As he was getting settled, a powerful change took place. The bright light coming from everywhere inside the ship suddenly went out, and then he felt like he was sitting in free space. He could see nothing of the ship and its equipment and when he raised his hand before his eyes he couldn't see it either. The ship rose up and apparently traveled through space since he saw from an opening, a blue-white greenish sphere, resembling planet Earth.

Soon the entrance door opened and he looked out, and was surprised to see that, completely unnoticed to him, the small ship had landed. He step out and found that he softly "floated" down to the ground and landed on hard, dry soil. The soil was warm and was a reddish color. Soon a larger luminous object appeared and landed nearby. After a while a beautiful female figure appeared from the behind the object. She walked confidently up to him and greeted him in a way that was familiar to him but he could not figure out why. She seemed strangely familiar. She wore a foot length pleated gown of a peculiar silver white color, girdled at the waist. Her long blond hair fell to her shoulders.

She invited Meier to join her in her ship, which he did, and that ship sped up into the sky and seemed to become invisible. The ship then landed in an area near what Meier could see were the pyramids of Egypt. Some nearby Bedouin Arabs did not seem to notice the landing of the ship. The woman identified herself as Asket and explained many things about his future mission on Earth to Meier.

HC addendum.
Source: Galactic 2. Net   Type: G
Comments: Cambodian diplomat to the United Nations, Phobol Cheng, later went on record, swearing that she and others had witnessed the extraterrestrial woman Asket (allegedly from another universe, an anti-matter twin of our own referred to as the DAL universe) and her spacecraft visiting Meier on multiple occasions the following year, 1966 in Nehruli, India, at the 'Ashoka' ashram. Photos were taken of the craft.

* * * * * * *

Location: Torrent, Corrientes, Argentina.
Date: February 11, 1965.
Time: Night.

A group of citizens in this neighborhood saw the landing of a strange transparent craft near their homes. Five creatures, a little larger than human beings, stepped out and the terrified witnesses saw that the visitors had, like a Cyclops; only a single eye in the middle of their foreheads. The witnesses ran back to the road. Then it was stated that one of the cyclopean figures entered a house. A few moments later, with his companions, it left the house and departed in the UFO.

Another report states, that in a field belonging to Mr. Souriou, two of his sons and several peasants met gigantic creatures whose stature was more than 8ft. One of the peasants had his right arm paralyzed when he tried to attack the creatures, and the automatic rifle of one of the sons of the owner of the field inexplicably failed to work. Frightened, the men ran to the house and shut themselves in. From outside, a light came in through the walls, illuminating the interior. At no time did they see any type of flying craft.

HC addendum.
Source: Dr Robert Banchs and Antonio Ribera.   Type: B & E

Location: Near San Jose, San Luis Potosi, Mexico.
Date: February 12, 1965.
Time: Unknown.

19-year old Francisco Estrada Acosta, encountered on the road to San Jose, a tall scaly creature that extended a cold hand as an attempt to possibly greet the witness. Panic stricken Jose fled the area on foot. He further described the being as having phosphorescent eyes, a large toad like mouth that suddenly appeared next to him on the road. Its hands were like "flippers" and it was well over 2 meters in height.

HC addendum.
Source: Ruben Manrique. Type: E

* * * * * * *

Location: Guarani, Minas Gerais, Brazil.
Date: February 14, 1965.
Time: Evening.

On a beach near Guarani, five local residents saw a large object land. Three went to look for other witnesses and while they were gone, the remaining two approached to within 60ft where, hiding behind a sand dune, they saw three beings that had left the object. They were tall and thin, nearly eight feet in height and wearing dark, tight fitting one-piece suits. Before the others could return, the object took off, leaving traces, including footprints, at the landing site.

HC addendum.
Source: Timothy Green Beckley, *Saga* UFO Special #3. Type: C

* * * * * * *

Location: Chalac, Formosa, Argentina.
Date: February 21, 1965.
Time: 9:00 p.m.

A group of UFOs were seen flying overhead for a while and then one landed. Three tall beings enveloped in luminous halos emerged, causing the local population; fifty Toba Indians, to go down on their knees. The beings approached slowly, with gestures dissuading one Indian from approaching the UFO.
Then a voice was heard telling the witnesses to remain calm, for there was nothing to fear, and that the space people would return to bring peace on earth. The humanoids then returned to their craft, bathed all

the time in beams of light emanating from small wing-like projections; it then took off with blinding luminosity. Photographs were said to have been taken by local police officers.

HC addendum.
Source: Local police and *FSR* Vol. 11 #4.   Type: B

* * * * * * *

Location: Silver Springs, Maryland.
Date: February 26, 1965.
Time: 3:30 p.m.

Madeline Rodeffer, a secretary for the US Air Force, was physically present when George Adamski sighted a bell shaped flying saucer at her home. She saw it for approximately ten minutes and at times could see human looking figures through the portholes. Adamski filmed the saucer using Madeline's camera when she was unable to film it herself due to difficulties from a recovering broken leg. Prior to the sighting, she saw three 'young looking men' arriving in an Oldsmobile who told Adamski to get ready to film the flying saucer.

Adamski told Rodeffer that they were part of a human looking contingent of extraterrestrials living among humanity. The film was subsequently analyzed by three independent photo/film experts. One was William Sherwood, who at the time worked at Eastman Kodak as an optical physicist. He traveled to Rodeffer's home and was able to determine that the flying saucer in the film was not a model but approximately 27 feet in size. Sherwood consequently concluded that the film was genuine.

Another visual imagery expert was Colonel Colman Von Kevieszky who worked at the time with the United Nations audio-visual department. He also traveled to Rodeffer's home to investigate the video and confirmed that it was genuine. Finally, Bob Oechsler, who worked as a physicist and NASA mission specialist, also independently concluded that the film was genuine and depicted a flying saucer.

HC addendum.
Source: Timothy Good, *'Above Top Secret: The Worldwide UFO Cover-up.'* Type: A

* * * * * * *

Location: Sorgues, Provence, France.
Date: Spring, 1965.
Time: 4:00 p.m.

The witness, Frank N. a 12-year old schoolboy was riding his bicycle and while coming out of the woods at Brante, saw to his left a small being no more than 50 cm tall, covered from head to feet in a shiny outfit. Its cranium was shaped like an egg, its eyes were very large, and its mouth very thin, no ears were seen. Realizing that it was not a normal 'human' he became frightened, but being even more curious he pedaled closer to the being.

The being remained motionless for a few seconds and when the witness put his bicycle down on the ground, it began moving away.

It walked with a peculiar stride, like someone with flat feet; raising its knees very high making it look like it was jumping. The witness thinks it also began emitting a strange noise resembling, *"hic...hic..."* It then suddenly ran with great agility as the boy followed meters behind. The being then stopped, looked back and made gestures to the boy, apparently ordering him to stop. The boy wanted to talk to it, and placed his hand on his heart saying to the being several times, *"I am friendly."*

Frank supposes that it understood his intentions because it did not appear frightened and took a step in his direction. At this point the boy noticed a craft which appeared to be made of a "flexible" material to him. The small being then approached the boy who apparently attempted to grab at it, but the being stepped back and produced a sort of small "hair dryer" type apparatus which he aimed at the boy, who immediately lost his balance and could not move any more. At this point a man who had apparently witnessed the whole scene, pulled the boy back and probably wanted to protect the boy, but this man became paralyzed also.

They then saw the small being enter the craft while seemingly uttering a loud shout. The top of the craft appeared slightly domed, and vaguely resembled a large matchbox with very rounded angles. On the top there was a round "cabin" which shone like a fluorescent tube. When it took off, the craft seemed to pass between the trees without breaking anything and it made no noise. It rose a few meters, moved a hundred feet and then landed on a meadow. A farmer then walked very close to the craft, which had started to glow, and onboard there seemed to be three silhouettes, identical to the small being that had been observed on the ground. The witness said that he recovered the use of his muscles little by little.

HC addendum.
Source: H. Julien, M. Figuet, *'OVNI en Provence,'* Raoul Robe.   Type: B

* * * * * * *

Location: Greenville, Texas.
Date: March, 1965.
Time: 11:00 p.m.

A woman had just helped haul her somnambulant husband to bed, and he was snoring when he hit the pillow. She crawled in beside him, kissed him goodnight, and rolled over on her side. There standing in her hallway was a being. "He had on a helmet type, clear type helmet. He did not look like one of these weird beings, he looked like we do, with kind of, I would say a ruddy complexion. He had on a gray type spacesuit with zippers down the arms, zippers down the front, zippers down the legs, and he held a glass round; all I could think of was a crystal ball, in his hands. I had a feeling he wasn't going to hurt us. It was just, I don't know; like mental telepathy or something, because it was like he would say, *'I am not going to hurt you. I am just here observing you.'"*

Our galactic peeping Tom was not all that reassuring, and she was constantly reaching back and trying to get her happily snoring husband to wake up (which he never did). When her daughter coughed in the other bedroom, the astronaut took his eyes from the glass ball and looked in that direction. That was too much, and maternal instincts took over, and she got up with, *"Don't hurt my children!"* in her mind. She got as far as the door and he disappeared. "Just like that."

HC addendum.
Source: Michael D. Swords, *'Grassroots UFOs.'*   Type: E
Comments: Bedroom visitation by time traveler?

Location: Weeki Wachi Springs, Florida.
Date: March 2, 1965.
Time: 2:00 p.m.

John Reeves, retired, was out hunting snakes when he saw a flying saucer, reddish purple, and bluish-green, standing on four legs on a sand hill, it was 20-30ft in diameter, with a clear dome on top and a row of vanes around the circumference. Creeping to within 100ft, Reeves saw a figure about 5ft tall, wearing a silver gray one-piece "space suit" with a transparent "fishbowl" helmet. His hands were gloved and his feet were in metallic looking boots. His eyes were far apart, and his chin pointed.

The humanoid raised to his chin a round dark object which emitted two bright flashes; the witness took it for a camera. He then re-entered his craft by waking up a small retractable stairway, and the object rose vertically with a whistling noise. Reeves found at the site many dumbbell shaped footprints, and four roughly equidistant 6" holes, left by the landing gear. There were also two folded sheets of thin tissue like paper that bore messages written in an unknown alphabet. Reeves subsequently had further sightings and contacts.

HC addendum.
Source: Marshall S. Cleaver, Robert M. Snyder and R. S. Carr for NICAP.
Type: B

* * * * * * *

Location: Red Rock, Pennsylvania.
Date: March 5, 1965.
Time: Early morning.

It was a cold and blustery morning as two Air Force technicians suited up to go outside. One was a young man named Walter, the other technician; Reed (pseudonym). They were stationed at Benton Air Force station in Red Rock at the borders of Sullivan and Luzerne counties. The facility was an air defense center that monitored the air for large-scale bomb attacks on the United States. Large radar antennas were stationed across the country as part of the Aerospace Defense Command Interior Radar Defense Zone. One of the large red and white radar antennas was the reason why the two young technicians had suited up. They had to go outside to repair a height-finding radar antenna that was positioned northeast of their location.

Walter and Reed stepped outside and made their way up the mountain to the antenna. They opened their tool kits, laid out the tools much like a surgeon would, and began to work. It was a routine operation and they had performed it many times before. Now they worked with

practiced ease, but the buffeting winds stinging their skin made them hurry. Suddenly one of the technicians caught sight of motion in the distant sky. A disc-shaped object was high above them, coming in their direction. The technician paused in his work,
"What in the world is that?" he asked aloud.

His partner followed the first technicians gaze and paused, too. They saw the disc-shaped object descending from the sky. The object settled to the ground not far from where Reed and Walter had been working. Both men were amazed by what they were seeing, and the craft was like nothing they had ever encountered before. The men laid down their tools and walked toward the craft for a better look. No doors opened and no pilot was visible. It was very puzzling. Reed and Walter were only a few feet away when a bright light suddenly shot out of the craft directly at the two young men. Inside the radar station, the other technicians and Air Force personnel continued to work. They weren't a bit concerned about the two technicians outside. But Walter and Reed did not return when they should have.

Walter and Reed never reported back to their command post that day. The Air Police were notified that the men were missing and they hurried on to the work site. They found the tools laid out as if Walter and Reed had been working on the antenna, and then simply walked away. The Air Police failed to locate Walter and Reed, and so they notified the Pennsylvania State Police. The police began a search of the area that continued for sixteen hours. Finally a state trooper driving down route 487 saw two young men in uniforms walking along the highway. They were staggering and seemed disoriented. The trooper pulled up to the men and saw immediately that they were Reed and Walter. The men were confused, dehydrated, and slightly injured. Both men had strange marks on their necks and they couldn't explain how the marks had gotten there. In fact the men were unable to answer most of the questions put to them. They did not know how many hours had elapsed, where they had been, or who or what had taken them. All they did know was that they were fixing the antenna when they saw a "small saucer shaped object" land nearby.

The men were transported to Williamsport Hospital, where they were treated for dehydration. The men were tested for drugs and alcohol but were found to have neither in their systems. Reed and Walter were then transferred to the Air Force hospital at Stewart Air Force Base in New York, where they were examined once more. Other than the marks on their necks, they were fine. Their clothes however were covered in trace amounts of alpha radiation that had no natural explanation. The men described what they remembered, but they had no memory of any events after they were shot by the beam of light.

HC addendum.
Source: *Filer's Files #36* and Patty A Wilson, *'UFOs in Pennsylvania.'*
Type: G
Comments: Incredibly, the two air force technicians at Red Rock were never hypnotized or regressed in order to explore what really happened during their missing time episode that did not receive proper attention (that we know of).

* * * * * * *

Location: Mobile, Alabama.
Date: March 6, 1965.
Time: 7:15 p.m.

    Mrs. B. S. Crutchfield was on her front steps when she saw a "basketball shaped" object come in from the southwest. It "looked like it was going to crash in the street." It was encircled around the middle by windows, through one of which she was able to see an entirely human appearing occupant, dressed in a silver garment.
    She was able to see a second figure as the object rotated, through another window, as he stood in front an instrument panel. Closest proximity was 150 feet, and lowest altitude about 60-70 feet above ground. Duration was about 2 minutes. The object disappeared in a westerly direction. The witness had subsequent sightings.

HC addendum.
Source: Ted Bloecher.   Type: A

* * * * * * *

Location: Jose de San Martin, Argentina.
Date: March 30, 1965.
Time: Unknown.

    Three objects were seen flying over the city. Outside of town one of the objects appeared to land. Local police responded to the site, and upon arriving, saw two humanoid type creatures standing 15 feet southeast of a landed bluish-white cigar shaped object.
    After apparently hearing the police car, the beings ran to the object and scampered up a ramp leading to one of the ends of the cigar. The object then rose straight up until it was lost to sight. An area of flattened grass was found on the landing site.

HC addendum.
Source: *Flying Saucer Digest*, summer 1969.   Type: B

Location: Monte Grande, near Macias, Entre Rios, Argentina.
Date: April, 1965.
Time: Various.

While hunting near Monte Grande a 37-year old shopkeeper named Felipe Martinez said he saw a large egg-shaped craft, hovering a few meters from the ground at a distance of 300 meters from him. It had some kind of 'rapid revolving ring' around it, and seemed to be quite silent. Rushing enthusiastically towards it and shouting, *"Amigo!"* he was suddenly struck by a paralysis which stopped him on the spot. A door opened in the craft, and a small man descended a ladder about 30 centimeters wide. The little man, who was not much above 1 meter in height, wore a helmet and there were two cables linking the helmet to the UFO. The rest of his clothing consisted of a 'diver's costume.'

They conversed, the little entity speaking slowly and with difficulty. He said that he and his people were friendly and that they 'came from near the moon.' He called his machine a 'sil' and said he would meet Martinez again on May 3, 1965. He also said that 'they' required some help from us. Martinez replied that he was not in a position to give them much assistance, but that he would report the meeting to the Mitre Radio Station in Buenos Aires. *"Yes we know,"* said the little man, extending a clammy hand and promising to see him again on May 3.

The second encounter allegedly took place on that date, but no details about it seem to have been published. The third meeting was at 23:00 on July 21, 1965 at Macias, near Guardamonte, when he allegedly saw the same little man. When Martinez explained the very great difficulty he had experienced in trying to find anybody to believe his story about meeting the little 'Martian,' the latter replied that they would soon be showing themselves to people everywhere on Earth. And he added, that Martinez must keep a further rendezvous with them, namely on December 3, 1965, when they would return, take away Martinez and his family, and then burn up the whole Earth as punishment for the failure to accept their existence.

In a later interview with a Buenos Aires Newspaper, Martinez gave some additional details about the alleged entities. For example, he said that he had once been inside the saucer in which four of the crew were less than a meter in height while the fifth member was a blond man almost 2 meters in height, on whose arms there were metallic plates with numerous small lights which looked as though they might be part of an electronic communications system. He added that on that occasion, the crew of the 'sil' had put a spacesuit on him, but this caused him to feel such a disturbance in his circulatory system and an acceleration of his heart that they took it off him.

HC addendum.
Source: *FSR* Vol. 13 #4.   Type: B

* * * * * * *

Location: Near Fortaleza, Ceara, Brazil.
Date: April 3, 1965.
Time: 11:20 p.m.

    Two traveling salesmen were driving toward Fortaleza when they saw something in the sky that looked like a bright infrared lamp. It shined a ray of light on the car. The object then descended just above the car, and the car then began to shake and its lights went out. They then saw a ray of light come down on the vehicle. At the same time the driver lost control of the vehicle; it skidded sideways and came to a stop.
    The object then landed in front of the car. Two humanoids, that resembled robots, came out from the object and began moving toward the car. Both men got out; one had a rifle and fired at the entities. Suddenly there was a terrible explosion and the two men were temporarily blinded, but they heard no sound. 15 minutes later they could see again, but the object and the two entities were already gone.

HC addendum.
Source: Bob Pratt, *'UFO Danger Zone.'*   Type: B

* * * * * * *

Location: Near Albuquerque, New Mexico.
Date: April 18, 1965.
Time: 4:00 p.m.

    Close to the bed of the Rio Grande, Paul Villa saw a craft about 150ft in diameter that projected a beam of light that caused a small bush fire, then another beam shot out and extinguished it. The craft also produced a "miniature tornado," causing the lower branches of some trees to appear blurred. The turbulence was so high, Villa reported, that he thought he and his truck would be blown away. Suddenly, the wind ceased, and the surrounding air became quite hot and there was dead silence. The ship landed on telescopic tripod landing gear. The three occupants had light-brown hair and tan skin and appeared to be about five foot, eight inches tall. Villa claimed to have talked to them for nearly two hours about personal as well as general matters.

HC addendum.
Source: Timothy Good, *'Alien Base.'*   Type: B

Location: Rivesville, West Virginia.
Date: April 23, 1965.
Time: 8:00 a.m.

Mrs. Ivan Frederick was cleaning up the breakfast dishes after getting the children to school and her husband to the day shift at the mine. She glanced out the small kitchen window and saw what she first thought was a child in the hillside pasture field above the house. Fearing the child might be injured if it tried to climb over the electric cattle fence, she ran out the front porch for a better look. There her concern turned to amazement and shock.

A saucer-shaped aircraft hovered near the ground and then landed. Running downward from it, through what appeared to be an elevator and doorway, ran a dark green colored cable. Attached to the end of the cable by a connection at its stomach area was a small black or dark green-colored creature. It appeared to be more animal, over even "satanic" than human. It was collecting grass and dirt and stuffing them into the small bag it carried and it didn't seem to be aware of her observing it. It was unclothed, had pointed ears and a tail. She could see no mouth or other facial characteristics, though it was only about 200 yards away. She was very frightened and watched it only a short while before feeling inside the house, getting into bed and pulling the covers over her eyes, "hoping it would go away."

She was able, however, to supply a few additional details. She estimated the craft was about 10 feet in diameter and about five feet in height, not counting the stem, or elevator, which was about the same height. It was cream and silver-colored, with rows of windows underneath a dome or "crystal canopy" on the upper surface which sparked in the morning sun. The machine rotated in a clockwise direction while emitting a loud humming or buzzing sound. After about 15 minutes, Mrs. Frederick recovered enough composure to venture another look out the kitchen window, just in time to see the creature step into the stern of the craft and disappear. The craft then rotated faster, the buzzing sound got louder, and suddenly it rose, "like a feather," straight up out of view.

When Jennings, the eldest son, came home from school and heard the story, he hastened to the hillside to investigate. There he found a depression in the ground where the stem of the craft had sat, and estimated that the weight must have been more than a ton. He also found claw-like tracks of the creature, which he estimated weighed about 45 lbs. He also found some hair samples in the footprints and sent these, along with plaster-of-Paris impressions and photographs of the area to the Air Force. The Air Force replied with an inane explanation; a weather balloon, and never returned the physical evidence.

HC addendum.
Source: Jacques Vallee, *'Passport to Magonia.'*

* * * * * * *

Location: Scoriton, Devon, England.
Date: April 24, 1965.
Time: 5:30 p.m.

Gardener Arthur Bryant was dramatically confronted with a situation completely beyond his comprehension; a huge flying saucer and its three occupants. Bryant had gone for a walk around 5:30 pm as he often did. Upon arriving at the Down, he turned to look back at Scoriton and as he did so, a large saucer-like object appeared out of thin air over a field. His first reaction was to turn tail and run really hard, but some influence seemed to suggest that he remain where he was. The saucer rose a few feet or so and then, swinging like a pendulum to the left then to the right and then to the left again before leveling out and becoming stationary thirty yards away over the field in front of Bryant; there it hovered about three feet above the ground. A door slid up into the roof from the center and three figures appeared from it all dressed alike in what he took to be a diving gear. After watching him for a few minutes, one of the three beckoned him, with both arms outstretched. Somehow he had lost his original fear and climbed over the iron-gate to the fence separating the field from the lane.

What followed then was completely baffling to Bryant. Two of the beings had extremely high foreheads which came to a point. Their features were thin and sallow and there was no facial hair. Eyebrows and eyelashes were fair and fine and their hair, which was longer than ours, and was between a blond and a mousy color. The nose was squat and the eyes very blue in color with a vertical cat-like pupil. Each had four fingers but no thumbs. The third person had a normal appearance; there was nothing to distinguish him from humans. He had short brown hair, very dark brown eyes and appeared to be a youth of between fourteen and fifteen years of age. The three wore suits of a silvery color that rustled like foil when they moved. "The young one's suit struck me as being too large and the belt too loose." Said Bryant. The boots were similar to ours in design having two straps, one at the toe and one at the ankle; the soles were very thick – approximately one and one half inches. When they moved no sound was heard.

The youth seemed to be in charge. He said to Bryant; *"My name is Yamski"* (or something close to that). Bryant thought he was Russian but he had an American accent. Yamski gave several messages but Bryant had no idea what they meant. The things Yamski said were completely foreign. The three also said they would bring proof of Capt. Thomas

Mantell's plane that had crashed while chasing a UFO (1948). They did bring parts that were identified as being of the same type of plane.

Later on the evening of June 7, Arthur Bryant was just going to bed in his home when he heard a sound like that of a ship's turbine. He looked outside and saw a pale blue light traveling west to east at an altitude of 300'-400'. He saw this come down, and then the light and noise disappeared. Next day he looked over the area and found strange pieces of metal, some like turbines with curved blades, and some looking like more complicated pieces of machinery. Also there was a glass phial with some silver sand in it, and the message; *"Adelphos Adelpho"* (brother to brother) in what appeared to be classical Greek script. There was also an evil-smelling patch of jelly-like substance where the object appeared to land, but this quickly evaporated.

HC addendum.
Source: Eileen Buckle and Norman Oliver.   Type: B & F?

* * * * * * *

Location: Byrd Station, Antarctica.
Date: May 7, 1965.
Time: Evening.

American scientist, Carl Robert Disch, twenty six, was assigned to the Byrd Station, operating equipment to investigate VLF radio noises for the National Bureau of Standards. He set out to walk from his hut to the main station a short distance away, following a hand-line that was strung as a guide for the path between the two points. When he failed to appear after forty five minutes, the other scientists went out searching for him in tracked vehicles. "If Disch had fallen and was lying in the snow,"

Ron Sefton the leader of the Byrd Station explained, "the huskies would have seen him long before the searchers did. Similarly, if he had fallen and was covered by drifting snow, the dogs would have sighted the mound and rushed out to investigate it. That's the way huskies are." The search went on for three days and covered a thirty five mile area around the hut. Disch's own dog, a husky called Gus, disappeared shortly afterwards. Some of the searchers claimed they saw mysterious lights and heard engine noises in the distance.

HC addendum.
Source: John A. Keel, *'Our Haunted Planet.'*   Type: G
Comments: Permanent abduction?

Location: Lake Mason, Washington.
Date: May 30, 1965.
Time: 2:00 p.m.

While sunbathing on her lake cottage roof, the witness saw a shiny disc shaped object approaching in a direct line from over the lake; she described it as metallic, about 40ft wide, and with a dome on top and a row of windows through which she was able to see first one, then two occupants. The object hovered over her cottage lot less than 200ft away, as tripod landing gear emerged from underneath. The witness, on the roof, was looking down on the landed object when she saw the first figure at the window. When he saw her on the roof, he beckoned to another figure that appeared at a second window; they seemed to be rather short with large, baldheads.

They stared at the witness for what seemed to be a long time. The next thing the witness recalled was watching the object move rapidly away in the direction of the setting sun. There was an apparent time lapse of at least four hours. Under self-induced hypnosis, the witness was able to recall walking up to the UFO and being led up a stairway and into the vehicle by the two occupants; they were under four feet tall and one of them held a small box which he then opened. Inside was a dark colored crystal that gave off a vapor or smoke; he held it in front of her face and the witness jumped back, but when he again passed it closed to her face she discovered that the fumes were odorless. The next thing she remembers was being back on her roof watching the object depart. There would be another encounter three months later.

HC addendum.
Source: Fred Merritt for CUFOS.   Type: G

* * * * * * *

Location: Omaha, Nebraska.
Date: Summer 1965.
Time: 1 or 2:00 a.m.

A family was driving in their camper (a pickup truck) near Omaha and the stockyards. Three beings raced across the road in front of them. The third stopped right in the road and they were going to hit it. It made a huge bounding thirty- to forty-foot leap from the Interstate and over a fence. The entities were small with large heads and eyes, no hair and very pale looking.

The stepfather was an ex-FBI man and wanted to stop to investigate, but the mother said, *"No. No. Let's get the hell out of here."* Later that morning they heard a radio report that some cattle had been found dead in the Omaha stockyards. The father then remarked, *"Well, they probably dissected them to see what they're composed of."*

HC addendum.
Source: Michael D. Swords, *'Grassroots UFOs.'*   Type: E
Comments: I pose this question; "Have Earth scientists dissected alien humanoid beings, to see what are they composed of?"

* * * * * * *

Location: Rio Hato, Panama.
Date: Summer 1965.
Time: Sundown.

During a spate of mysterious animal killings in the area, the main witness, Eddie Melvin and several other locals stayed up one night, hidden behind the darkened windows of the house and kept watch on the nearby woods. Soon they saw a bizarre creature step out of the woods. The creature was described as being 4-feet tall, covered in dark stringy hair. Its head was shaped like a large oval, with a pointy chin, with huge glowing red, almond-shaped eyes. It seemed to have what appeared to be fangs protruding from its mouth.

The being walked on two muscular legs that terminated in claw like feet. It had two small, thin arms, terminating in four-fingered hands with powerful looking claws. It had a peculiar feature described as some kind of a crest running down its back. This sharp crest appeared to be fluorescent, giving off multicolored hues. The creature at one point lifted its arms revealing a web-like membrane under them. Suddenly it apparently sensed their presence and ran into the woods rapidly disappearing from sight.

HC addendum.
Source: Jorge Martin, *Evidencia Ovni* #12.   Type: E

Location: Bray-sur-Seine, Seine-et-Marne, France.
Date: Summer 1965.
Time: Late night.

While on the farm, the witness Michel G. (involved in other encounters), was suddenly awakened by voices coming from the guest room. Upon investigating, he is confronted by several luminous "and beautiful" beings; both male and female. The beings were very friendly towards Michel and they wore bright clothing with high collars. Using telepathy, the beings invite Michel to go with them. Even though they insist, Michel refused and then lost consciousness when one of them wearing "a great dress decorated with a large sun" shined a pipe-like instrument at him. After this encounter Michel suffered from fatigue and a strange skin disease that lasted for several weeks.

HC addendum.
Source: Georges Metz. Type: E

* * * * * * *

Location: (Undisclosed Air Force Base) Brazil.
Date: June, 1965.
Time: 10:00 p.m.

The witness couldn't sleep and felt very restless. Somehow he found himself riding a bicycle from his barracks around the outside perimeter of the base. In an isolated field his bicycle would not go on anymore, it slowed down. Then a beam of light came down from above and he was lifted up, bicycle and all, into a large disc-shaped object. Inside he was met by several short, gray colored humanoids that communicated via telepathy assuring him that everything was going to be all right. He then sensed that the craft was moving at a very rapid speed.

He was given a tour of it and was shown stars, planets, and celestial bodies. The craft appeared to stop and the humanoids then examined him in a large room. Soon after, he was returned to Earth. He was escorted out of the craft but quickly realized that he was at the wrong military base. He communicated this fact to the humanoids apparently by using telepathy. They then returned and walked outside, grabbed him by the arms and took him back onboard. The craft then landed again, this time at the correct base. He walked to his barracks and went to sleep.

HC addendum.
Source: Peter A. Schlesinger, Orion Investigating Group. Type: G

Location: Valensole, Basses Alpes, France.
Date: July 1, 1965.
Time: 5:30 a.m.

Maurice Masse, 41, had just reached his lavender field, 'L'Olivol,' when he heard a whistling noise. Walking around a hillock, he saw an oval shaped object with a dull metallic finish about 30 yards away resting on a central column and with four legs splayed out; it reminded him of a big spider. Beside it, examining the lavender plants, was a being the size of a 6-year old child, dressed in an orange coverall or suit but with bare head and hands. His baldhead was twice the size of a normal human head; his chin was pointed, and the mouth was merely a small hole. Inside the craft was another of these beings; they were talking to one another with a "gurgling" sound.

The witness approached to within 15-18ft, when the little man pointed a tube at him and he found himself paralyzed. The being then re-entered the object through a sliding door and it then took off with a whistling noise, seeming to vanish in mid-air. Where the craft had rested, there was later found a central hole 20" deep surrounded by four others, and the soil was hardened like cement. Several days later Mr. Masse became inordinately sleepy, a condition which lasted for several days. No lavender plants would grow at the site at least five years later.

HC addendum.
Source: Victor Nathan, Aime Michel and Charles Bowen.   Type: B & A

* * * * * * *

Location: Monte de los Curas, Villa Florida, Argentina.
Date: July 20, 1965.
Time: 8:00 a.m.

Ramon Eduardo Pereyra, 38, was driving when he saw something like a "luminous parachute" fall from the sky. On walking into the woods, he found a metallic ovoid craft, 12ft in diameter. Inside its upper portion, which was a transparent dome, were two "form fitting" chairs, back to back, and a humanoid figure wearing a spherical plastic helmet, who did not see the witness, occupied one. About thirty yards away from the object stood another man, about 6ft tall, looking up at the sky; he was blond, similarly clad in a lead gray, one-piece garment with a monk-like hood. He was holding a piece of paper in his hand.

When he saw Pereyra, the man hurried back into the craft. As he passed, the witness asked him if there was some sort of trouble, but got no answer. The man was carrying a pair of large binoculars and he had a sort of cartridge like pouch on one leg. When he got back in his seat, the vessel took off vertically with a slight humming sound, becoming luminous as it gathered speed. There was no mention in the report of traces at the site.

HC addendum.
Source: Fabio Zerpa and Omar Pagani.   Type: B & A

* * * * * * *

Location: Macias, Entre Rios, Argentina.
Date: July 21, 1965.
Time: 11:00 p.m.

    Felipe Martinez for the third time met the little humanoids he had contacted earlier, and was told that the space people would soon show themselves to people everywhere on Earth. He was told also that on December 3, 1965, they would return to take away Martinez and his family, and would then burn up the whole Earth as punishment for disbelieving in their existence. Martinez also said that on some unspecified occasion he was received inside the UFO. Four of the crew were little men, less than 3ft tall, and the fifth man was blond and 6ft tall, who bore on his arms metallic plates with numerous small lights.

HC addendum.
Source: *FSR* Vol. 18 #4.   Type: G

* * * * * * *

Location: La Plata, Buenos Aires, Argentina.
Date: July 22, 1965.
Time: 7:20 p.m.

    Ruben Angel Napoli spotted an object hovering in mid-air and next to it, two human like figures also floating about. Apparently he was able to take two photographs of the scene. One of the photos supposedly shows a glowing object and a "robot-like" figure next to it.

HC addendum.
Source: Fabio Picasso.   Type: C

Location: Fragosa, Spain.
Date: August, 1965.
Time: Afternoon.

Brother and sister, Juan and Isabel Dominguez, were returning home with a load of peaches, when they noticed what appeared to be a tall shadowy figure moving back and forth in front of a nearby garden wall. Curious, they approached the figure and were horrified to see a tall, translucent human-shaped figure that was now moving over a vegetable patch near the river.

They could see that the entity had very long arms that moved in harmony with its body, the rest of the body was proportional and "gelatinous" in appearance. The creature was well above 2 meters in height. When the giant turned and walked in the direction of the witnesses, these dropped their bundles of peaches and fled in terror. During the whole encounter both witnesses heard a sound resembling that of a "rattler."

HC addendum.
Source: Iker Jimenez, *'El Paraiso Maldito'* (Cursed Paradise).   Type: E
Comments: Translated by Albert S. Rosales.

* * * * * * *

Location: San Pedro de Los Altos, Venezuela.
Date: August 7, 1965.
Time: 4:00 p.m.

Three anonymous witnesses, two area industrialists and a well-known gynecologist, were visiting the through-bred horse-breeding establishment owned by friends of theirs at San Pedro de los Altos, a place in the district of Los Teques and distant some 50 or 60 kilometers from the Venezuelan capital, Caracas. They were out inspecting the grounds, pastures, and surrounding terrain, and had arrived on a low-lying plateau. Their conversation was concentrated entirely on economic and financial matters, investments, and thorough-bred horses, and on the beauty of the surrounding countryside.

Suddenly a brilliant flash of light in the sky attracted their attention. Then this flash of light resolved itself into a ball which began to increase in size as it slowly descended and moved towards them. They thought at first that it must be an aircraft or a helicopter, but they could hear no sound.

The object continued to descend, and when it was at a height of approximately 300ft, they could see that it was a huge discoid apparatus, emitting a brilliant yellowish glow, with a round dark patch underneath. They could still hear no sound of the kind made by aircraft but were aware of a peculiar humming, almost inaudible, which penetrated their ears. At this point the youngest of the three men turned with the intention of running away, but the gynecologist seized him by the arm saying, *"Don't run away, man! Let's stay here and see what it's going to do."* The huge disc was now swaying slowly downwards, until it became stationary at a height of hardly 5ft from the surface of the ground. By this time they knew that they were witnessing something extremely unusual. They were frightened, but as the disc was still at a distance of some 100ft or so from them, they wanted to wait and see what was going to happen.

Suddenly from the underside of the apparatus (which they estimated to be about 90ft in diameter) a shaft of light shot out, and it seemed to them that in this light, which contacted the ground, two beings were descending. These beings were about 7 or 8ft in height. They had long yellow hair which fell to their shoulders, large penetrating eyes, and were dressed in a type of one-piece which showed no seams and shone with a metallic luster. Still standing their ground, but trembling with fear, the three witnesses now watched the two tall beings approach to a distance of some 10ft from them. Here the two beings halted and simultaneously all three witnesses heard a voice telling them, *"Do not be afraid; calm yourselves."*

The peculiar feature of this voice was that the witnesses did not perceive any movements of the lips or of any other part of the bodies of the two strange beings. They heard the message inside their heads, or, rather, inside their brains. This confused them, and the two blond creatures seemed to perceive their confusion, because they now began to hear a second voice saying, *"We are speaking to you directly."* The three witnesses then understood that they were receiving a telepathic communication. The following are the replies which the three men heard inside their own brains in reply to questions asked by the gynecologist (who had recovered his composure more quickly than the other two, who simply stood there passively watching the proceedings).

Witness: *"Who are you? Where do you come from? What do you want here?"*

Humanoids: *"We are from Orion. Our mission on this planet is one of peace. We are studying the psyches of the humans, to adapt them to our species. There are seven inhabited planets: namely Earth, two satellites of Saturn; Epsilon; Kristofix (of which none of you know); Kelpis; Orion; and a small planet in the Outer Dipper (Ursa Extrema)."*

Witness: *"Can you tell us how your flying saucers operate?"*

Humanoids: *"(In an imperative tone of voice as though irritated) 'They' are not "flying saucers." They are "Gravitelides" and operate by means of nucleus of concentrated solar energy which produces an enormous magnetic force."*

Witness: *"Have you managed to master gravity?"*

Humanoids: *"Undoubtedly."*

Witness: *"By whom are these ships piloted?"*

Humanoids: *"Some are piloted by Espacitomeles and others by Mecanisoteles."*

Witness: *"What to these names mean?"*

Humanoids: *"Beings from outer space and mechanical automata."*

Witness: *"Are the inhabitants of all seven planets equal or alike?"*

Humanoids: *"No. There are the Morphous and the Amorphous. We, the Morphous, possess greater similarity among ourselves, with the exception of those that originate in the Outer Dipper, who are diminutive beings approximately 35in in height."*

Witness: *"Have you bases on Earth?"*

Humanoids: *"Each planet that sends an expedition to investigate the Earth has a ship almost half the size of your Moon, which they leave behind in the planet Mars. This is the reason why more of us are seen when this planet is near to Earth."*

Witness: *"Are there any beings, like you living among us?"*

Humanoids: *"Yes. Two million, four hundred and seventeen thousand, eight hundred and five (2,417,805)."*

Witness: *"Have you undertaken interbreeding with us?"*

Humanoids: *"No, but we are studying the possibility, which will create a new Species."*

Witness: *"Have you interbred among yourselves?"*

Humanoids: *"Yes."*

Witness: *"Have you carried any beings from Earth away with you?"*

Humanoids: *"No, only animals. On Kristofix there exists the 'Fitozoolopanetologeico,' which is the richest in the Galaxy, and in which there are species of animals totally unknown to you."*

Witness: *"What do you use for food?"*

Humanoids: *"Prepared artificial elements."*

Witness: *"What did you mean to say when you mentioned 'amorphous' beings?"*

Humanoids: *"You will not understand this form of life."*
(The gynecologist insisted at this point on some further explanation, and the following reply was given):
They're entities, living by means of 'Kriso-stelic' ascending neural evolution."

Witness: *"What do you think of our achievements as regards space-flight?"*

Humanoids: *"They are primitive experiments."*

Witness: *"Have you any powerful weapons?"*

Humanoids: *"Yes, we possess a wave-compressor capable of disintegrating the Moon with only one discharge."*

Witness: *"Have you brought this compressor with you?"*

Humanoids: *"No, we repeat that our mission is one of peace; but we have brought diminutive portable ones powerful enough to halt a plutonium explosion."*

At that point the general conversation ceased but the witnesses remembered snatches of other things that the beings said, such as:

"That we (here on Earth) are their beginning, and that they in turn are the beginning of the Amorphous."

"That outside of the Galaxy, the Life of Contrasts exists."

"That they will continue to leave evidence of their presence in various parts of the world."

HC addendum.
Source: Horacio Gonzalez Ganteaume.   Type: B

* * * * * * *

Location: Smithville, Ontario, Canada.
Date: August 9, 1965.
Time: Night.

The Hamilton Spectator reported on August 16, 1965, that a truck driver from Lakeview claimed to have seen a half-human, half-animal beast, six or seven feet tall, on a side road near Smithville. The man estimated it weighed 500 pounds. A secondary source reports that it was covered with hairs, had powerful shoulders, a head that seemed too small for its body, and inordinately long arms. The truck driver went back to look for tracks but found none.

HC addendum.
Source: http://ufologie.patrickgross.org/indexe.htm   Type: E

Location: Lima, Peru.
Date: August 9, 1965.
Time: 10:00 p.m.

The anonymous witness, a sober music teacher and "high public official," was driving in the outskirts of Lima when his car's motor started to miss, and then stopped. At that moment the car, surrounded by a beam of light from above, rose up from the road and was then carried through the sky for an unknown distance, at an altitude such that the witness could see the coastline and a peninsula, La Punta, west of the city. He was paralyzed.

The car was returned to the ground at a place he could not identify (but near the coast, for he could hear waves breaking), where a voice speaking perfect Spanish asked him to get out. He did so, and "could barely make out" little men with big ears. Apparently no UFO was seen, but there was a luminous screen nearby, on which he read; *"We are using calming rays on you to remove your fear."* He then asked several questions, in response to which the spokesperson told him that they came from a place more distant than Mars, that they had visited Earth on various occasions in the past, and that they did not appear in public because that might cause panic.

Asked if they knew music, he caused the witness to hear "something that might be considered as music, but that had the power of raising the feelings to the highest exaltation." Then his car was transported back through the air to the spot from which he had been picked up. He told his story to an uncle, an official in the Peruvian police, who informed reporters.

HC addendum.
Source: Humcat quoting Newspaper source.   Type: G

* * * * * * *

Location: Cruzeiro, Santa Catarina, Brazil.
Date: August 14, 1965.
Time: Daytime.

A railway worker named Joao de Oliveira, (known as Joao do Rio) of the village of Cruzeiros, was quietly fishing in the river Paraiba when a flying saucer landed nearby. From it there emerged a strange little man, some 70 centimeters in height, with large luminous eyes, who addressed the fisherman in perfect Portuguese and said that he was from a flying saucer from another world, and authorized Joao do Rio to relate the occurrence to his fellow countrymen.

Before re-entering the saucer, the little man gave him a strange piece of metal, of a kind that does not exist on Earth. The piece of metal was now undergoing examination at the laboratories of the Brazilian National Railways Coach building Works, with a view to the determination of its composition. Meanwhile a neighbor was quoted as saying that he had always been regarded as a very serious and entirely reliable individual.

HC addendum.
Source: SBEDV 54. Type: B
Comments: Apparently nothing was ever heard about the supposed alien piece of metal.

* * * * * * *

Location: Sedalia, Missouri.
Date: August 16, 1965.
Time: 11:00 p.m.

The witness, an anonymous woman, was driving home at 23:00 and was within a mile of her house when she saw a light in a field, with "smoke" around it. In the ditch she noticed two large "birds," one of which flew at her car. She arrived home at 00:25 a.m. unable to account for the lapse of time. Under hypnotic regression she recalled that the "birds" in the ditch were in fact two entities wearing space suits; one carried a sack on its back, into which the other was putting clumps of grass and soil samples. They were "bouncing up and down, their arms flopping at their sides" in a stiff manner suggestive of robots.

One started to come out of the ditch, slipped back, then emerged and stood in front of her; its helmet began to glow brilliantly, and she could now see that its head was wrapped up in tape like a mummy, with only the eyes visible. It stood slightly over 5ft tall. At this point, a 'thing;' a football shaped UFO, landed on the road ahead of her car. Two beings with slightly pointed heads and "wrap around" eyes emerged from it and opened her car door. They conducted her into the object, assuring her telepathically that she would not be hurt. The air inside the UFO was "heavy" and difficult for her to breathe.

Once she was inside, they flew the ship over a nearby field, which caused its interior lights to change from white to red. One of the entities, who did most of the talking, appeared to be a scientist or doctor; he wore an insignia of three rings on his chest. Another had a red lighting flash symbol on his uniform; she took him to be the pilot. A third entity appeared to be a woman. All these stood 5'10" tall. The "doctor" put an object of some kind over her head; she felt as if something were going into her brain. A round black object was then taken out of the wall, and with it "pictures" were taken of her; the object glowed blue when the pictures were taken.

On a screen on the wall appeared a pattern; seven vertical lines with markings between them, which she thought must be a tabular representation of her brain and body. The two figures, about a foot shorter, made their appearance; resembling "gnomes," they aroused fear in the witness. They appeared old; their foreheads were wrinkled. She was told by the humanoids that they and the "mummies" came from different planets. Finally she was led back to her car; the UFO ascended, and then vanished while still at low altitude.

HC addendum.
Source: Ron Owen and Jerome Clark. Type: G

* * * * * * *

Location: Lima, Peru.
Date: August 19, 1965.
Time: Night.

A young man, Alberto San Roman, reported going up to the terrace on the roof of his house and encountering a strange greenish, dwarf-like being, with very wrinkled skin and about 90cm in height. It had large slanted eyes, and oval-shaped head and large pointy ears. It walked over the roof in a strange 'duck-like gait.' It came very close to the terrified witness who was able to further see that the creature had short stubby legs and long dangling arms.

The creature's skin seemed to emit dim flashes of light and apparently attempted to communicate with San Roman using friendly gestures. Apparently since the attempt of communication was unsuccessful it climbed a nearby antenna tower and entered a hovering round object that emitted bright reddish light. Once this was done, the craft left at high speed.

HC addendum.
Source: SBEDV 55-59 quoting Instituto Peruano de Relaciones Interplanetarias (IPRI). Type: B

Location: Near Cuzco, Peru.
Date: August 20, 1965.
Time: 11:50 a.m.

A group of people, including Mr. and Mrs. Alberto Ugarte, and Edwin Voter, observed a small disc, only 5' in diameter, and of a vivid silvery color, land on a terrace of Sacsahuaman. From it there emerged two small beings "of strange shape and dazzling brightness." They at once went back inside into their vehicle, which then flew off.

HC addendum.
Source: The Humanoids and *APRO Bulletin* Jan/Feb 1966.   Type: B

* * * * * * *

Location: Near Mexico City, Mexico.
Date: August 21, 1965.
Time: Unknown.

It was reported that two independent groups of students, three from La Salle University and a party of high school boys, had separate but identical meetings with strange visitors. Each group had come upon a huge landed metallic disc, 150ft wide, emitting intense white light. Its blond and blue-eyed crewmembers, entirely human in appearance but 7ft tall, wore seamless one-piece garments of metallic appearance.

The students were invited into the craft and taken for a 3-hour journey to a huge space station. The humanoids communicated entirely by telepathy, and operated their instruments by thought-power. Many varieties of beings were seen at the space station; the student's hosts were from the Jovian moon Ganymede. They said they knew 700 languages, and informed their guests that they would make mass landings, for "peaceful conquest," in October of 1965.

HC addendum.
Source: *'The Humanoids'* citing newspaper source and UPI Dispatch.
Type: G

Location: Between San Jose de Jachal and San Juan, Argentina.
Date: August 22, 1965.
Time: 8:00 p.m.

An anonymous witness reported that while driving that Sunday night on Route 40 a luminous sphere about 20 meters in diameter suddenly appeared ahead of his vehicle and about 100 meters above the road. Stunned, he stopped the car and waited a few minutes. He then continued on and noticed that the luminous sphere was now following him closely at a lower altitude. Concerned he again stopped the vehicle on the side of the road and exited the car. The sphere or craft now hovered above him, illuminating the area all around. Terrified, he noticed what appeared to be a pair of large plier-like robotic instruments, come out of the object which grabbed him and lifted him up; at this point he loses consciousness.

Upon waking up, he finds himself on the floor, presumably inside the object, facing up and surrounded by several beings that were watching him closely. At the same time these were pushing luminous buttons located within several indentures on the walls. The entities were human in appearance, wearing metallic clothing, shiny without any seams. Their heads were covered by diver-type helmets and they moved around at very high speed. The craft was apparently circular and luminous with a main column in the center. The witness remained on the floor without being able to move, looking through a window located on the ceiling of the object right above him. Noticing his impatience, one of the entities approached and touched his face, rendering him unconscious once again. When he woke up again he was now sitting next to his car. He looked at his watch and it was 00:10 a.m., he had been gone for four hours.

HC addendum.
RAO Casuistica Argentina, citing *Diario de Cuyo San Juan*, August 1965.
Type: G

* * * * * * *

Location: Near Cuenca, Ecuador.
Date: August 26, 1965.
Time: 1:30 a.m.

Hector Crespo, a highway engineer, his son Urgenio and Francisco Lopez, were approaching Zhulleng, 11 miles from Cuenca, when they saw two beams of bright light shining up into the sky. Upon going to investigate what they believed was a car wreck; they found a circular object 20ft in diameter, with a transparent dome on top. A bright amber light kept flashing around the edge, and flickering red and blue beams were shining downwards. The three witnesses approached within 60ft of the UFO and could see through an open door instruments and lights inside it. Three human-like figures were seen outside the object, one apparently adjusting the light beam projector and the others handing him tools. All moved very slowly, "as if under water." They were dressed in metallic looking, silvery white close-fitting coveralls, with wide white belts, dark epaulets, and shiny helmets.

At one point two of the "men" turned and looked directly at the spot where the witnesses were watching, as though knowing the operation was being watched, and then returned to the repairs. The object was standing on telescopic legs with curved, dish-like footpads, although they were uncertain as to whether there were three or four legs. Crespo's son became so frightened that he was nauseated, so they went back to their car. After some time they saw the object take off, the light moving around the edge now a brilliant red and the vertical white beams now extinguished. Just before it "took off like lighting," it became too bright to look at.

HC addendum.
Source: Wendelle C. Stevens, *Saga* UFO Report Spring 1975.   Type: C

* * * * * * *

Location: Rio De Janeiro, Brazil.
Date: August 27, 1965.
Time: Unknown.

Gabriel Rubens Hellurg reported encountering a landed, disc-shaped object on a rice field. He reportedly communicated via telepathy with several human-like occupants that informed him that they hailed from another solar system. Hellurg asserted that he was able to communicate telepathically and understood what he was being told. No other information.

HC addendum.
Source: Fabio Picasso.   Type: C?

Location: Gunnison River Valley, Colorado.
Date: September, 1965.
Time: Evening.

The witness saw a black triangle from the highway heading toward the mountains in the northeast. It flew about 40 mph not more than 300ft off the ground, made no sound and had no outside lights. If the moon had not been out full he would have never noticed the object. He got out of the car and watched it gliding almost overhead, on its left side nearest to the witness, he noticed a number of porthole shaped windows.

A yellowish light was emitted from within and he could see the outline of a number of small humanoid creatures with large heads coming to the windows to peer down at him. It continued on and out of sight in a few minutes. The object was very large and very black.

HC addendum.
Source: Norm Buckallew, CAUS. Type: A

* * * * * * *

Location: Huildad, Chile.
Date: September, 1965.
Time: Midnight.

The witness; Augustin Alvarez, was about to close the kitchen door on his way to his bedroom, when he heard a strange sound coming from the ocean. He turned around and beheld one of the strangest sights he had ever seen in his life. A large section of the ocean appeared to have 'evaporated' leaving behind an empty channel in which he could see whole schools of fish and other sea creatures in the bottom, the fish seemed to float and shine with a silvery brilliance, and were completely still as if sleeping, the whole scene resembled the famous parting of the Red Sea in the bible tale. In the center of the dry channel he could see an elongated object and on top, several tall men wearing golden metallic suits who appeared to be giving orders among themselves in a language that Alvarez could not understand, to him it sounded like inhuman grunts.

The men onboard the strange craft appeared to be collecting bags and crates from a smaller launch-like object next to it. He also saw what appeared to be the cooks in the galley of the strange object washing their dishes. At the same time they did this the dishes seemed to emit a strange musical type sound. The whole operation seemed to have been directed by a very tall man. On the fore section of the craft he could see a 'flag' shaped like a fish tail and replete with phosphorescent colors from all shades of the rainbow.

Augustin Alvarez watched the incredible spectacle for at least half an hour and then thought to wake up his wife so she could see what he was seeing and to prove to himself that he was not going crazy. His wife got up immediately but when both went to look, the whole scene had vanished, the water seemed to be back in place but there was a strange glow deep under the waters, besides that, every else appeared to be normal.

HC addendum.
Source: Antonio Cardenas Tabies, Pacifico Sur.   Type: A?
Comments: A dream? Or was the witness privy some a brief glimpse of some alien realm?

* * * * * * *

Location: Green River Gorge, Washington.
Date: September 4, 1965.
Time: Unknown.

In an isolated area a man named Salsbury encountered a landed craft from which a powerful voice resembling a "loud speaker" originated. It told him not to be afraid, and to put down his gun. Once he did that, an oval shaped door opened under the lower part of the white disc-shaped object and a man came out, walking slowly towards the witness. The man was described as six foot tall, about 30 years of age. He was dressed in a one-piece tight fitting suit made of some sort of metallic coating resembling aluminum or chrome, dull reflecting. He also wore a helmet that was very close fitting on his skull.

On his side he carried an odd-looking sidearm with a barrel about the size of a regular flashlight, but instead of a hole in it, it had some sort of oval lens of a purplish-bluish color. He spoke to the witness in a very refined voice telling him, *"Don't be alarmed, I am not here to cause you any injury or harm."* The man told the witness that he was the captain of his craft and invited him onboard for a brief tour. No other information.

HC addendum.
Source: Andy Page, UFO.   Type: G

Location: Pease Air Force Base (closed in 1991), New Hampshire.
Date: September 7, 1965.
Time: Evening.

Carl Moore was an Airman Second Class with a top-secret clearance in the Air Force. His main duties was to guard boxes in a warehouse which by his own account was the most boring job anyone could have. Part of his duties was taking shipments off the rail head and many of the other Airmen didn't like going down there. It was on this rail head that a craft appeared. It was off in the distance and he tried to copy what he saw by drawing it on a small sheet of paper. Before he could finish it, the craft was directly above his head.

It was close enough that he couldn't see the sky because it took up the whole of his view. When he gasped, *"Holy mackerel!"* at the sight of the sudden appearance of the ship, he heard the phrase verbatim echoed back to him from the craft in his own voice. He tried to run but the ship remained over him. Hearing it repeat his further exclamations, he decided to face the vessel and said, *"If you can copy that, try copying this."* He pulled a card from his pocket and to his surprise the ship opened. He was expecting it to be a slot to put the card but what really happened caught him even more off guard as the ship's entry was opened up and the occupants exited. They grabbed him and touched a "wand" to his back of his head and he no longer struggled.

As he was taken onboard, his commanding officer told him that the visitors had been around for years and that they were interested in "testing us." He claimed they weren't going to hurt him and that this was, in fact, a pretty "regular situation." This was the first time he was taken aboard and his "visit" was comprised almost totally of medical examinations. The occupants were the "typical Greys," which were actually broken down into two types, one a "worker class" and the other the "bosses." The larger "bosses" were smarter. Both of them he said have eyes like us only their pupils were so large that you couldn't see the whites. He described their forehead like a melon. A small hole for ears and a walnut-shaped feature immediately behind the hole. He says that when they communicated with him, it was with thought and it seemed as if they were purposely flooding his mind with images to hide what they looked like but he was able to "ignore" what they were saying. He was gone for the entire weekend.

HC addendum.
Source: http://whofortedblog.com/2013/06/13/dad-alien-abductee-sweet-truth-extra-terrestrials/   Type: G

Location: Sao Joao, Pernambuco, Brazil.
Date: September 10, 1965.
Time: 8:30 a.m.

Antonio Pau Ferro, a 45-year old peasant farmer, was working in his field of maize when he heard a strange rushing and whistling noise. Turning around, he saw two luminous discs about 1-1/2 meters wide and 60cm thick landing slowly, a little further down the hill from him. When they were about 30 centimeters from the ground, they stopped and shot up again to about 5 meters, leaving below them two small beings of 70 or 80 centimeters who had apparently emerged from them. The little creatures were man-like, well-built and proportioned with beardless faces and amazingly smooth reddish-brown complexions, 'just like wax,' and normal eyes. They wore tight-fitting one-piece garments, but he was too disconcerted to take in more details.

In terror he stood clutching his mattock in one hand and hanging on to a tree with the other. The creatures approached but apparently perceived his fear, and turned away. He heard them talking in an unintelligible language. Just as he was thinking to himself; *"Can these be the flying saucer people of whom we have been hearing?"* they both suddenly turned around, smiled, and began edging back towards him, examining a tomato plant on the way and picking one of its fruits. But they soon turned away again; the hovering discs descended over them, and apparently took them aboard, for when the discs shot vertically into the air with a high-pitched whistle, the little men were gone. Two people in the village had heard the strange loud hum.

HC addendum.
Source: Dr. Walter Buhler, SBEVD.   Type: B

* * * * * * *

Location: Jalapa, Veracruz, Mexico.
Date: September 10, 1965.
Time: Night.

A hovering object was seen in a Jalapa street which discharged yellow, blue, and orange lights from slits around its circumference, as well as "a black-clad being with eyes glowing like a cat's, holding a gleaming metal rod." This entity vanished suddenly after being seen by four witnesses, a local reporter, a bullfighter, and two taxi drivers.

HC addendum.
Source: Humcat quoting Reuters dispatch.   Type: C

Location: Warminster, Wiltshire, England.
Date: September 26, 1965.
Time: Afternoon.

On that afternoon, Arthur Shuttlewood received a phone call from someone claiming to be from another planet; 'AENSTRIA,' calling himself 'Karne.' Shuttlewood wanted proof, so he invited the man over. Seconds later there was someone at the front door. This man looked like any ordinary man, except for an apparent absence of pupils in his eyes; he also had blue blotches on his cheekbones and lips. He spent a total of nine minutes with the journalist. He also acted in a manner that unnerved Shuttlewood, who felt that if provoked, this man could instantly destroy him.

The stranger spoke of an imminent war in the Middle East and of further UFO appearances. He said a third world war was almost inevitable at some point in the not so distant future. Shuttlewood noticed that sometimes Karne would have difficulty breathing. At other times he would glance at a pale gold disc on his wrist. At the conclusion of the meeting Shuttlewood gripped Karne's wrist and left thumb in what he intended as a gesture of good will, but the visitor winced in pain. The stranger walked away in a slow and deliberate gait.

HC addendum.
Source: Arthur Shuttlewood, *'The Warminster Mystery.'* Type: E

* * * * * * *

Location: Bonnert, Arlon region, Luxembourg.
Date: September 26, 1965.
Time: 7:00 p.m.

A farmer living alone in an area called Ligenthal saw, coming low on the horizon, a luminous globe that resembled the 'solar disk.' It was approximately three feet in diameter and was moving erratically, wobbling on itself. As it approached it changed from yellow to a pale golden 'apple' color. Then it landed on the ground and nine revolving bands of blue color fanned out from its center by twisting anti-clockwise until they covered its whole surface.

Then in a rounded cone of light appeared a creature of feminine appearance standing on a globe. Immediately identified by the witness as the "Holy Virgin Mary," the creature was dressed in a neon colored golden cloth with two blue stripes similar to the 'Lourdes apparition.' The whole effect resembled a "jewelry store display" and was illuminating the entire valley. The cattle under his custody remained undisturbed and didn't react.

After ten minutes of the face to face encounter, the globe progressively changed to a red, sunset type color and began to lift upwards in the northeastern direction, flying low like a hawk in complete silence. It remained visible until about a distance of about 400 meters when something like "hand" passed four times in front of it and it faded away. After that, from the heavens flashed an iridescent light beam of purple-pink in color that was very beautiful.

During the 10 minutes of the 'face to face' meeting, the witness received the following instructions from the entity:

1. She urged that war be ended and peace prevail on Earth.
2. Explained how to properly harvest the fruits of the Earth.
3. Asked for peace to reign between families in every home.
4. Gave instruction on how eliminate accidents of all kinds.

The apparition so impressed the farmer that he immediately sent communication to the Vatican, The King of Belgium, The State Council, The UN security council, the Belgian, French, English, American, Russian and Chinese embassies and also to the International Red Cross. However it appears that this communication which was handwritten was not taken seriously since the sender did not receive any acknowledgements of its receipt.

The farmer called his message an *"Honorary Secular and Public Message, Legal and authentic form in aeternum."* The document concludes, *"Oppositely to some people actually alive or dead, who only were given a limited basic education, the highest authority of this world did not display any sign of haughtiness in my presence. That affidavit should stay in open and public reading prohibited from being interned into any secret archives, unless a copy in lieu thereof exists."*

This amazing document consists of eight recto-verso handwritten sets of pages covered with tiny characters, bearing the words written in blue ink above.

HC addendum.
Source: Franck Boitte quoting J. L. Vertongen.   Type: F or X?

Location: Morales, San Luis Potosi, Mexico.
Date: October, 1965.
Time: Daytime.

Francisco Estrada Acosta had gone out on a small game hunting expedition near a local mining area; he followed the local Santiago River and arrived at the San Jose dam. There while bending down collecting rocks for his slingshot, he felt the presence of someone standing next to him. Getting up, he was startled to see a tall figure with a large, oval-shaped head, huge reddish phosphorescent eyes and a large toad-like mouth.

The strange humanoid extended a "flipper" like hand to Acosta and touched one of Acosta's hands on his palm, the touch felt cold and scaly like that of a reptile or an amphibian. Terrified, Acosta stepped back and ran like a man possessed from the area. Looking back he noticed that the creature had membranous wing-like protrusions on its back and was apparently preparing to leave the area also.

HC addendum.
Source: Luis Ramirez Reyes, Contacto Mexico.   Type: E

* * * * * * *

Location: Mogi-Guacu, near Pinhal, Rio Grande do Sul, Brazil.
Date: October, 1965.
Time: 9:00 p.m.

At her house located about 700m from the grounds of a huge local warehouse, 17-year old Aparecida Correa da Silva and her cousin Neide, saw a green light passing over their house and then landing in the yard. It was the size of a Volkswagen but it had a round and luminous body, which had what appeared to be three 'wheels' on its underside. Three man-like figures about 1.1m in height came out of the object and appeared to bend down, looking at the ground, apparently collecting samples. When somebody approached the area, the men quickly entered the object through a sort of hatch.

The machine then rose vertically and was suddenly gone, since everything was now dark. The light from the object had illuminated the walls of the nearby storehouse and it also illuminated the 'men' which wore one-piece bluish clothing which apparently reflected the light. The men seemed to be rather 'stout' for their small size. They had clear skin, but two seemed to be more 'tanned,' and on their heads they wore large transparent helmets. The next night the whole family saw a green light fly over their house.

HC addendum.
Source: SBEDV-54.   Type: B

* * * * * * *

Location: Mexico City, Mexico.
Date: October, 1965.
Time: Evening.

At 4:30 a.m. a man and his wife had stepped out to empty an ashbin on a nearby empty lot when they saw a bright orange, disc-shaped object flying low over the area. Two days later at the local Tacubaya Plaza; witnesses saw four, tall humanoid figures, 2 meters in height. They wore tight-fitting silvery clothing, with knee high boots. They had long silvery hair and large slanted eyes. They remained silent and did not speak to anybody. Several witnesses followed the strangers until they disappeared from view. They were apparently seen again around 8:00 p.m.

HC addendum.
Source: Contacto Ovni.   Type: D

* * * * * * *

Location: Navsjon, Sweden.
Date: October, 1965.
Time: Evening.

Daniel Glantz (involved in other contacts) was on the outskirts of Navsjon when he saw a two hundred meter sized disc-shaped craft come down and land nearby. A sort of hatch or opening became visible and an individual wearing a "protective suit" stepped out. This individual was very tall, and was wearing a belt with flashing lights. The figure stood 2 meters away from Daniel as he could hear a faint buzzing sound, the figure wore a helmet with a faceplate. Soon the covering of the faceplate slid down and Daniel was able to see a pair of "synthetic eyes and eyebrows." No verbal communication took place, however the individual motioned to Daniel using hand signals and then returned to the landed object. The huge ship had three, ball-like protrusions on the bottom, which began to rotate right before it took off and left.

HC addendum.
Source: http://www.galactic-server.com/rune/stenlindgren.html
Type: B

Location: Pocomoke Forest, Maryland.
Date: October, 1965.
Time: Night.

Several men were in a wooded area near a local poultry farm when they noticed a glow among the trees. Their dogs began barking and then they noticed four or five whitish glowing figures with large egg shaped heads. The witnesses fled the scene in terror.

HC addendum.
Source: Mark Chorvinsky and Mark Opsasnick, *Strange Magazine* #5.
Type: E

* * * * * * *

Location: Hualpencillo, Chile.
Date: October 6, 1965.
Time: 4:20 a.m.

An Air Force sergeant (AFB) heard some interference on his radio equipment while at Concepcion Airport. He tried to call out without success. He then goes outside to have a look and sees a silent luminous saucer-shaped object which had landed about 300 or 400 meters away, at the end of the landing strip. The craft was 20-30 meters in diameter and 3m high, like a 'parachute.' The semispherical object emitted a strong orange glow.

Three figures then came out; they looked like 'divers' and walked slowly. On profile one of them had his head elongated forward, "perhaps a gas mask." The witness then decided to stand still and not approach. Two or three minutes later, the figures returned to the disc. It then took off vertically and flew away. The radio interference lasted for about 45 minutes or more. His own watch stopped at 4:22 a.m. The next day the witness and some reporters located a small circle (150 cm) in diameter at the landing site.

HC addendum.
Source: *'Visitas de Otro Mundo?'* Cronica, Diario de la tarde (Concepcion) 6 October 1965. Last page and *'Bajaron tres siluetas Cronica: Diario de la tarde,'* 8 October 1965, pp. 2-3 in Luis Gonzalez Manso's "Firsthumcat" quoting Diego Zuñiga.   Type: B

Location: Long Prairie, Minnesota.
Date: October 23, 1965.
Time: 7:15 p.m.

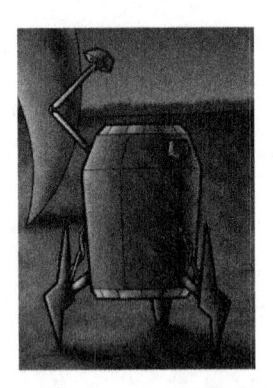

James F. Townsend, 19, was driving outside of Long Prairie when his engine failed and his headlights went out. 20ft ahead, in the middle of the road, was a metallic, rocket shaped object, illuminated "as bright as sunlight," 30-40ft high, and standing on leg-like fins about 10ft wide. He got out of his car to walk up to it, but stopped upon seeing three tiny entities emerge from behind the object and approach him. Not more than six inches high, they looked like tin beer cans with matchstick legs and arms.

After a confrontation of about three minutes, they went back to the object, and a few seconds later it began to rise slowly. When it had attained some altitude, the car's lights and motor both came back on. Three streaks of an oil-like substance were later found at the site.

HC addendum.
Source: Sheriff James Bain, Jerome Clark in *FSR* Vol. 10 #3 and APRO.
Type: B
Comments: "Townsend left Long Prairie before I came here in 1969. Nobody seemed to know where he went. He was living in a basement apartment in a farm home and was visited by a man in a blue Air Force uniform. The lady upstairs could hear them talking but could not understand most of what was said. The conversation was carried out in a normal volume with no raised voices. Townsend left town shortly thereafter. I talked to Sheriff Jim Bain about the case when I came to Long Prairie. My recollection is that Bain told about Townsend coming into the Sheriff's office white-as-a-sheet and trembling."
-Richard Moss, Long Prairie.

Location: Alto dos Cruzeiros, Canhotinho, Pernambuco, Brazil.
Date: October 26, 1965.
Time: Noon.

A saucer was seen flying over the area and at about noon, a 56-year old mechanic named Jose Camilho Filho, a man of some education and of excellent repute, ran into two entities that may have belonged to its crew. Passing along a road through a belt of scrubland containing many banana trees, he suddenly rounded a bend and beheld two young people sitting on the stump of a fallen banana tree. This in itself at once struck him as odd, for even small children know better than to sit on such things, as they leave ineradicable stains on clothing.

But when the two people jumped to their feet, he saw that they were only 80 or 90 centimeters in height and certainly not normal folk. Their complexions were brown and their faces 'shriveled' and furrowed like those of old people. Their hair was white; their heads rather large in proportion to their bodies and very round, and their eyes were 'slits' like those of Orientals but, he thought, proportionately larger than in human beings. One of the little men had a sparse beard and wore a dark, peaked cap. The other was bare-headed. Both appeared to have white hands (possibly white gloves?). One was carrying under his arm a rod-shaped object about 50 centimeters long and about as thick as a flashlight.

When he saw the witness and jumped up, he "looked so astonished that it seemed his eyes would leap from their sockets," and he made a gesture with the other hand towards this apparatus under his arm as though thinking of using it against him. The other little man, who seemed much less alarmed, wore a blue shirt-like garment, olive green trousers, and 'shoes which looked like tennis shoes.' The material of his clothing looked 'tropical' and 'shiny.' But the most remarkable feature was his 'luminous belt.' This covered the upper part of his chest, from shoulder to shoulder, and from it there flashed out vivid lights, bluish-red, yellow, and green, 'like the flashes from an electric welding kit, so bright that you could not look at it.'

Between the entities stood a cylinder about 1 meter 20 centimeters high and 15 centimeters in diameter. The man with the flashing lights, who was closer, now jumped to his feet also and grabbed this cylinder by a handle in the middle of it, and began running off, staggering as he did so, and he collided with his companion so that both nearly fell to the ground. The witness meanwhile had also taken to his heels, but looked back in time to see them vanish among the trees.

HC addendum.
Source: *'The Humanoids,'* quoting Walter Buhler. Type: D

Location: Near Navsjon, Sweden.
Date: November, 1965.
Time: Evening.

   After receiving telepathic communication for a pre-arranged meeting with the "space visitors," Sten Lindgren, Daniel Glantz and three other persons, drove to the agreed upon location outside of Navsjon. Soon after arriving, some in the group felt a sort of weak electrical sensation in their brains, that felt like a "scanning" similar to electrical hairdryers. It was very subtle but it was clearly felt. At the locations there was already one ship on the ground, the ship was emitting a powerful white light. Eventually the lights dimmed and the group could now see the shape of the craft. It was a metallic bell shaped craft with three spherical protrusions on the bottom.
   The ship on the ground was between twelve and fifteen meters in diameter and about five meters in height, the other two were much bigger, approximately three hundred to six hundred feet, these two bigger ships were hovering and rotating slowly above the lake, emitting bright orange flashes of light.
   Sten and one of the others retrieved a flashlight from the car and after a minute, a figure was seen to exit the landed ship. The figure was human-like and stood in front of the ship, it was bareheaded and was about 1.70m in height, with long hair down over the shoulders and wearing a sort of blue ski-suit with a polo collar, he also wore a wide belt. Sten felt that this individual was a man. Daniel then flashed the light three times at the individual and this one took something from his belt, and answered the signals with a bright light. The object he used cast a type of solid beam of light that was very accurate and stopped at variable distances from the witnesses. The distance from the ship to the witnesses was only five to ten meters. Daniel and the other two then walked towards the ship. One carried an envelope, apparently to give to the space visitors. However the figure motioned the trio to stand back, and instructed them to return to the vehicle. Once back by the car they noticed that the envelope was now missing.
   The group was then instructed to drive away from the area and drove about 5 km away and stopped the car. They then saw above some woods, a hovering object emitting an orange colored light. The sky was starlit that evening, and as the group looked up at the stars they experienced a strange phenomenon as if the whole sky was now ten times magnified and they could see all the stars much closer, they saw more stars than normal, and seemed to have experienced a sort of expansion of their consciousness. After that they drove home and had dinner, very inspired by their recent experience.

HC addendum.
Source: http://www.galactic-server.com/rune/stenlindgren.html
Type: B

* * * * * * *

Location: Near Durango, Mexico.
Date: November 3, 1965.
Time: Unknown.

In an isolated desert area a man and his 15-year old son encountered a disc shaped object that stopped and hovered close to the ground nearby. After a few minutes, a round opening became visible on the top of the object and reddish vapor or smoke was seen coming out. A strange being then emerged, it was described as short, reptilian in appearance with very long ears, six tubular arms like protrusions and a long greenish tail. It carried a strange object, resembling a metallic umbrella that it moved around as if making signals, the being spotted the witnesses and jumped to the ground. At this point both witnesses ran away from the area in a panic and did not see the object and being's departure.

HC addendum.
Source: Peter Kolosimo, *'Sombra en Las Estrellas.'* Type: B

* * * * * * *

Location: Manhattan, New York City, New York.
Date: November 10, 1965.
Time: Night.

A widespread power failure blacked out New York City and much of the northeastern United States late on the afternoon of November 10, 1965. By dawn of the following day, power still had not been restored. Movie and television actor Stuart Whitman, who was staying in a Manhattan hotel, heard a "sound like a whippoorwill whistling outside my twelfth story window." When he stepped to the window, he was startled, so he told Hollywood reporter Vernon Scott two months later, to see two UFOs hovering nearby. According to his account;

"One of them was orange, and the other was blue. They gave off a strange luminescent light, so I couldn't see if there were portholes or who was in them. Then I heard them speaking to me as if they were on a loudspeaker. They spoke to me in English. It may not have been audible to anyone else. They said they wanted to talk to me because I appeared to have no malice or hate. They said they were fearful of earth because Earthlings were messing around with unknown quantities and might disrupt the balance of the universe or their planet.

The people in the UFO said the blackout was just a little demonstration of their power and that they could do a lot more with almost no effort. It served as a warning. They said they could stop our whole planet from functioning. They asked me to do what I could to fight malice, prejudice, and hate on Earth, and then they took off. I couldn't say how big the objects were, but when they took off I felt elated. I wasn't even shocked. And I know I wasn't asleep because I was standing by the window and wide awake the entire time. I don't know why they picked me as a contact. But I'll swear on a Bible that I saw them out there and that they talked to me."

Whitman insisted that he had not been drinking. Scott, who thought the story was absurd, nonetheless acknowledged that Whitman seemed sincere. It was not, after all, the sort of tale likely to advance his career. He never spoke publicly of the incident again.

HC addendum.
Source: John Keel. Type: F

* * * * * * *

Location: Mogi Guacu, Sao Paolo, Brazil.
Date: November 13, 1965.
Time: Night.

Two nights following the above incident, Mr. Dario Anahaua Filho alerted neighbors and associates to the appearance of the objects. On hand this time were the director of the local bank, their priest, Longino Vartbinden, two police officers and, in addition, several neighbors. As darkness approached, an object appeared, hovered briefly, and then landed 100 yards away, focusing a light beam upward.

The local sheriff and a police clerk had observed it independently as they drove nearby. The bank manager became so excited at the object's appearance that he dropped his camera and could not find it in the dark. At this time, two beings the size of a 7-year old child were seen at 20 yards distance; one was wearing overalls, the other chocolate colored pants and a gray collarless shirt. A third entity, seen through the mirror-like beam of light, had a square, flat head, and was wearing a surgeon's apron. Both the UFO and the beings were brightly luminous.

HC addendum.
Source: Prof Flavio Pereira, Dr Leo Godoi and Dr Renato Bacelar.
Type: C

* * * * * * *

Location: Shasta Lake, California.
Date: December, 1965.
Time: 1:00 p.m.

    Several students from the local Deer Creek middle school were outside meeting the principal or something similar which called for most of the student body to attend. The weather was clear. Suddenly a silver, disk-shaped craft flew over the school grounds without noise. It flew north to south, very low, just above the tall pine trees. Over 45 witnesses watched, which included, teachers, students, etc. As the object went over them it appeared to land in back of the school grounds, behind some trees. The area was wooded, without houses.
    The students were immediately sent back to their classrooms until 14:00. While in the classroom, the main witness observed a man walk by the class window. He was not a sheriff, as they had been told that the sheriff had been called. The man wore a black suit, and carried a black briefcase. He did not see any others. He was walking towards the craft, to the south. At 14:00 the dismissal alarm sounded and the students were told that they could go. The main witness and a girl then headed towards the direction of where the craft had landed. The tall pine trees had covered its descent, but they did not see it leave.
    They then met other students coming back from behind the school from the landing site; some had gone to find the ship. They were told that it was gone, but they still went to the site where they found a large, approximately 40ft diameter ring. It appeared to be burned all around the edge. (Later on the main witness would return to the scene to find that for years nothing grew there). At the landing site they saw nothing else, so they left. Something then scared them and they began to run, the main witness could not recall what scared them. The main witness told his mother who went to see the ring.

HC addendum.
Source: NUFORC. Type: D?
Comments: Who was the mysterious stranger carrying the black briefcase?

Location: Birmingham, England.
Date: December, 1965.
Time: Night.

A young man was returning home after dark, along a lane on the outskirts of Birmingham after an evening spent with his girlfriend. He had not partaken of anything alcoholic and was in perfectly happy and normal state of mind. Suddenly he looked around to find that he was being followed by something he describes quite adamantly as a luminous man emitting a green glow from head to foot. His immediate reaction was of disbelief fear and then panic, he ran to his home, which was nearby, as fast as he could.

When he arrived there in a sweat of fear, his mother would not believe his story, but she did in fact peer out of the window and admits seeing a green glow coming from behind nearby bushes. In spite of this she still found her son's story incredible. The witness stated that the figure was that of a man of normal size.

HC addendum.
Source: Charles Bowen quoting BUFORA in *FSR*.　　　　　　　Type: E

* * * * * * *

Location: Nairobi, Kenya.
Date: December, 1965.
Time: Night.

Michael Mudachi was sitting in his home near Eastleigh Airport when he saw a point of light approaching from the horizon. As it neared he saw it was an elliptical object with transparent windows. It landed vertically and three humanoid figures emerged from it, wearing what looked like tall hats. They had human appearance, seemingly a synthesis of all races.

They spoke in an incomprehensible language but were able to make Mudachi understand that they were not hostile and wanted to take his photograph. To get him to agree they first photographed his brother and another witness, and then they put him on a platform where there was an implement like a birdcage, which emitted a white light, like sunlight. A powerful ray shot out from a red bulb at the center of this contraption, which hit Mudachi on the chest leaving him spluttering and fighting for breath, suddenly the beings left without the witness seeing how. After the incident he fell into an unusually deep, dreamless sleep. Later he suffered from hallucinations, depression, loss of appetite and general malaise.

HC addendum.
Source: Peter Rogerson, quoting Kenyan news sources.　　　　　Type: B

Location: Nykoping, Sodermanland, Sweden.
Date: December, 1965.
Time: Night.

Danie Glantz, arranged for a group of people including his wife, UFO researcher Sten Lindgren, Christer Jansson and another man, to meet "the aliens." He told them to urinate before they went and to not bring any metal with them. They drove out to Lake Navsjon where they encountered a large metal object on the beach. Daniel, his wife and the anonymous man approached at which time a humanoid appeared out of nowhere and signaled at them with a light like a laser, warning them away. They drove away and then stopped to calm down, at which time a strange object passed over them, calming them and giving the impression that the thing was scanning their brains. The stars seemed to come closer during this experience. Mrs. Glantz was so frightened the couple divorced.

HC addendum.
Source: Anneli Engstrom in *INFO Journal* #72, p44.   Type: E?
Comments: Glantz had been involved in other encounters.

* * * * * * *

Location: Uddevalla near Gothenburg, Sweden.
Date: December 9, 1965.
Time: 3:00 p.m.

52-year old rock hunter Richard Hoglund was taking a stroll with his dog on the frozen lake Grindhultsjon, 5 miles east of Uddevalla. Richard had a lingering kidney stone problem and was undergoing surgery the next day. Suddenly he heard a whining sound in the air and Richard observed a saucer-shaped, semi-translucent object land on the ice. A dark tube was then lowered down from under the object. Richard assumed that it must be a Russian aircraft.
From the tube, four entities floated down to the ground and walk over to him. There were three men and a woman. Except for the translucent space suits they are wearing, they are completely naked. They were of normal height with very dark, somewhat slanted eyes and perfect teeth. Their skin had no blemishes and there was no hair on their bodies, not even genital hair. Richard is fascinated by the large and pointed ears of the entities. The orifice in the ear was very large, like a cat. They have a slight Oriental look. The space suits looked like they were held away from the body by air pressure.
Richard felt very confused but not afraid. They started a conversation through sign language and drawings in the snow-covered ice. The

entities didn't want Richard to touch them. With a small black device they sprayed a gas-like matter on everything, before touching it, even the dog. The dog doesn't like the spray. It has a strong smell of hyacinth. The entities seemed friendly and the girl played with the dog. When it got darker, Richard could see that the craft was surrounded by a blue phosphorescent glow. One of the men, who seemed older and appeared to be the leader, took a metallic object shaped like a microphone and 'scanned' Richard's back with it. Richard then suddenly felt relieved from his kidney pains. The object was warm and vibrated. After this healing, the entities enter the craft which took off.

The next day, when Richard was X-rayed prior to his operation, medical personnel were puzzled to discover that his physical problem had been cured. Not long afterwards a Stockholm based Ufologist interviewed him about his encounter.

In August 1966, Richard experienced a second contact. Again drawn outside by some mysterious instinct, he once more observed the UFO hovering above the lake. This time however, the older entity stood outside in mid-air, and he spoke, but his words were not coordinated with his lips; they seemed to emanate from the ship, moments after the mouth movement. Richard was given a metal plate and instructed to wear it always. The being instructed him to go to the Bahamas (and specifically to the Bahamian island of Little Exuma) as their representative. Richard declined on the grounds that he could not speak English, was uneducated, and had a wife to care for. All to no avail; he was told that he had no choice in the matter.

Afterwards, Richard buried the plate, a small rectangle made of an aluminum-like material, about three inches wide by two inches thick, with three rows of symbols on one side. The following March, leaving it behind, he and Anna (his wife) nonetheless went to the Bahamas to live. On the flight there, they noticed 14 men who, because of their black dress, they assumed were Catholic priests. The "priests" however were nowhere in sight when everyone else left the airliner. Beyond that curious little incident, nothing of significance happened. Too embarrassed to return to their hometown, Richard and Anna moved south of Stockholm to an apartment arranged for them by a small UFO group that knew something about his experience. A wealthy member of the club offered to finance further trips to the Bahamas.

Richard drove to Uddevalla and dug up the plate. Heading back to Stockholm, he stopped at a gas station, where an oddly dressed old man, sporting black slouch hat and black cape, approached and asked if he could accompany him. Richard agreed to take him. On the way the stranger revealed himself to be one of the "priests" on the flight, identifying himself as Father Rapas. He worked for the "overlords," as he called them, who had contacted Richard earlier. He directed Richard to return to the Bahamas and to bring along the plate this time. Rapas took over the driving, and Richard dozed off. When he awoke, the car was parked near its destination, and the driver was gone.

The couple stayed at a hotel in Nassau as 1967 turned to 1968. This time Richard was taken alone in a boat with two others to a small Bahamian island. Through an opening they entered a mountain, and inside it they found themselves in an extraterrestrial base where they observed several kinds of entities, including giants, dwarfs, and hermaphrodites. From then on, however, Richard would deal with the sorts of nordics who occupy more typical contactee literature; beautiful and golden haired. Richard came back with orders to found a group to be called the New Generation, which was to attract young people to work for peace and justice.

The core was the small UFO group that had formed around Richard, who showed its members what he alleged, was a letter from Rapas. Its language was blunt to the point of rudeness; *"We detest you. This is why we believe in the youth; they are the only ones whose hands are not soiled with the blood of others...Your catchword shall be; Freedom from violence; from hunger; we are all brothers and sisters...You who have supported (Richard) shall not be forgotten; you shall reap a hundredfold, but if someone hurts him or his devoted wife, I say, they shall be avenged sevenfold."* Rapas also produced a list of 65 rules members were obliged to follow; or else. Richard himself was to stay in the background.

The New Generation fell apart within months. Its members, unenthusiastic from the start, felt anxious about the threats, and the group's wealthy benefactor expressed displeasure at being asked for large sums of money whose purpose was never explained to him. Richard Hoglund died of a heart attack in 1977.

HC addendum.
Source: Hakan Blomquist, UFO Contact, *Igap Journal* February, 1986.
Type: B

* * * * * * *

Location: Kecksburg, Pennsylvania.
Date: December 9, 1965.
Time: 7:30 p.m.

In the late afternoon, many people witnessed a large orange-colored light in the sky above Lake Erie and several other locations to the north. Small lights were seen breaking away from the larger object and smoke was reported as far away as the bordering New York State. The emergency services had been contacted with reports of an aircraft, which was possibly in trouble and a Mrs. Jones from Mount Pleasant reported that an object had crashed into the woods near her home. Soon State Police cordoned off the area.

Soon the military took command and the local Kecksburg Fire Department headquarters became a temporary base. Military vehicles, including a flatbed truck and a crane, were seen heading towards the woods, and there was talk that a high-level team of military and scientific personnel had arrived on the scene. Later that night a large truck was seen leaving the area at high speed. It carried flashing lights to signal its importance. A large tarpaulin concealed an unknown cargo.

An 18-year old firefighter, James Romansky recalled seeing the object on the ground, after being called on duty following concerns that an airplane had crashed. He described the object as bronze colored and shaped like an acorn. Some 12ft long and 25ft in diameter, it had a slightly raised "blunt" end and strange markings. "It had writing on it, not like your average writing, but more like ancient Egyptian hieroglyphics." It had a sort of a bumper on it, like a ribbon about six to 10 inches wide, and it stood out. It was elliptical the whole way around and the writing was on the bumper. Another witness, Don Sebastian, who ventured to the area to check on the commotion reportedly, heard two unearthly screams coming from the woods. The screams did not sound human and frightened Sebastian so much that he left the area immediately.

HC addendum.
Source: Stan Gordon, PASU. Type: H
Additional info: In 1998, investigator Linda Moulton Howe interviewed "Myron," a truck driver hired by the government to deliver bricks one day to Wright Patterson Air Force Base soon after the Kecksburg incident. Myron said after his delivery of bricks to the base one day, he in fact saw the acorn-shaped craft retrieved by the military. But that wasn't all he saw. First he saw Navy and Air Force men dressed in white outfits, with masks on, and rubber gloves and rubber boots. He said he saw in the corner of the garage an acorn-shaped craft that was 10ft in diameter and 13ft high. It was dark colored with a copper top. There was writing near the bottom (triangles with + characters and X characters which appeared to be welded on the surface of the craft.)

Myron stood standing in the garage until they ran him out of there. He returned a second time after unloading the bricks and noticed a ladder leading to the top of the craft. He then said he saw something that was covered in a sheet being removed from the craft. It appeared to be four feet tall and was then placed on a stretcher. Trucker Myron said one of the creature's arms became exposed from under the sheet and it appeared like "a lizard's arm" or in other words, Reptilian. Myron corroborated other people's descriptions of reptilian aliens by saying that the arm was dark greenish/reddish in color. The truck driver was then threatened by military personnel when they told him, *"You have seen nothing and you have heard nothing!"* and that they could easily "lose him" in the spaces around that area. Myron talked to a friend since then who had been on the base and he says that particular building is bricked up and that is the part of the base no one ever goes any more. What happened to the body of the alien creature is unknown.

* * * * * * *

Location: Herman, Minnesota.
Date: December 20, 1965.
Time: 11:45 p.m.

15-year old Edward Burns was driving his father's pickup truck toward home late at night, when his headlights picked up a dark, oval shaped craft hovering about six feet over the road ahead of him. The object covered the entire road and looked like a huge light, a mixture of red, and white. He came within a telephone pole distance of the object and then immediately the engine and lights of his pickup went out. He felt his truck moving and wound up in a ditch. He claimed he saw something inside moving. It was shaped like a "man" but green in color.

HC addendum.
Source: Dr. James McDonald, etc, Brad Steiger, *'Flying Saucers Are Hostile,'* 43-44.   Type: A

* * * * * * *

Location: Panama Canal Zone.
Date: Late 1965.
Time: Unknown.

While several US military personnel were out on a field, a large disc shaped object reportedly descended and landed, apparently paralyzing all the soldiers on the spot. Several orange-colored, thin humanoids, with long arms, four-fingered hands and heads slightly larger than humans, emerged from the object and apparently examined the soldiers.
The beings had huge yellow colored eyes and wore tight-fitting outfits. The moment the beings returned to their craft, it flew away. The soldiers were then able to move again.

HC addendum.
Source: Jorge Martin, *Evidencia Ovni* #12.   Type: B or G?
Comments: Translation by Albert S. Rosales.

1966

Location: Peter Bottom, Arkansas.
Date: 1966.
Time: Late afternoon.

Two boys were traveling on horseback in an isolated area, when a man on a tractor suddenly emerged from the valley, moving at full speed in their direction. The man was extremely agitated and told them to leave the area, that a "monster" was living in the Bottom, he had seen it only moments before. The two boys, unafraid, decided to investigate as the farmer drove away. As they entered further into the wilderness area, the horses refused to go any further, so they continued on foot.

A few minutes later they found themselves in a gorgeous mountain meadow lush with flowers and sweet smelling grass. One of the boys then noticed what appeared to be clumps of white fur lying near the trunk of an old tree. It looked like a dead dog or animal. Suddenly the clump stood up and ambled toward them. It was a creature nearly 9-feet tall, and almost completely covered with thick, snow white fur. Where the skin was exposed it was a strange, pinkish color. Its face and posture was human like.

It also emitted a powerful odor, and made a sound like a radio signal as it slowly approached the two boys. The signal sounded like *"beep, beep, beep!"* The terrified witnesses fled the area immediately. A posse was formed to hunt the creature down, but it was never found. Dead and mutilated cows were found in the area and also a human corpse, missing its limbs from its battered torso.

HC addendum.
Source: D. Douglas Graham, *Fate,* November, 1995.   Type: E

Location: (Undisclosed military base) Texas.
Date: 1966.
Time: 2:00 a.m.-3:00 a.m.

An employee at a base used for overhauling aircraft was on a late shift to strip a C-133 to be moved out. He was on his way down to the pit with the crew, when a workmate (already there) radioed, *"Call security!"* "As I started to go in the entrance door of the aircraft somebody pushed me down and ran out into the bushes." When they all arrived on the scene, the radioing worker said that a "small guy" pushed him over. He believed the person was an alien and that the push was accompanied by an electric shock.

The crew saw a flattened silver, ball-like object rise up out of the trees in the direction that the small man was said to have run. "Just sort of like a silver cloud-type thing." It went straight up, and then moved slowly away to the east. As to the friend who had been pushed down, his girlfriend told the witness that the incident had screwed her boyfriend up regarding their relations and she wasn't happy about the alien interference with their love life.

HC addendum.
Source: Michael D. Swords, *'Grassroots UFOs.'* Type: C

* * * * * * *

Location: Blowing Cave, Arkansas.
Date: 1966.
Time: Late afternoon.

Several spelunkers, among them George D. Wight, were exploring the cave when they spotted a light at the end of the tunnel. As they approached it, Wight noticed a narrow crevice, just big enough for him to squeeze inside it. Then he found artificial steps. He called to the others and they climbed through the opening. The tunnel expanded and they suddenly came into a large corridor, 20 by 20. The walls and the floors were smooth and the ceiling had a curved dome shape.

Soon they encountered blue skinned but otherwise human-like individuals. The strangers communicated with the witnesses, telling them that they had instruments that could measure people's emotions. They learned that the tunnels went on for miles. They were led to underground cities populated by entities that included serpent-like creatures and large hairy bipeds. Later, using an elevator-like device they were taken to a glass-like city. Soon after this incident, Wight apparently returned to the cave and was never seen again.

HC addendum.
Source: Richard Toronto.   Type: G?

* * * * * * *

Location: Vereeniging, South Africa.
Date: 1966.
Time: Night.

M.B. was lying in bed when she suddenly became aware of a far-off whirring vibration. Suddenly a small metallic Saturn shaped object appeared and hovered quietly over her bed. It seemed to have numerous oval shaped portholes around its rim. As she lay there staring at the object, she suddenly found herself inside of it. She was seated on a stool next to a porthole looking outside at what appeared to be ploughed fields and fences.

Suddenly the craft swept up and nothing more was visible except for the interior of the object. She noticed sitting on a seat facing her, a very handsome man. He appeared to have perfect looks, build and immaculate in dress. He wore green "spectacles" with square frames and a hat. He stared intently at the witness. Besides him, were three more men and a woman. The woman wore a silk scarf tied around her head; a pleated woolen skirt in brown tones and a finely knitted woolen twin-set and a pair of brown brogues. She saw in the pit of the craft machinery and several crewmembers operating machinery. One of them operated a central steering column, which stood upright in the middle.

Then she found herself inside a large room, empty but for a white painted dining room table, oval shaped, and six tall backed chairs around it. From the wall protruded an elbow-arm with a large green disc light over the center of the table. She was alone in the room and noticed several white painted closed doors. She went to one of the doors then opened it, there was a long passage, and she went in and then found herself back in the central control room of the craft. When she became aware that they were returning to Earth, she panicked and pleaded with the crew not to take her back. But without any knowledge how she got there, she suddenly found herself lying in her bed again.

HC addendum.
Source: *UFO Afrinews*, July, 1988.　　　　　　　　　　　Type: G

* * * * * * *

Location: Near Marrakech, Morocco.
Date: 1966.
Time: 2:00 a.m.

 A local shepherd who slept near a window in order to keep watch on his animals, was awakened by the sounds of his dogs barking. The witness, Mohamed, who believed the dogs were barking at a cat or some other wild animal, called his dogs back into the courtyard, trying to reassure them. They were silent for a few minutes but began stirring again once Mohammed was in his room.
 Mohamed then looked out a window overlooking the rear of the house, the side opposite to the driveway to see if there was anyone on this side of the house. Surprisingly, the landscape was illuminated as if there were a full moon (but the night was supposed to have been moonless) and noticed a dark mass, slightly shiny, somewhat resembling aged aluminum. This mass (or object) was large, round and elongated. Mohammed also noticed that the object appeared to be suspended at 1m above the ground on what he described as a barrel-shaped object, very dark, approximately 70cm wide.
 The object did not exceed 5 meters in width and its height was 2m at the center and was about 80 to 120 meters from the house. It was a perfectly oval-shaped craft, with no doors or windows. Suddenly he saw a being which he likened to the beings spoken of in the Koran (the Jinn) which suddenly appeared and approached the object and then seemed to disappear again. This being was the size of a 15-year old child, about four feet high and walked on two legs, it had two arms that moved as it walked and a head that looked "extremely large."
 Given the dark, Mohammed could not provide any additional details on the creature. It seemed to have been wearing some sort of tight-fitting dark outfit. Its gait was normal as it walked to within 2 meters of the object and then disappeared behind it. Mohammed expected it to come out the other end of the object but it never did. He woke his wife but she saw nothing. The object also disappeared "as if becoming invisible." The children slept soundly throughout the whole incident. The observation lasted from 2 to 3 minutes.

HC addendum.
Source: Files of Ufologist Gerard Lebat. Type: C
Comments: Date is approximate.

* * * * * * *

Location: Alamogordo, New Mexico.
Date: 1966.
Time: Night.

Because of his high clearance, Air Force Sergeant Bill Holden was assigned to top-secret flights and special air missions. One trip took him to the above location on a mission as part of Project Mercury. It consisted of Air Force officers and civilian scientists.

Although ordered to remain at a distance, Holden said he could see a vehicle shaped like a saucer parked on three legs. And to his surprise he said he also saw two aliens wearing silver/gray metallic coverall uniforms. Before the mission he had to sign a 20-year non-disclosure statement and was asked if he objected to being involved in other similar projects.

HC addendum.
Source: UFO Chronicles. Type: H?

* * * * * * *

Location: Near Essex, California.
Date: January 23, 1966.
Time: 11:45 p.m.

The anonymous witnesses were changing a tire when they saw a flying saucer land 200 yards away. On investigation they found an object 75-100ft in diameter and 25ft high.

A door slid open and a 7-foot spaceman appeared. He called them by their names, and conversed with them by telepathy. He said his race was from another star and that 400 American citizens are actually of his race.

HC addendum.
Source: NICAP. Type: B

Location: Malaga, Spain.
Date: February 3, 1966.
Time: 12:30 a.m.

Trinidad Gomez Sanchez was getting ready to go to sleep late at night when she decided to go out to her terrace to check the doors and the garden. As she looked around and without knowing how, a strange creature appeared in the patio area, which had no access to the street.

She described the creature as very thin, gaunt, and covered with long black hair; it was a little bit over a meter in height. It had a round hairless head, like that of a "newborn." Terrified, she screamed and ran into the house. A later search for the creature proved fruitless.

HC addendum.
Source: *FSR* Vol. 13 #2, Iker Jimenez.   Type: E
Comments: Other sources give the date as February 1968.

* * * * * * *

Location: Near General Madariaga, Pinamar, Argentina.
Date: February 25, 1966.
Time: Evening.

Hilda Torper and her husband were on their way to a nearby movie theater, driving on a strangely empty road, which usually had more traffic at that time. Near some cornfields they noticed an object resembling a "tower" flying low over the ground and approaching the road. Excited, she yelled at her husband and he began signaling the object with the headlights. Concerned she yelled at him to slow down since it could have been some type of farm equipment and she was afraid of an accident. He argued with her and instead went faster. Those were the last words she heard. Suddenly she heard a sound like that of a giant vacuum cleaner and an uncanny force sucked both of them out the car. At the same time she felt a blow on her chin that threw her head back violently; at this point she lost consciousness.

An intense light woke Hilda up; the light was blinding and was bothering her. She pleaded to whoever was with her to shut off the light, but her request was ignored. However, slowly she was able to open her eyes again. She saw a small disc-shaped device hanging from a "ceiling" by what appeared to be a chain; this object emitted the blinding bursts of light. She fell asleep once again and soon woke up lying on a cot or stretcher, there were five men milling around her, she could not see her husband anywhere. She then heard a voice in her head that said, *"Don't attempt to remember, it is useless."* A figure then appeared next to her cot, it was a tall blond man, wearing a metallic blue coverall, he spoke to her in her mind, *"I am Turnelde, and I will be your guide."* He grabbed her arm and she noticed that he had six digits. Later she remembered being taken on a trip to the Brazilian Matto Grosso, more precisely "El Roncador Mountain." There the craft entered a huge tunnel where she saw immense shiny or metallic walls.

HC addendum.
Source: Proyecto CATENT, Argentina. Type: G

* * * * * * *

Location: Quipapa, Pernambuco, Brazil.
Date: February 25, 1966.
Time: 10:15 p.m.

Three young women were walking home after dark when they came upon an object hovering just above the road which resembled an upside down dish, 9-12ft wide, with two large "headlights." Beside it were three small individuals the size of 9-year old children, wearing "large headgear," who seemed to be conversing; all wore one-piece garments with an extremely luminous band across the chest, whose colors constantly changed. There was also a man more than 6ft tall, wearing a brightly luminous headgear likewise of varying colors, whose face could not be seen. The girls ran past the object and the beings, but soon found it had landed in front of them again, though the beings could no longer be seen. They had to run past it again. They arrived home, and then they returned with the mother of the Da Silva girls, but met the object flying toward them, 18ft above the ground. The UFO, its luminosity waxing and waning, flew in circles above the house before rising and vanishing.

HC addendum.
Source: Rubens do Couto Soares, SBEDV. Type: C

* * * * * * *

Location: Rome, Italy.
Date: February 26, 1966.
Time: 2:00 a.m.

Postal employee and painter Luciano Gasbarri woke up in the middle of the night when a bright light illuminated his bedroom and a loud voice called his name. Standing in front of him was a humanoid almost 2 meters in height wearing a silvery helmet and a coverall. On his chest area he had a scintillating multi-petal "daisy" that appeared to be moving and emitting flashes of light.

The humanoid said his name was "Nicodemo" and that he was an extraterrestrial that could materialize into a tangible body whenever he needed to. The helmet had a transparent visor and inside Gasbarri could see an "anatomically diverse" human face with glowing red eyes. The humanoid suddenly disappeared. After this encounter the witness would go into trances and paint bizarre scenes.

HC addendum.
Source: Moreno Tambellini, Archivio S.U.F. Type: E

* * * * * * *

Location: Near Drogheda, County Louth, Ireland.
Date: Spring 1966.
Time: Night.

John Farrell and Margaret Johnson were driving along a remote country road passing a local estate, when suddenly a huge figure appeared on the road ahead. They stopped the car and one of the witnesses looked out and saw a creature resembling a huge horse with a man's face with large bulging eyes.

Both witnesses were paralyzed with fear and could not move. The being had a huge hairy, man-like face and was standing across the road completely blocking the car's path. The creature stood there for a few moments then left.

HC addendum.
Source: Graham J. MacEwan, *'Mystery Animals of Britain and Ireland.'*
Type: E

Location: Point Pleasant, West Virginia.
Date: March, 1966.
Time: Daytime.

A housewife, who did not want her name to be used, was waiting in her car for her children near Point Pleasant School, when she observed a glistening metallic disk hovering low over the school playground. At an opening on its circumference a man was standing outside the object in mid-air. He wore a silvery skintight suit. He had very pointed features and very long silvery hair. He was looking into the schoolyard "intently."

She watched the object and being until her children arrived, then when she looked again, both the object and being had disappeared. Later a similar object and being landed in the woman's backyard, these were also seen by her two teenage children. There were electrical disturbances and "poltergeist" effects in the house. The woman did not tell anyone about the original incident, believing it to be a religious vision.

HC addendum.
Source: John Keel, *FSR*, Vol. 17 #3.   Type: B

* * * * * * *

Location: Edinburgh, Scotland.
Date: March, 1966.
Time: Afternoon.

A man talking a walk in the Royal Botanical Gardens suddenly experienced a state of heightened perception. He then became aware of a figure or nature spirit resembling the God "Pan" standing nearby. The being had a pointed chin and ears, shaggy legs with cloven hooves with two little horns on his forehead. He was apparently naked. The witness saluted the being that seemed startled by the intrusion.

During a brief conversation the being told the witness that he lived in the garden and that his task was to help the growth of trees. He also stated that they no longer were interested in humans since we no longer believed in them.

HC addendum.
Source: Colin Wilson, *'Poltergeist.'*   Type: E

Location: Brooksville, Florida.
Date: March-April, 1966.
Time: 1:00 a.m.

During a 'flap' of UFO activity in this area, a woman reported that local residents were being disturbed by inexplicable 'shrill screaming sounds.' She heard her dogs barking one night and when she looked out the window she saw a 'big hairy thing standing in the yard."

The thing was swinging its arms and the dogs were yapping to beat hell trying to get it. It started going back into the woods with the dogs still chasing it.

HC addendum.
Source: Mark Moravec, *'The UFO Anthropoid Catalog.'*   Type: E

* * * * * * *

Location: Los Alcazares Army Base, Murcia, Spain.
Date: April, 1966.
Time: 2:00 a.m.

A soldier at the local military base observed two little figures crossing a nearby highway and disappearing in a grove of date palms. They were 65 cm tall, humanoid in form but with pronounced stomach and buttocks, short legs and very long arms.

Their heads were shaped like inverted pears, and they wore what appeared to be goggles of a phosphorescent yellow color. The figures appeared to be unclothed and green in color; no sexual organs could be discerned. The soldier was in a state of panic and nervous excitement as a result of his observation.

The figures were similar to the one reported at San Feliu de Codines in September 1967.

HC addendum.
Source: *Center for Interplanetary Studies*, Barcelona, Spain.   Type: E

Location: Newport, Oregon.
Date: April, 1966.
Time: Afternoon.

16-year old Kathy Reeves and a girlfriend came upon a dome-shaped object "as high as a room" with a ruddy glow and smoke boiling around it, looking as if on fire. After this she saw in a meadow near her home, three creatures described as resembling tiny "tree stumps," orange, blue, white, yellow and pink colored. The three beings walked silently across the meadow and soon disappeared from sight.

By mid-October, a total of five persons in the vicinity had reported seeing moving stump-like creatures, at two locations east of Toledo Oregon. During the same time there was other phenomena reported in the area, including low level UFO sightings, strange globes of bluish light, poltergeist like phenomena and the reported sighting of a group of cyclopean beings by a local elderly couple.

HC addendum.
Source: Loren Coleman, Mysterious America and Humcat quoting Newspaper source.   Type: D?

* * * * * * *

Location: Near Corpus Christi, Texas.
Date: April, 1966.
Time: 11:15 p.m.

The witness was camping near a lake with a fellow scout. At night he was suddenly awakened by splashing noises and a strange odor. He looked out his tent door and saw a bright light gliding over the lake, sucking up the water. He was curious but frightened at the same time. He lay face down and watched the light move over the water. Worried, he tried to wake up his tent partner but could not wake him. He then moved back to the tent door but stopped quickly when he saw what he described as "two legged hairy monsters."

He backed away from the door but could still see their images because the light was now closer. He doesn't remember much more except that he has unending dreams of being pulled into the lake and emerging inside a cavern under the lake. There was air but it was hard to breathe and he could see moving shadows. The inside of the cavern had some kind of light source. In his 'dream,' he pulled out his scout flashlight with the rubber seal and pointed it toward the shadows and saw spider-like creatures, hairy with tall thin legs. His light appeared to bother them. The creatures then moved to his left and right as though they were trying to surround him. He could see their 'wet black eyes.' He held back his tears and tried to shout but couldn't hear himself.

Exhausted and with little light left they stick him with their pointy legs and smother his breath. He woke up soaked with sweat or lake water; he couldn't tell which. He is scared every night to sleep because he knows they come in his dreams and he can't stop them. The witness believes he was abducted but can't prove it. He has had medical problems ever since the encounter by the lake.

HC addendum.
Source: NUFORC. Type: G?

* * * * * * *

Location: Clayton, Victoria, Australia.
Date: April 6, 1966.
Time: 11:00 a.m.

In a confusing and covered up incident, numerous independent witnesses including dozens of schoolchildren and teachers from the local Westall High school, watched a metallic, disc-shaped craft land in a nearby field, then take off again, while several Cessna-type aircraft and other silvery "plane-like" objects circled the area. Some witnesses found a perfect circle of flattened grass on the ground while others encountered military or government personnel in the area who warned them to stay away.

Some witnesses described seeing a cow in the paddock, where the object came down. It was alleged to have been in such a distressed state that it eventually had to be put down. One student who arrived before the others was found to be in a dazed, trance-like state. Other schoolchildren saw the object on the ground and a normal looking man in white coveralls walking around it, telling everyone to stay back. Another man appeared, this one wearing a dark uniform with an emblem or a logo on it. One of the men was seen entering the object, while the other disappeared. The object emitted a loud humming sound then took off.

HC addendum.
Source: Bill Chalker, *'The OZ Files.'* Type: B

Location: Greenbush, Ohio.
Date: May, 1966.
Time: 1:00 a.m.-2:00 a.m.

13-year old Robert Carter was sharing a bedroom with his sibling, when one night his brother awakened him and asked if he felt an odd humming sensation, which he did. They both jumped up and ran to the window. Both then saw a large saucer shaped craft which covered an entire 25 acre field, (!) moving from west to east very slowly. Its altitude was approximately 15-20 feet over the field. From their vantage point on the second story window, they saw a side view of the craft. The craft was very bright and luminous silver/white in color and at the most it was approximately 100-150 feet from the witnesses.

They could see what appeared to be portals with creatures that appeared to be facing and staring at them. The craft slowly covered the distance of the field and then when it started going over a second 25 acre field directly to the east it accelerated at an extremely high rate of speed, going at a 40 degree angle. At which time they could see the perfectly round shape of the craft as it accelerated to a very high altitude. It then performed a 150 degree reversal, then a 70 degree angle towards the rear fields. All of this accelerated activity taking no more than 1-2 seconds. They woke their parents up and they found it very hard to believe, admonishing the boys and telling them to get back to bed.

The next day there were reports of a low flying object in the area on local television and newspaper sources. In an area near Milford Ohio, it flew so low that it broke tree branches. The witness claims that within three days an officer from Project Blue Book came to the farm and asked for an interview with them, but their parents refused. He told them that their neighbors directly to the east of them reported the same craft and that it had landed in their field. When they went back there the same day there was a large circular depression that appeared to be slightly burnt and covered almost the entire 25 acre field.

HC addendum.
Source: http://www.etcontact.net/newsite   Type: A

Location: Marisela-Caracas, Venezuela.
Date: May 10, 1966.
Time: 4:50 p.m.

A man observed the landing of an oval object and two beings, which came out of the object through a system of light beams. They used strange instruments to examine a number of objects, especially plants. They were 6ft tall, had oversized heads, and appeared bright and "transparent." Their eyes were slanted, their shoulders very broad. They wore no apparent weapon, but their belts were very wide and emitted light rays. They did not touch anything without first illuminating it with these beams. They went back aboard the craft "as if carried by the light."

HC addendum.
Source: Jacques Vallee, *'Passport to Magonia.'*　　　　　　　Type: B

* * * * * * *

Location: Cordoba, Spain.
Date: May 16, 1966.
Time: 7:30 a.m.

Farmer Manuel Hernandez was returning home from the fields walking on Los Morales County Road when at about 100 meters away from him he observed a disc shaped object. The craft was metallic and had a protruding rim that reflected the early morning sunlight. Carefully, he approached to within several meters of the object, which appeared to be about three meters in diameter. Suddenly out of nowhere and without any opening becoming visible on the object, several bizarre beings appeared. The humanoids flew around the object and over the nearby field.
　　Afraid, Hernandez began moving away from the area and noticed that the creatures appeared to be short in stature with bird-like wing protrusions and gray-green skin color. He could not distinguish any facial features, but did see that the strange humanoids wore dark coveralls and transparent glass helmets that covered their heads. Terrified he ran all the way home.
　　Later, upon returning to the site with several family members, the object and the bizarre creatures were nowhere in sight.

HC addendum.
Source: Jacques Vallee, *'Passport to Magonia'* and　　Iker　　Jimenez Encuentros, *'La Historia de Los Ovni en España.'*　　　　　Type: C

Location: Nizhnyaya Tunguska River, Siberia, Russia.
Date: May 17, 1966.
Time: 9:00 p.m.

At the time, Alexander Severov was head of a geological expedition tasked to research the banks of the river in search of the presence of cobalt. On May 12, a group of eight persons including Severov disembarked by helicopter in the area. The next day they walked a long distance during their search. On the evening of May 17, four of the group had stopped to spend the night. They pitched their tents, made a bonfire and began preparing dinner.

The sun had almost set as Severov finished entering notes into his diary when he suddenly heard a strong whistling sound, and felt a large object fly at a low altitude over the camp. The craft landed silently at about 100 meters from the camp. At first the group was filled with fear but in about 20 minutes it changed into curiosity and dared to approach the strange object. The object was described as shaped like a blunt cone about 30 meters in diameter. The surface of the cone was smooth with what appeared to be appreciable traces of burns and no visible apertures or openings.

When the group approached to within 40 meters of the object they felt warmth emanate from the craft. At this point the geologist took readings with a Geiger counter for possible radiation but found none. They then approached even closer to the object to about 10meters. Suddenly they heard a rustling sound and saw an opening in the form of an ellipse become visible in the bottom of the object; it was illuminated, shining a strange lifeless bluish-violet light.

In this aperture there was something similar to a person in a "spacesuit." The figure was a little above human height. In the bottom section of the aperture (hatch) was something similar to a ladder and it rested on the ground in front of the cone. The figure in the spacesuit walked down this ladder and moved in the direction of the witnesses. Strangely they didn't experience any fear, but the witnesses felt paralyzed, in a state of catalepsy unable to move their hands or feet. Behind the first figure appeared two more humanoids, these two walked down the ladder and approached the witnesses.

At about 5 meters from the witnesses, the first humanoid made an uncertain hand gesture which could have been interpreted as a greeting or as an order to approach. Then by using additional gestures, the humanoids invited the witnesses to follow them into the craft, the two other humanoids walked by the witnesses and stood one of each side of the group at about 5metersr away. The witnesses were now able to move and felt they had no other choice than to follow the humanoids into the craft. The first humanoid in the spacesuit entered the craft followed by the four witnesses (including Severov) and then by the other two humanoids. Alexander and the other witnesses then found themselves in an empty square room hardly more than 2 meters in height and 5 meters in width.

The room was completely empty; there was no sign of the humanoid that walked inside the object first. The walls were absolutely smooth without any traces of doors and the room was lit by a bluish-violet light from an unknown source. After the last geologist (witness) entered the room, the hatch closed slowly behind them, leaving outside the two other space-suited humanoids.

Suddenly a milky, colored gas began filling the room. As the odorless gas reached up waist level to the witnesses the room suddenly became extremely dark. The witnesses became terrified but after a while the room became light again. The gas was already gone and they could now see a rectangular-shaped aperture directly in front of them on a wall and inside they could see some entities which were watching the witnesses with interest. These entities were described as human-like but with leathery-blue skin tones and the size of their heads was a bit larger than humans. In strongly accented Russian the entities offered the witnesses a tour of their ship.

The witnesses were then led through a narrow corridor about 1.5m in width. Through this corridor the witnesses entered another room which had sparkling crystal white colored walls. In this room, the aliens asked the witnesses to undress and then subjected them to a careful examination of their bodies using a silvery plate over, apparently some type of scanning device. The witnesses felt a strange prickling sensation over the areas of their bodies were the silvery plate scanned over, according to Alexander it felt as if they were being pinched by hundreds of tiny needles.

After the examination the aliens somehow knew that Alexander was the leader of the group of geologists and he was then separated from the others and taken into another room where a conversation between the aliens and Alexander took place. During the conversation, the aliens explained to Alexander that they had made an emergency landing due to a malfunction in their propulsion system. The purpose of their expedition was to study humans, their ability to live (survive), and their social structures without direct intervention into their lives. They were especially interested in the increase of radiation in the environment of planet Earth which, as it seemed to them, could bring Earth's civilizations to complete ruin.

At the end of their conversation, the aliens told Severov that he must never talk about this meeting with them, since anyway, nobody would ever believe him and furthermore his comrades will never confirm the encounter since their entire memory of the episode would be completely erased from their memories. The aliens then released Alexander and warned him not to come closer than 100 meters to their ship.

When Alexander descended the ladder from the ship, the ladder was at once sucked back into the ship and the hatch was closed, leaving no visible seams. Near the bonfire, Alexander noticed his friends apparently sleeping on the ground and he rushed to them and attempted to rouse them. They finally came to their senses not remembering anything of what had occurred, their last memory was of sitting by the fire ready for supper. Alexander tried to explain to them what had occurred but they would not listen to him and made fun of him. In the morning Alexander visited the site where the UFO had landed but found not the slightest trace of the mysterious craft. After returning from the expedition, Alexander told the entire story to his supervisors, but his story was not believed since the other members of the expedition could not confirm it. After the incident all the members of the expedition except for Alexander suffered from repeat headaches and doctors could not determine the cause.

HC addendum.
Source: *'UFOs, Myth and Reality,'* September 1971, Mikhail Gershtein.
Type: G
Comments: Interesting early abduction account which has just recently come to light.

* * * * * * *

Location: La Serena, La Serena, Chile.
Date: May 21, 1966.
Time: 8:30 p.m.

Staff at the ENDESA hydroelectric plant, saw three very bright bodies approach the site of the Las Tres Cruces Mountain and land there. When the operator wanted to communicate the event to the Los Molinos substation, inexplicable interference prevented contact. Other people came to observe the three devices, that appeared to be changing color and form and which lost themselves in the firmament. Meanwhile La Serena hospital chauffer Manuel Muñoz Carvajal, 25, and another hospital employee Luis Hernan Astudillo Maria, had taken a medical team to a school high on the mountain, where Manuel developed altitude sickness. Luis apparently drove him back to Desvio Norte, where he received medical advice.

Driving back to Las Tres Cruces early the next morning, as they were driving on the steepest part of the route, a ball of fire flew across the sky in front of them. As they neared a ridge an object approached them, making a terrific racket. At first they thought it was a truck. When they stopped and switched their lights off, they saw it was a sphere blazing with light. With not much further to go they decided to continue on, the light from the sphere illuminating the interior of the truck. The object now had the appearance of a walnut, with two large projections on top. Tired, with his illness, Mario stopped, at which point the object came in close.

Mario could see six smaller objects, in pairs, with it, and in a cabin beneath the main object, the outlines of three motionless heads. Mario tried to go for a walk but felt paralyzed and fell asleep. He dreamt that a number of beings 1-1.2m tall were walking around the truck. They had large eyes, green skin, large round heads with long necks, broad chests and narrow waists, thin legs and skin tight clothing. He woke up and drove on and, as he rounded a bend, saw a little man with pointed "dog-like" ears, similar to those in his dream and pointed him out to his companions. The next night back at the school, he had yet another dream in which three of the beings entered the school and "placed in his head" the idea that he should not tell anyone.

HC addendum.
Source: Richard Heiden citing Antonio Ribera, *FSR* 14, 4, p. 16 citing DIOVNI Bulletins 8+9 and Petrowitch catalogue of Chilean landings.
Type: A & C?

* * * * * * *

Location: Near Fort Knox, Kentucky.
Date: Summer 1966.
Time: Daytime.

The witness was alone, sitting in a wooded area, when a man wearing a peculiar outfit suddenly confronted him. The man wore a one-piece outfit closed at the neck, long sleeves, and pants that seemed to go right into the boots. The beige outfit had a single metallic belt with a silver box attached on the front.

A small blue light flickered occasionally on the box. The man had very fine blond hair, and friendly pale blue eyes. He communicated with the witness; telling him he was from a world a great distance from Earth and that his name was 'Zo.' Eventually the being left, leaving behind a low buzzing sound that lasted a few minutes. The witness claims additional contacts.

HC addendum.
Source: Joseph Randazzo, *'Witness ET: The Contactee Manuscript.'*
Type: E

Location: Gambrill State Park, Maryland.
Date: Summer 1966.
Time: Evening.

On the outskirts of Gambrill State Park, a man only referred to as 'Jim A.' encountered a creature known as the "Dwayyo," as he was heading toward a camp site. It was described as a shaggy, two-legged creature the size of a deer; that had a triangle-shaped head with pointed ears and chin.

It was dark brown in color and when approached it made a horrid scream and backed away from the man. Jim described it as having an odd walk; as it retreated, its legs "stuck out from the side of the trunk of the body," making its movements appear almost spider-like as it backed away.

HC addendum.
Source: *'The Michigan Dogman: Werewolves and Other unknown Canines across the USA.'*   Type: E

* * * * * * *

Location: Grafenwoehr, Germany (West Germany at the time).
Date: Summer 1966.
Time: Late night.

The main witness was at the time, serving in the Army and stationed at what used to be a major N.A.T.O. training area located close to the Czech border. He was in the weapons platoon, made up of four armored personnel carriers, which were 13 ton, lightly armored, tracked vehicles (M113). Three of the APC's were 81mm mortar gun crews, and the one he was in was the fire directions center. He was a driver at the time. The group, approximately fourteen men, were on a training mission out in the fields by themselves.

The gun crews had set up their mortars and the fire directions center had laid in the guns, which is sighting them, using aiming stakes for the gun crews to put their sights on. He was tired at dusk and rolled out his sleeping bag in a nice grassy area under a tree and beside his APC. Another sergeant did also. He went to sleep quickly. Three men, one on guard duty, were watching a star or light in the sky apparently pulsing with different colors. Two of the men went on to their sleeping bags and the guard stayed up. His squad leader was on radio watch because they had been warned they might have aggressors trying to sneak up on them that night.

The next morning he awoke to find several men talking in a group about not being woken up for guard duty. Just then his squad leader emerged from the APC and said he had fallen asleep at the radios for some strange reason. This had never happened to him before. His platoon sergeant, one of the three watching the light the previous night, told of being in a dream state and hearing the guard yelling frantically for help. The sergeant said he couldn't move but could hear. About 9am they heard and saw the guard that was on first watch coming down a hill about 200 yards away. When he reached them he was hysterical and crying. He said; *"I thought all of you were dead."* He then recounted his story.

When two of the three men watching the 'star' the previous night went to bed, the guard went toward the tree-line, where they had set up camp. The guard then turned toward a clearing to the west of camp and said a craft had landed there in front of him. It had numerous lights of changing colors all down its side. The guard saw three figures emerge from the craft. The figures didn't walk on the ground, they seemed to be floating just above the ground and bobbed side to side. The guard yelled for them to halt. When they didn't stop, he thought about turning on his flashlight, but something in his head said "no." The guard grabbed an aiming stake and tossed it at them. (He was carrying a rifle but no live rounds were issued because they were not on a range at the time). He kept hearing a voice in his mind that said, *"Don't be afraid, we won't hurt you."*

The guard heard one of the beings in the woods behind him and felt he was being trapped so he ran away. He came upon another group of GI's some distance away and told them his story. He pleaded with them to come to his position and they wouldn't. They assumed he was intoxicated or something. He stayed with them until morning then came back toward his position. Looking down a hill he saw a silvery cigar-shaped craft still where it had landed the night before. He ran back to the other GI's and again begged them to come with him. They again refused to come. He waited a few more hours and then came back to his camp when all of them saw him. He told them the story, and someone found the aiming stake he had thrown.

The sergeant that slept a few yards from the (reporter) said he had the strangest dream of being examined in a brightly lit operating room. He also said he had an awful headache in the top of his head. Along with this, the grassy area where they slept appeared to have had a core sample taken from it. A round spot of grass and dirt a few inches deep was missing. The platoon sergeant recalled hearing the guard yelling desperately for help but he could not move. The reporter's APC had the infrared lenses cracked and everything electrical was burned out. He remembered the maintenance crew in the company asking what happened. They had never seen this kind of damage to a vehicle before. The APC had to be towed to base that night, later to be sent back to Ordinance.

The Colonel, their battalion commander, wanted some explanation for all of the damages. When he was told, he said he could not file an official report, because only one person was a witness to the event. The reporter's personal experience that night involved a watch he was given for graduation. It was anti-magnetic and glowed in the dark, but that night it stopped working and glowing. He knew the guard who was on duty that night and after the incident he was very emotionally disturbed. He was sent away and they never saw him again. The outfit involved was the US Army A Company 2nd Battalion 21st Infantry 24th Division.

HC addendum.
Source: MUFON CMS. Type: G?

* * * * * * *

Location: San Benito, Texas.
Date: August, 1966.
Time: 1:00 a.m.

The witnesses, Tony and his wife-to-be Maria, had been sitting in the car outside his mother's house when they saw this thing standing on a telephone pole. It was dark so they couldn't see well but he could see enough of it to know he had never seen anything like it. It was a weird big bird, bigger than a man, a yard wide, with wings folded around it, it was black in color. They could see that it was staring at them. They ran over to his mother's house. He has not seen it or heard it since.

HC addendum.
Source: J. Clark, and L. Coleman, *'Creatures from the Goblin World,'*
Comments: Interestingly, this incident occurred before the first events in connection with the Mothman began to occur in Point Pleasant, West Virginia (not all). Type: E

* * * * * * *

Location: Near Arhus, Denmark.
Date: August, 1966.
Time: 8:00 p.m.

On a Saturday evening, the witness was home alone and decided to go to the city and watch a movie. It was early and he bought a ticket for the 21:00 showing. He walked over to the theater at around 20:00 and stood at the crossroads next to the cinema. There he was met by two very tall men with long blondish air, and wearing strange long gray coats somewhat old-fashioned. He noticed that they had distinctly blue eyes.

He approached the man who seemed to know who he was and spoke to them in Danish. He had the feeling that the men were indeed of extraterrestrial origin. Strangely they seemed to answer the witness' questions before he would ask them, as if they had the ability to read his mind. He was asked to follow them to the city outskirts. It was already getting dark as they walked northwest of the city until they arrived at a pretty deserted location.

At this point he noticed a lighted area in the distance and when the witness (accompanied by the tall men) approached the area he saw a huge lighted and rotating vessel which was sitting on the ground. He estimated the craft to have been about 40 to 50 meters in diameter. A large ramp was lowered to the ground from the object and the witness was told to go up the ramp while the two tall men remained behind. When he walked up the gangway he saw two people waiting for him at the entrance to the object. He approached them and seems to have recognized them "from another reality." They hugged each other and there was joy and tears.

Once he went inside the object it was it he had been immediately transported to another world. He seemed to be now in a gigantic city somewhat resembling those depicted in the 'legends' of Atlantis. He saw huge buildings and all sorts of vessels flying around in all directions. He could not see any windows on the buildings but was somehow able to see 'magnificent views' within. His next memory was of waking up in Arhus where he lived and it was already Sunday. He found an unused theater ticked in his jacket pocket.

HC addendum.
Source: http://www.galactic.to/rune/ Type: G

* * * * * * *

Location: Segamat, Johor, Malaysia.
Date: August, 1966.
Time: Night.

The Malaysian Territorial Army has received orders to the be alert and to shoot on sight a "giant" which has frightened the town of Segamat, situated 160 kilometers to the southwest of the capital, according to a story in the "Utusan Melayu." In this story the so-called "giant" gave a good scare to several soldiers in their camp. One of the men said that he heard steps when he was on guard duty at night, and in the light of a bonfire, saw a monster six meters tall (over 18 feet).

The "giant" disappeared immediately on being seen by the sentinel. The inhabitants of the state of Kampong Bangis, 15 kilometers from Segamat, reported last week that they encountered footprints 45 centimeters (18 inches) long, 15 cm. (six inches) wide, and 12.5 cm. (5 inches) deep in the earth. A guard at a game preserve stated that the "giant" caused no danger to anyone.

HC addendum.
Source: Janet and Colin Bord, *'Unexplained Mysteries Of the 20th Century,'* also *'Diario de Las Palmas,'* The Canary Islands, Aug. 9, 1966.
Type: E

* * * * * * *

Location: San Diego, California.
Date: August 1966.
Time: Late night.

The witness was sleeping alone in her apartment when she was suddenly awakened by three beings that appeared in her bedroom. There were two men and one woman. They were human-like with bright fluorescent skin. The woman had long red hair and violet eyes. They communicated telepathically with the witness and told her to follow them.
She was floated out the window into a hovering "spacecraft." She was then placed in a "mind probe" chamber and the witness was examined with a glass-like cylinder that came down from the ceiling and covered her. Somehow the witness resisted their mind "probing," and next found herself back in her apartment.

HC addendum.
Source: Brad Steiger, *'The UFO Abductors.'*   Type: G

* * * * * * *

Location: Near Melbourne, Australia.
Date: August 11, 1966.
Time: Night.

Marlene Travers, 24, visiting friends "in the country," was outdoors after dark when a luminous silvery disc, 50ft across and 10ft thick, landed in a field only 30ft away. A door opened and a tall, handsome man wearing a metallic-green tunic stepped out. She felt compelled to obey him, and entered the UFO. Here he told her telepathically that she had been chosen to be the first Earth woman to bear a child by their race.
He had intercourse with her, and then escorted her out of the ship, but she accidentally tripped over some kind of switch, causing a flash that burned her ankles. She passed out and then found herself laying in the

field. When she returned to her friend's house she found that she had been gone for several hours. Later she was found to be pregnant.

HC addendum.
Source: Hans Holzer, *'The Ufonauts,'* quoting Frank Edwards.   Type: G

* * * * * * *

Location: Malvern, Arkansas.
Date: August 22, 1966.
Time: Night.

Six days after several UFOs were seen in the area; local residents reported seeing an eight-foot tall "thing," humanoid in shape that changed color from red to orange to yellow. A witness named Mr. Niles reportedly was able to snap a picture of the "thing" from his window as it passed by the house.

HC addendum.
Source: John Keel, *'UFOs: Operation Trojan Horse.'*   Type: D
Comments: The alleged photo has never surfaced.

* * * * * * *

Location: Stephensport, Kentucky.
Date: Autumn 1966.
Time: 1:30 a.m.

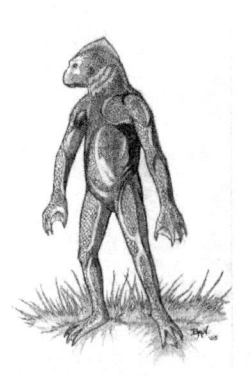

Joe, a 9-year old boy at the time, woke up to a loud thrashing noise outside of his bedroom window at approximately 1:30 a.m. He went to his window to peak outside, but there was nothing in view. Naturally, Joe went to his living room to investigate the sound that continued to bang against his house. When he came to the living room, he pulled back the curtains of the front door window. To his surprise, he was staring at a 5'6" to 6" tall man of amphibious characteristics, with dark brown scales covering its entire body.

The creature had webbed feet and hands, and little dark eyes. Joe recollects that the brief moment he seen the creature's face, it appeared to have huge rows of gills that flared out on both sides of its face, resembling that of a lizard. Jose doesn't remember the creature having nose, lips, muscles, or genitals, but there was a ridge-like feature starting from its forehead and running back over the top of its head.

After the brief moment Joe peered at the creature through the window, it quickly ran for the creek next to Joe's house. Joe, yet shocked, ran to and adjacent window to catch a glimpse of it as it ran away on two legs toward a creek about 75 yards from his house.

HC addendum.
Source: Michael Newton, *'Hidden Animals,'* and Charlie Raymond
Type: E

* * * * * * *

Location: Island Lake, Manitoba, Canada.
Date: Late Fall, 1966.
Time: Unknown.

A homemaker of Island Lake said that for several days, dogs had been barking ceaselessly and little children had been disappearing for hours at a time. The children told of "little men" who had been entertaining them, 3.5 tall, with large egg shaped heads and long arms. These little men, who wore shiny silver suits, reportedly gave the children candy which could be chewed on for days and still retain its flavor.

HC addendum.
Source: Wade D. Rowland and NICAP.   Type: E?

* * * * * * *

Location: Vardo, Norway.
Date: September, 1966.
Time: 4:00 p.m.

Near the Svartnes Ferry area an anonymous witness experienced total car engine failure. He then noticed a large reddish round object that appeared to be on the road just ahead of the vehicle. Two man-like figures wearing blue clothing and wide belts stepped out from behind the object and approached the witness, who by now had stepped out of the car. The witness described the aliens as having yellowish skin and six fingered hands.

In apparent perfect Norwegian, the aliens spoke to the witness about the poor conditions on earth and man's constant warfare. The humanoids then began to ask several questions on different subjects. The communication was done completely via telepathy. After warning the witness about the bleak future of humanity, they walked back to the landed object and boarded it. The UFO then rose and quickly left the area. His vehicle then restarted without any problems.

HC addendum.
Source: Ole Jonny Braene. Type: B

* * * * * * *

Location: Near Latacunga, Ecuador.
Date: September 3, 1966.
Time: Sunset.

Manuel Pereira, 15 and Jose Sotuyo, 14 were walking along a path high in the mountains when they saw strange lights maneuvering in the sky. Manuel frantically signaled the UFO with his flashlight. Using International Morse Code he sent the following message:
"Friend, please land."
He repeated this message several times. A few seconds later they heard a faint whirring sound and the UFO descended to within a few feet from where the boys were standing. The craft settled just above the ground and three long tripod-like supports telescoped downward. The glowing of the UFO dimmed until it was a dull white light, and then a ramp opened and lowered to the ground. Then three tiny man-like figures emerged from the craft and began to walk stiffly down the ramp.

The frightened boys were tempted to run but remained there. Just then they heard a loud voice that sounded strangely metallic speak; *"Do not fear us. Stay and talk."* Manuel and Jose, speechless, nodded. They stared in utter astonishment as the three little men in their suits of shiny brass-like material came toward them. A voice that seemed to come from all directions at once, asked them; *"What are you?"* The boys asked the little men where they were from but the question was ignored. For nearly an hour the questioning continued. The boys answered whatever the voice asked but whenever they asked a question they got no reply.

Finally the voice inquired, *"Would you like to come aboard our space craft?"* Both boys agreed to go inside. The little men in their gleaming brass-colored uniforms and pear shaped helmets led the way up the ramp. They kept turning around as if looking to see if the boys were following. Their features in the helmets were obscured because of a cloudy vapor, which they seemed to be breathing, so the boys had no idea what they really looked like. When they entered the craft they were surprised at the roominess of the interior. All around the craft were hexagon shaped sections like small cubicles. Tiny lights and buttons were to be seen on a console panel in the exact center. They saw no other little beings, although they had a strong feeling that other eyes were closely observing them.

The little men asked the boys if they would like to go with them, and added that they would not be harmed. But the boys replied that their parents would be worried. After several more questions by the little men, the craft began to make a loud humming sound and the voice announced that it was time to leave, that perhaps they would visit them again. Manuel asked for a souvenir from them to prove their encounter. There was a peculiar high pitched humming noise and one of the little men came forward and held a small cylinder in his hand. They were told to take it as a token, that it was a small hand held light, that whenever they wished for the light to come on, they merely had to squeeze it. The little men demonstrated. There was a brilliant light from the lens. Manuel removed its own flashlight and gave it to the little men, as an exchange.

Several minutes later on the ground, the boys watched the saucer-shaped object rise up noiselessly and vanish in a wink. Just as the boys began to hurry toward their homes, several helicopters swooped down from the night skies overhead, playing searchlights over the area. At the same time three Army jeeps came down the path at breakneck speed. They were interrogated numerous times by the military personnel and their strange flashlight device was examined and then taken away. Manuel Pereira and Jose Sotuyo vanished from their homes about a week before Christmas 1966, and were never seen nor heard from again.

HC addendum.
Source: Robert Tralins, *'Children of the Supernatural.'*   Type: G
Comments: Permanent abduction?

* * * * * * *

Location: God's Lake, Manitoba, Canada.
Date: October, 1966.
Time: Various?

A local teacher reported that flying saucers had been observed many times in the area and also around Island Lake, often landing and leaving behind imprints in the muskeg and grass. In addition, the teacher had been told of the "little people" often associated with these objects. These "people" were about a meter in height, dark-skinned, and wore close fitting dark coveralls suits with hoods. They carried a rod that gave off a beam of light, and they often "poked about" in the mud for unknown reasons.

Along with this, there were rumors of some of these "aliens" trying to snatch children in their sleep, causing more than a little fear in the area; some people were afraid to leave their homes at night.

HC addendum.
Source: Chris Rutkowski in *'Unnatural History, True Manitoba Mysteries,'* quoting APRO. Type: D or G?

* * * * * * *

Location: Palmer, Massachusetts.
Date: October 31, 1966.
Time: 7:20 p.m.

Stella Lansing (involved in other encounters) went to park her car and when her headlights were on the water, she saw a bobbing head or figure emerging from the water; it had a black skullcap. It scurried along the shore to get to the peninsular (approximately 60 meters from Mrs. Lansing's house). She backed up the car, put on the dim lights, and she saw a fuzzy mist by the house on the peninsula.

Then she saw an orange ball of light as big as a baseball or basketball there. She felt as if the hairs were raised on her arms, her body and the back of her neck and head. Then suddenly, this huge light, object or whatever it was swooped down in back of the house and swished over the lake. She waited to hear a splash, or a crash, but heard nothing. It was a reddish orange mass of light. A pair of neighbor boys had seen a large flash of light come down to the lake around the same time.

HC addendum.
Source: Berthold Eric Schwarz M.D. *FSR*. Type: C?

* * * * * * *

Location: Point Pleasant, West Virginia.
Date: November 1, 1966.
Time: Unknown.

A National Guardsmen at the armory near Camp Conley Road, saw a brown humanoid figure perched in a tree.

HC addendum.
Source: John A Keel. Type: E

Location: Cedar Grove, West Virginia.
Date: November 2, 1966.
Time: Evening.

Woodrow Derenberger was driving his panel truck home in Mineral Wells, West Virginia and was rearing the state Route 47 exit when he noticed a metallic gray object resting on the highway in front of him. He later described it as being somewhat similar to "the shape of a glass chimney of an old fashioned kerosene lamp lying on its side with a dome-like top." One peculiar aspect of the craft was that it did not touch the ground, but floated eight to ten inches above the road. Derenberger claimed that a tall man climbed out of the hovering craft and started walking toward his truck.

As the stranger approached, the alien craft immediately climbed into the air to a height of approximately 50 feet. The man appeared to be between 35 and 40 years old. He was fairly tall, and looked as if he weighed about 185 pounds. He had a dark complexion and dark brown hair that was combed straight back. His dark and shimmering clothing was covered partially by some sort of overcoat. The stranger reassured Derenberger that he would not be harmed and not to be frightened, but oddly, his lips were not moving at all. The peculiar looking man was apparently communicating telepathically. (Although this is rather common in contemporary contactee accounts, a statement such as this was not usually associated with UFO cases of the time.)

After introducing himself as *"Indrid Cold,"* the visitor said that he was from "a country less powerful" than the United States. Cold held a lengthy conversation with Derenberger, discussing topics such as politics, West Virginia climate, and family ties. All the while the visitor flashed a beaming smile, keeping his arms crossed with his hands under his armpits. This was a bit distracting at first, but no more so than conducting a conversation with somebody who did not move his lips when he spoke. At the end of the conversation, Cold told Derenberger that "at a correct and proper time, all of this would be revealed." The visitor then turned away from the truck and walked back to the craft, which by this time had once again settled to its former position. Derenberger claimed that he saw the arm of an unseen second occupant appear from the doorway of the craft to help Cold in. The object then flew away at an incredible rate of speed.

As soon as the UFO was out of sight, Derenberger started his vehicle and traveled; also at a fabulous rate of speed; directly home. After calming down and explaining his unbelievable experience to his wife and children, Derenberger called the authorities and the local media. Derenberger pointed out that Indrid Cold repeated to following sentence to him several times, *"We eat, breathe, and sleep, and bleed even as you do. We wish you no harm. We wish you nothing but happiness."*

HC addendum.
Source: Kevin D. Dee for NICAP.   Type: B

* * * * * * *

Location: Gallipolis, Ohio.
Date: November 2, 1966.
Time: 8:00 p.m.

 The witness was out behind her building getting ready to go home, when there was a sudden flash directly above her. A large cylinder shaped object then appeared and landed in the nearby parking lot. The object was completely silent and the witness was unable to move as two men descended from the object and walked towards her.
 The men were normal looking but heavily tanned with pointed noses, pointed chins, and high cheekbones, they wore coverall like uniforms. They asked the witness several mundane questions using a singsong high-pitched voice. They then walked back to their craft, which took off at high speed. The witness lived on a farm and had been having problems with missing cattle around the same time.

HC addendum.
Source: John A. Keel, *'The Mothman Prophecies.'*   Type: B

* * * * * * *

Location: Near Parkersburg, West Virginia.
Date: November 2, 1966.
Time: Night.

 Two men traveling by car on highway 77 watched an elongated object descend from the sky directly in front of their vehicle. They stopped the car and saw a man emerged from the object and walk over to them. The man was human looking and was grinning broadly. He was wearing a black coat and kept his arms folded out of sight under his armpits.
 The black-garbed stranger asked them several pointless questions before returning to the dark cylinder shaped craft, which quickly rose and disappeared into the sky. This incident occurred on the same night as the Woodrow Derenberger contact-landing case in the same general area.

HC addendum.
Source: John A. Keel, *'The Mothman Prophecies.'*   Type: B

Location: Clendenin, West Virginia.
Date: November 12, 1966.
Time: Daytime.

Five men were digging a grave in a cemetery near Clendenin when something that looked like "a brown human being" fluttered from some nearby trees and maneuvered low over their heads. It was in sight for about a minute.

HC addendum.
Source: John A Keel.   Type: E

* * * * * * *

Location: Salem, West Virginia.
Date: November 14, 1966.
Time: 10:30 p.m.

Newell Partridge was sitting at home when suddenly the TV blanked out. A real fine herringbone pattern appeared on the tube, and at the same time the set started a loud whining noise, winding up to a high pitch, peaking and breaking off, as if you were on a musical scale. It sounded like a generator winding up. Outside on the porch, his dog Bandit began wailing. Partridge picked up a flashlight and went outside to investigate. The dog was sitting at the end of the porch, howling down toward the hay barn in the bottom.

Partridge shined the light in that direction, and it picked up two red circles, or eyes, which looked like bicycle reflectors. There was something about the eyes that was difficult to explain. The eyes were huge, plainly visible at a distance of 150 yards. As soon as the flashlight picked out the "eyes" Bandit snarled and ran toward them. A "cold chill" swept over the man and he felt a wave of fear, which kept him from following the dog. That night he slept with a loaded gun beside his bed.

The next day he went looking for his dog. They found tracks. At the approximate position of the "eyes," he found a large number of dog tracks. The tracks were going in a circle, as if the dog had been chasing his tail. Then the tracks vanished, the dog was never seen again.

HC addendum.
Source: John A. Keel, *'The Mothman Prophecies.'*   Type: E

Location: Point Pleasant, West Virginia.
Date: November 15, 1966.
Time: Midnight.

Two young married couples, Steve Mallette, Mary Mallette and Roger and Linda Scarberry on a cold, clear and crisp night were out on a lark in the desolate TNT area, located on the Ohio River off Route 62, about six miles north of town. In 1966, it was a favorite with couples who liked to park and neck. On this night they were looking for friends and "chasing parkers," as Linda Scarberry related later. They made the rounds through the ghostly igloos without success and headed back to the unlocked gate at the old generator plant. They went over a small rise in the road, and the car headlights caught something that made Roger slam on the brakes.

Illuminated in front of them was a slender but muscular man-like creature, six to seven feet tall, with huge round red eyes, wings, and large hands. It had no definable head. The circular eyes looked more like they sprouted from the shoulders. The eyes about 2 inches in diameter and about six to eight inches apart, stared at them with hypnotic intensity. The creature was gray, or as Linda described much later, flesh colored with ashen wings. One of its wings appeared to be caught in a guide wire near the road, and it pulled at the wing with its hands. Later, Linda thought the creature was frightened, but in the heat of the moment it was the occupants of the car who erupted in fear and panic. While they screamed, the creature wiggled its wing free and wobbled with an odd shuffling gait into the generator plant through an open, broken door.

Roger hit the gas and tore out of the gate onto the road, heading for Route 62 back to town. Suddenly, the creature was in sight again, standing on a little hill, as though it had instantly teleported itself. The car headlights struck it again, and it spread its ten foot wings and took off straight into the air. It began following the car, matching its speed. Roger pressed the gas pedal down harder and harder until they were flying along Route 62 at 100 to 105 miles per hour. The creature effortlessly kept up, banging down on the roof of the car two or three times as they fled.

It made a high-pitched squeaking noise like a mouse. Somehow they careened down the road and its dangerous curves without mishap. As they grew closer to the bright night lights of town, the creature peeled off. They saw it once again crouched on the Ohio River floodwall, its legs and wings tucked in. Roger drove to the Dairyland and they tried to calm down and decided what to do. They could not agree on whether or not to report the creature to police and they argued over whether or not they would be labeled crazy or drunk or both. A decision was made to return to the TNT area, but partway back they decided against it.

When they turned back around they saw the body of a large dead dog by the side of the road. According to one of the witnesses, the winged creature jumped out at them as they passed the dog, went over the top of the car, and went through the field on the other side.

Back in town, the couples decided to notify the police and told their story to Deputy Millard Halstead. Seeing their genuine fright, Halstead took them seriously. He got in his patrol car and the two vehicles went back to the TNT area. The body of the dog was missing. There was no sign of the red-eyed monster, but when Millard turned on his police radio a strange garbled sound screeched out at high volume, as though someone were playing a tape recorder at fast-forward speed.

HC addendum.
Source: John A. Keel. Type: E

* * * * * * *

Location: Mineral Wells, West Virginia.
Date: Mid-November 1966.
Time: Various.

After Woodrow Derenberger had met Mr. Cold, supposedly from 'Lanulos,' on 2 November, two salesmen visited Mineral Wells and went from house to house with their wares. They weren't very interested in making sales. At one house they offered bibles. At another, hardware.

At a third they were "Mormon missionaries from Salem Oregon." One man was tall, blond, and looked like a Scandinavian. His partner was short and slight, with pointed features and a dark olive complexion. They asked questions about Woody and were particularly interested in opinions on the validity of his alleged contact.

HC addendum.
Source: John Keel, *'Visitors from Space,'* p. 56. Type: E

* * * * * * *

Location: Point Pleasant, West Virginia.
Date: November 16, 1966.
Time: 9:00 p.m.

Marcella Bennett, her two year old daughter Tina, and her brother Raymond Wamsley and his wife Cathy, had decided to visit family members who lived near the TNT area. They had read about the strange being in the newspaper, and they even thought it might be fun to go out and look for it. They paid a visit at the home of a sister and brother-in-law and decided to depart around 9 p.m. They walked out to the car, Marcella in the lead, holding a cigarette and her car keys and cradling little Tina in her arm. Raymond was the first to see the creature, coming toward them out of the sky. Brilliant lights filled the area. Marcella kept on walking toward the car, oblivious to Raymond's shouts to stop and return to the house. She started to unlock the passenger door, and as she looked down, she saw a man's legs that looked like they were covered with gray feathers. She did not see any feet. Like a slow-motion horror film, she pulled her eyes up. Standing only a few feet away from her was a giant man-bird, its head sunken into the shoulder area and tilted to one side. She saw no red eyes, but later said she might have been too frightened to notice.

Marcella thought her life was over. She had never before seen anything so monstrous. Raymond screamed at her to run. Marcella turned, took four steps, and fell down on top of Tina. She felt paralyzed. Another, distant part of her thought the creature would scoop her up by her back. She heard the sound of flapping wings. Marcella was at last able to rise and stumble to the porch with her daughter. She was skinned, bruised, bleeding, and burned by having also fallen on top of her lit cigarette. They all hurried into the house, where the children inside were screaming and crying in panic. Raymond called the county sheriff's office. It took about fifteen to twenty minutes for deputies to arrive; while The Mothman lurked outside the house causing more terror. It came up on the porch, pushed on the door, and looked in the windows. But the creature was gone by the time the deputies got there. The officers searched the area and found nothing.

Marcella was so traumatized that she could not sleep. Somehow, she felt the creature now had a link to her and would come back. After several days she went to the hospital and was treated for shock. She was unable to drive at night. Once she had to go pick her husband up from work late at night. Suddenly, she was certain that "it" was in the backseat, and she nearly wrecked the car.

HC addendum.
Source: John A. Keel. Type: D?

Location: Gaffney, South Carolina.
Date: November 17, 1966.
Time: 4:00 a.m.

Two police officers, C. Hutchins and A. Huskey, were driving in an outlying section of Gaffney known as the West Buford Street Extension when as they neared a right angle bend in the road, they suddenly saw a metallic object directly in front of them. This object was descending when they first saw it, Hutchins said, and was about twenty feet above the ground. He described it as being spherical, like a ball, with a wide, flat rim around it. There were no lights or portholes visible on it. It was completely dark, reflecting a dull gold color in the headlights of the police car.

The car did not stall as the object settled to within a few feet of the ground, both men got out of their car in a state of benumbed amazement. Later Hutchins estimated that the object must have been about twenty feet in diameter. A small door suddenly opened noiselessly on the underside of the sphere, he said, and a short ladder, four to six feet long, dropped down. White light poured out of the opening, but neither man could see anything in the interior. A figure appeared in the doorway, descended the ladder, and walked slowly and deliberately toward the two police officers. When the figure reached a point about fifteen to twenty feet from the two men, it stopped. "He didn't move stiffly," Officer Hutchins said. "He moved just like anybody else, but kind of slow...like he was taking his time. He wasn't scared of us or anything like that."

In appearance, the humanoid was about the size of a twelve-year-old boy, maybe four feet. He wore no helmet or headgear and was dressed in a gold suit with no buttons or zippers. His costume was shiny, like metal, in the reflection of the headlights; it was not self-luminous. The humanoid asked numerous questions and ignored the witnesses when they asked any questions. Hutchins could not remember seeing the feet of the creature. It was standing on high grass and the feet must have been hidden. Both men could not really remember the full context of the "conversation." Hutchins claimed the alien spoke perfect English "Didn't have any accent or anything. He acted like he knew exactly what he was saying and doing and didn't make any quick moves or false moves. He just stood there and talked to the witnesses." He wanted to know why both men were dressed alike. His speech was very precise. He pronounced each work very carefully.

When asked where he was from he just laughed. The meeting was brief, perhaps only 2 or 3 minutes. Then, Hutchins said the creature announced, *"I will return in two days"* he turned, walked slowly back to the ladder and climbed into the object. The door closed quietly and the craft began to hum, a soft whirring sound, like an engine with a muffler on it. The object rose slowly and vanished into the sky. A local councilman found numerous footprints at the site where the little man had stood. There was no return visit by the alien.

HC addendum.
Source: John A Keel. Type: B

* * * * * * *

Location: Cheshire, Ohio.
Date: November 17, 1966.
Time: Night.

On Route 7, a gray man-shaped creature with red eyes and a 10-foot wingspan pursued a boy's car. No other information.

HC addendum.
Source: John A Keel. Type: E

* * * * * * *

Location: Point Pleasant, West Virginia.
Date: November 18, 1966.
Time: Night.

Capt. Paul Yoder and B Enochs saw a huge bird-like creature, with big red eyes, in the TNT dump area. No other information.

HC addendum.
Source: John A Keel. Type: E

* * * * * * *

Location: Campbell's Creek, West Virginia.
Date: November 20, 1966.
Time: unknown.

Six teenagers saw a gray man sized creature with red eyes flying over the area. No other information.

HC addendum.
Source: John A Keel. Type: E

Location: Charleston, West Virginia.
Date: November 21, 1966.
Time: 10:15 p.m.

Richard West called police to report that a "batman" was sitting on a roof next to his house. "It looks like a man 6ft tall and has a wingspread of 6-8ft," he said. "It had great big red eyes. It flew straight up like a helicopter."

HC addendum.
Source: John A Keel. Type: E

* * * * * * *

Location: Point Pleasant, West Virginia.
Date: November 24, 1966.
Time: 7:15 a.m.

Mr. Thomas Ury was driving home in daylight when the 'Mothman,' a bird-like creature 6ft tall and with a 10ft wing spread, circled over his car. He speeded up to 70-75 mph, but it kept up with him. He had been in the area of the TNT dumpsite.

HC addendum.
Source: John A. Keel. Type: E

* * * * * * *

Location: Point Pleasant, West Virginia.
Date: November 24, 1966.
Time: Night.

Mary Myer, a reporter, saw the glowing red eyes of the "Mothman" when she visited an abandoned power plant in Point Pleasant, where it had been seen before.

HC addendum.
Source: John A Keel. Type: E

Location: St Albans, West Virginia.
Date: November 26, 1966.
Time: Evening.

Mrs Ruth Foster saw the "Mothman" standing on her front lawn. It was about 6ft tall and had a "funny little face" with "big red eyes that popped out." She screamed and ran into the house.

HC addendum.
Source: John A. Keel. Type: E

* * * * * * *

Location: New Haven, West Virginia.
Date: November 27, 1966.
Time: 10:30 p.m.

Miss Connie Joe Carpenter saw the "Mothman," a tall figure in gray, standing on a golf course. It unfolded 10-foot wings and flew directly at her windshield; she saw its red eyes; then it veered off and disappeared. Her eyes were red, swollen, and itchy for two weeks afterwards.

HC addendum.
Source: John A Keel. Type: E

* * * * * * *

Location: St. Albans, West Virginia.
Date: November 27, 1966.
Time: Night.

13-year old Sheila Cain and her sister were walking home when they saw a being standing by the road. It was 7ft tall, and gray and white with big red eyes. They screamed and ran home. It flew low over them.

HC addendum.
Source: John A Keel. Type: E

Location: Near Brooksville, Florida.
Date: November 30, 1966.
Time: Night.

A young woman was changing a tire on a lonely road when she was approached by a huge hairy, biped creature with large green eyes and encased in an eerie greenish glow. No other information.

HC addendum.
Source: *Fortean Times* #51, quoting John Keel. Type: E

* * * * * * *

Location: Tlalpan, Cerro del Ajusco, Mexico city, Mexico.
Date: December 1, 1966.
Time: Evening.

Housewife Cristina Leguizamo (involved in other encounters) was performing some domestic chores when suddenly a very brilliant light briefly illuminated the house and its surroundings. She then heard a humming sound and saw a bluish light outside. Upon opening the door she saw a humanoid that was floating at about 30cm from the ground. The humanoid had refined human features and was more than 2-meters in height, his skin was had a dark orange tint. He had long silvery hair down below his shoulders, was athletic in built with green eyes and double eyelashes that curled upwards. It wore a scaly outfit that emitted a greenish phosphorescent light.

In later contacts, Mrs. Leguizamo would learn that the supposed "scales" were part of the alien's body. She also noticed that the humanoid's fingers were connected by a membrane-like tissue. She was briefly invited into the UFO (not described) and reported that onboard she could see a pinkish mist and there was a sulfur like odor prevalent.

HC addendum.
Source: *Contactos Extraterrestres* Magazine #50, November 29, 1978, and 'Galeria Extraterrestre,' Carlos Guzman and Francisco Dominguez.
Type: G
Comments: Translation by Albert S. Rosales

Location: Gallipolis, Ohio.
Date: December 4, 1966.
Time: 3:00 p.m.

At the Gallipolis Airport, five pilots saw what at first they took for an airplane. It was a winged form about 300ft up, traveling at 70 mph without flapping its wide wings; it had a long neck and was turning its head from side to side.

HC addendum.
Source: John A Keel. Type: E

* * * * * * *

Location: Point Pleasant, West Virginia.
Date: December 6, 1966.
Time: Night.

Two adults, one a high school teacher, were driving near the local TNT dump site when they saw a giant gray man like figure with glowing red eyes.

HC addendum.
Source: John A. Keel. Type: E

* * * * * * *

Location: Cheshire, Ohio.
Date: December 7, 1966.
Time: 4:00 a.m.

Charles Horn (or Hern) was walking his dog by the Ohio River when he saw a red light across the river. At first he thought it was the light on the boat of a muskrat trapper and then realized that it was on the opposite bank. In the glare of the light he could see some very small figures moving to and fro. He called his wife and they both watched for several minutes before waking their neighbors Mr. and Mrs. Walter Taylor. Mrs. Taylor, a schoolteacher, also saw the red and orange lights, which flashed on and off, one light being directed towards the water most of the time.
After the others had gone in, Mr. Horn remained watching and saw the lights go out to be replaced by a bright green light. The object then rose straight up into the air and disappeared into the sky. The Horns were so stunned that they did not talk about the incident and sat silently through breakfast.

HC addendum.
Source: John A. Keel, *'The Mothman Prophecies,'* MUFORG Bulletin April 1967, p2 citing UAPRO Bulletin January 1967 citing Athens Messenger 12, December, 1966. Type: C

* * * * * * *

Location: Near Gallipolis, Ohio.
Date: December 7, 1966.
Time: Night.

Four women driving on Route 33 saw a brownish silver, man-shaped flying creature with glowing red eyes. No other information.

HC addendum.
Source: John A. Keel. Type: E

* * * * * * *

Location: Near Point Pleasant, West Virginia.
Date: December 11, 1966.
Time: Night.

An adult woman saw a huge gray creature with glow red eyes fly past her car.

HC addendum.
Source: George Mitrovic, *'UFOs an Atlas and History 1800-1977.'*
Type: E

* * * * * * *

Location: Near Leticia, Amazonas, Colombia.
Date: Late 1966.
Time: Daytime.

Ludwig Pallmann a health food sales representative and expert on nutritional plants was searching the jungles deep within the rain forest. Near the Mari River, his boat paddlers told him the next district was "very mysterious" and not well known. They mentioned that the tribe living there was secretive and was thought to be working with some "Americans" up there. While he was exploring the area, several indians armed with crude, hand-made weapons approached him.
He was then conducted to a small village of plastic like cones, resembling American Indian teepees, but the material was firm, like

metal. There he saw a couple of persons dressed in calf-length toga like garments. They were light skinned and seemed to be of a white race stock. Pallmann addressed them in English, which they seemed not to understand. He tried other languages without any results. Then one of them went in a hut for something and came out with a translating device. It was adjusted and they began to understand him. These Aryan looking light-skinned humans told him that they came from a planet much like Earth in many respects. They were operating this plantation site with local indigenous people in an attempt to develop hardier and higher yield species of plants and fruits. Pallmann stayed with them for nearly a month.

The strange visitors, that called themselves, Itibians from the planet 'ITIBI-RA,' traveled in 30-foot diameter disc shaped objects, ceramic in appearance. These ascended and descended vertically, and flew in horizontal flight with prodigious speed.

HC addendum.
Source: Wendelle C. Stevens.   Type: G?

1967

Location: NORAD, Cheyenne Mountain, Colorado Springs, Colorado.
Date: 1967.
Time: Unknown.

According to researcher William F. Hamilton III he met a certain M.J. in California who had been a captain with the office of Naval Intelligence. M.J. said he held a C-4 clearance. It, along with P-4 and S-4 was a specialty clearance. "S" stands for scientific. In 1967, his superior reportedly sent him to an underground facility (8 levels down) in the vicinity of NORAD headquarters at Cheyenne Mountain to check on the recovery and examination of discs that had crash-landed in the southwest. He had entered a corridor or tunnel to a larger area where he saw two discs through a large window.

One craft had a large opaque dome sitting on a ring atop of a disc with a flat metal finish. This particular craft had a symbol on its flange. He was amazed to see ladders and scaffolding all over the discs and men crawling on these, making various studies and measurements. Nearby were two alien-looking bodies encased in glass. The bodies were no more than 4.5ft tall, had slits for eyes, and normal proportioned heads (unlike the enlarged cranium humanoids). They were dressed in flight suits and appeared to be preserved cadavers. The entrance to the examined craft was out of his view.

Suddenly while absorbed in looking through the glass a sergeant major and a member of security challenged him for being in a restricted area. A lieutenant, observing this, also came over and asked to see M.J.'s credentials and his authorization for being in the area. M.J. showed his ID and authorization but he was still asked to leave the area. He stated that this incident sparked his further interest in the subject and when he had returned to his post, he often kept an eye out for any documents referring to aliens. One document he saw described an incident in which a live human-like alien was picked up in Death Valley, California (date unknown, probably in or after 1967). M.J. believes that Naval Intelligence has some authority in the secret UFO program.

HC addendum.
Source: William F. Hamilton III, *'Cosmic Top Secret: America's most secret UFO Program.'* Type: H

* * * * * * *

Location: Sayward Beach, Cordova Bay, British Columbia, Canada.
Date: 1967.
Time: Evening.

An adult housewife who lived at the shore was walking the beach and was beginning to come up on a "girl sun-tanning" at about 200 feet away. But she then noticed that the topless blonde sunbather had a tail for a "bottom." The lady tried to run to get closer, but the mermaid spotted her and slid over the rocks thereby and was gone when she arrived. Perhaps in an attempt to maintain her own sanity, the witness believed that it had not been an actual mermaid but rather someone playing a joke of some kind.

HC addendum.
Source: http://thebiggeststudy.blogspot.ca/ Type: E

* * * * * * *

Location: Manhattan, New York City, New York.
Date: 1967.
Time: Evening.

Professional violinist and soon to become UFO researcher Timothy Good was staying at the Park Sheraton Hotel and on a whim, he decided to conduct an experiment. For about an hour, he stood in the lobby sending out the mental message, *"If there are any space people around let your presence be known."* Good was amazed when suddenly his request appeared to be fulfilled. Says Good, *"Finally, as I was about to give up, a very healthy-looking man, about 5'10" came over, sat down beside me, and took out a copy of The New York Times from his attaché case."*

Stunned, Good mentally requested, *"If you are a spaceman, touch your finger to your nose."* The response was immediate and positive. Without once looking directly at Good, he did exactly as Good had requested in his silent message. Good was amazed and unable to react as the man quickly stood up and walked away. To this day he is convinced that he made contact with a human-looking extraterrestrial right in the middle of New York City.

HC addendum.
Source: Preston Dennett, *'UFOs over New York,'* p. 113. Type: E?

* * * * * * *

Location: Chartak, Uzbekistan.
Date: 1967.
Time: Night.

Tamara Smirnov and a friend were leaving the local cinema when they spotted a red light descending over the area. The light increased in size and as it approached their position, they could see that it was a capsule shaped object that as it descended meters from them appeared to create a strong air displacement.

The object seemed to have a transparent glass-like compartment on the front and inside, two helmeted figures sat, apparently operating some controls. One of the figures was a man the other a woman and both were human-like and very handsome. After flying above the cinema and shining a beam of light towards the ground, the object disappeared towards the east.

HC addendum.
Source: UFO Ukraine. Type: A

* * * * * * *

Location: Eldorado, Belo Horizonte, Brazil.
Date: 1967.
Time: Night.

Luis Muzio Ambrosio (a known medium involved in other encounters), was one night on the verandah of his house, when he observed a luminous object moving slowly across the sky at an altitude of about 1,000m. He knew it wasn't an airplane, nor was it anything known to man, since it was emitting light such that he had never seen before. Suddenly it came nearer to within 150 meters; and then stopped, swaying gently in the air for a moment as if it were trying to attract his attention and that of two friends who were present.

Afterwards it flew off rapidly towards the south of Minas Gerais. Two days later he saw another strange object near his house. It was not a celestial body, since it moved with an oscillating motion. Then it came down to within 300 meters and as it came closer, it grew bigger and the constant bluish-green light increased in brightness. It stayed in the sky for an hour. Then it began to flash on and off as if trying to transmit some message. He got a flashlight and exchange flashes with the ship and noticed with surprise that it responded to his signals. It was then that the object seemed to descend to land. In doing so it vanished from Muzio's sight, since it was at an angle he couldn't follow.

As the same thing continued to happen on the following nights, he went to his friend Jose Custodio de Oliveira, a town official in Contagem and told him about it all. One night round 19:00 they saw the object coming closer and flashing its light on and off continuously. They set off in the car towards Contagem and saw the object come down to a very low altitude; almost touching the ground. On this occasion they did not get really close. On another night near the town of Betim, they saw the machine at a distance of 400 meters. From their position they felt that the local temperature; normally about 20C; had suddenly dropped to about 5C and they seemed to be 'turning to ice.' After the object had flown away, they discovered that the place where it had landed was burnt and a circle of vegetation was dried out.

The next night they again saw the strange machine heading towards a deserted region not far from his house. An area which he believes to be a landing ground for these objects. When they got there, the object was about 1 meter from the ground, swaying in the air, and they approached to within 50 meters. They flashed the car lights and the object responded, but when he tried to get out of the car and go towards the object, it emitted a brilliant green light which shone directly on his chest and reflected on the car bonnet. There was a strange thing about this beam of light, it had a marked effect on one's cerebral control, dominating thought and movements.

Even though Muzio had the intention of getting out of the car and approaching the object, as soon as the light came on and struck him, his will power was completely dominated. The beam worked directly on his brain. The light was cold steel and magnetic; rather line neon, but much more intense and beautiful. Suddenly it crept up his chest to his head and this was when he heard the voice for the second time, saying,

"We are friends and we come from the planet Venus. Do not be afraid, we are on a peaceful mission and desire the well-being of the people of Earth. Be calm. Be calm."

For three months running they kept coming back, and once the ship became transparent (this was his impression), enabling him to see the crew using a sort of lever or control column, and one of them seemed to be luminous. The ship was round and more or less 15 meters in diameter, with a sort of cupola on top with six windows around it. Beneath there were three spheres set in triangular formation in a cavity in the fuselage.

When it came down towards the ground, it was of a reddish-orange luminosity, and when it flew up towards the sun it got redder until it was blood-red with aluminum tones.

HC addendum.
Source: Nigel Rimes, *FSR*.　　　　　　　　　　　　　　　　Type: A & F

* * * * * * *

Location: Near Caracas, Venezuela.
Date: 1967.
Time: Midnight.

 Mandy Klark was out late, watering his garden when he suddenly heard a whistling sound and looking up, saw a large, disc-shaped craft descending overhead. Afraid, he ran to the house but then heard a voice coming out of the object that instructed him to be calm and not to be afraid. He was told to approach the object.
 Now completely unafraid, he approached the now landed craft and saw an opened door and went inside. As soon as he entered, the door closed behind him and he found himself in a small room. Another door opened and he entered a larger room where a human like figure wearing a tight fitting white coverall awaited him. He was then given a tour of the craft and onboard he met ten men and eight women, all very human like. Only the first man he met spoke to him, the others were busy at controls and just stared and smiled.
 He was then invited into a large circular room by the "captain" and there saw a great lens and through it saw a large hovering cigar shaped craft apparently in space. He was then shown numerous complicated machines and was taken into a blue room where there appeared to be some form of static energy floating in the area. There he spoke to the "captain" for two hours.
 Later the craft landed on top of a mountain and there he was shown the outside of the craft. Nearby was a cave entrance and he was told that it was one of their earth bases. Soon Klark was brought back to the field outside his home and was told that they would meet him someday again.

HC addendum.
Source: Contacto Ovni.　　　　　　　　　　　　　　　　　　Type: G

Location: Rio Grande area, Minas Gerais, Brazil.
Date: 1967.
Time: Late night.

A local attorney fishing on the banks of the Rio Grande (a tributary to the Parana River) suddenly found himself enveloped in a very bright light, immediately after that he was in a strange room accompanied by three different women, all three human like with very fine human features. Emitting strange grunts, one of the women approached and grabbed the witness's shirt, clearly showing her intentions. At the same time he was overcome by an irresistible urge to mate with the woman. He had sexual relations with the woman and says he felt "unimaginable pleasure."

After he was done, he felt very tired and was later found by friends sleeping on the ground in the river bank. No other information.

HC addendum.
Source: Carlos Alberto Millan *UFO Especial 45*.   Type: G

* * * * * * *

Location: Miami, Florida.
Date: 1967 (or 1968).
Time: Various.

Two men turned up at a Miami hotel, were they befriended a chambermaid, telling her that they were from "the north of the continent," taking great care in specifying that they did not mean the lands of north of the United States, i.e. Canada. In a letter written to investigator Salvador Freixedo, the chambermaid and her husband detailed their experiences. One of them was tall, blond and amazingly knowledgeable, with a command of many languages and a mind-reader, to boot. His companion was short, Asian-looking and wearing an orange uniform; his general demeanor was that of a bodyguard to the tall blond.

According to the chambermaid, the blond produced what appeared to be a ball and stuck it to the wall in defiance of gravity. He then asked the woman to address it, which she did, noticing swirling waves of light within the device, which would follow her in the air every time she made a move. The chambermaid and her husband were able to see the tall blond and his companion on the beach during stormy weather, pointing what appeared to be cameras and other devices at the rough seas. While cleaning their rooms (the pair refused to leave their rooms while she cleaned), the chambermaid was able to see a suitcase filled with "billiard balls" pulsating with light, as if filled with electricity.

The two strangers disappeared as suddenly as they had come. Freixedo points out a similar case in the city of Puebla, Mexico, where exactly the same circumstances were repeated but with a destructive outcome; a house was almost entirely demolished as if by a battle so fierce that even the power conduits were torn out of the walls.

What did the strangers mean by "the north of the continent?" Due to the curvature of the Earth, is it reasonable to assume that they might have meant the lands to the north of the Americas; the polar icepack and Asia? Freixedo supports the view that references to the "Inner Earth" and subterranean kingdoms are to mean other-dimensional planes of existence accessible through certain underground mat-de-mat points.

HC addendum.
Source: http://inexplicata.blogspot.com/2012/03/realms-below-where-fact-meets-fiction.html   Type: E

* * * * * * *

Location: Frome, near Warminster, Wiltshire, England.
Date: January, 1967.
Time: Afternoon.

An 80-year old widower was standing in the garden of his secluded cottage smoking his briar pipe and contemplating the woods beyond when his reverie was suddenly interrupted by the arrival of a disc-shaped craft. It descended into a clearing and silently hovered four feet above the ground. Two figures clad in shiny blue-gray jumpsuits and black plastic helmets jumped down from the craft. They walked into the woods with a stiff gait "as if weighed down" and stood deep in conversation. Thinking that the craft must be "some new-fangled contraption of the air force," the old man hobbled towards the pilots to ask if they would like a cup of tea.

Seeing him approaching, one of the figures raised its gloved hand and promptly vanished into thin air along with its companion. The widower turned around to look at the flying saucer, and saw that it too had disappeared. In its place was a swirling cloud of mustard-yellow smoke. A shapeless light shot up from the smoke and streaked away through the sky. "I wondered if I was dreaming," the old man recalled, "but my pipe was still alight and hot. I took an extra big puff at it and pressed it against my cheek to make sure I was still awake. I don't believe in ghosts or any of that nonsense. It did not make sense to me, and it still doesn't!"

HC addendum.
Source: Arthur Shuttlewood.   Type: B

Location: Cape Canaveral, Florida.
Date: January, 1967.
Time: Unknown.

A NASA scientist from Cape Kennedy was fishing in a small boat off the Florida coast, when an object emitting a humming sound made several passes over his boat, coming so close he could have touched it with his fishing rod. The object hovered, giving off an intermittent flashing light. Then a sort of 'robot' floated down toward the boat, whose crew accelerated away.

HC addendum.
Source: Gabriel Green 1967, citing report by the Amalgamated Flying Saucer Clubs of America. Type: C

* * * * * * *

Location: Malmesbury, near RAF Hullavington, Wiltshire, England.
Date: January, 1967.
Time: 6:00 a.m.

Mr. H. Tyrell, 64, was taking his usual way to work on the A429 and had turned his car right onto the main road, just past Burton Hill House School for Physically Handicapped Children. His headlights were not full on and he suddenly saw the figure of a man appear in the middle of the road; he seemed to be dressed in gray coveralls and a bright buckle shone near his waist.
Fearing he might hit the man, though he was not driving fast, he tried to pull up, but said it seemed he could not stop the car. Suddenly the man in gray turned and his face could be seen. He seemed a sharp-featured man of about 40, with a very white face. He turned sideways towards the verge, raised his arm, and just vanished in plain sight.

HC addendum.
Source: Mike Rogers, *'The Warminster Triangle.'* Type: E

Location: Vienna Woods, Austria.
Date: January, 1967.
Time: Evening.

A woman was walking in a wooded area when suddenly she became paralyzed, unable to even move her eyes, as a strange object descended. It resembled two saucers edge-to-edge, with a domed top and three spherical "landing gear." Three thin but strong men, 1.5–1.65m tall descended via a ladder. They wore dark brown one-piece suits and transparent helmets, through which humanoid faces could be seen.

One held a small box, which flashed a red beam at the witness. When the figure pressed a button on it, it enabled the witness to hear them speaking in English. They asked if she would like to visit their planet. Then flashed another light and gave a warning about the wickedness of humanity. They warned her she might die of cancer as she was of no further use to them, then re-entered the craft "with a smile of either mockery of pity."

HC addendum.
Source: Peter Rogerson in *Magonia*. Type: B

* * * * * * *

Location: Near Elfers, Florida.
Date: January, 1967.
Time: Night.

Four teenagers parked in an isolated area suddenly noticed a terrible smell around them. Moments later a short hairy chimp like creature jumped onto the hood of the car. The hairy creature was greenish in color and had glowing green eyes. The witness started the engine and the creature ran back into the woods. Later a sticky green substance was found at the encounter site.

HC addendum.
Source: John A Keel, *'Strange Mutants...'* Type: E

Location: Point Pleasant, West Virginia.
Date: January 11, 1967.
Time: Daytime.

Mrs Park McDaniel was outside her home when she saw what she first took to be a small plane approaching; as it drew closer, she saw it was man-shaped and had wings. The creature swooped low over the witness and circled above a nearby building before going out of sight.

HC addendum.
Source: John Keel. Type: E

* * * * * * *

Location: Near Howard Lake, Minnesota.
Date: January 25, 1967.
Time: 4:30 a.m.

Harold Lenz was driving to work in Winsted, when the engine of his pickup truck stalled. He got out to check under the hood and saw a brightly lit luminous object, 75 feet long by 30 feet wide, approach and land on three legs on the highway. It made a loud whirring noise.
Something like an elevator descended from the bottom, and a man walked out dressed in a silver-blue, tight-fitting coverall suit with a "fishbowl" helmet over his head. He was about average height and human appearing. The occupant seemed to examine something on the object, and then got back into the UFO, which took off. Duration was 3-4 minutes.

HC addendum.
Source: USAF Blue Book Files. Type: B

* * * * * * *

Location: Pittsfield, Pennsylvania.
Date: January 25, 1967.
Time: Around 6:00 p.m.

On January 20 at 2330 Mrs. Walter J Kushner and her two daughters, Susan 17, and Tanya 14, and a close friend of the girls, Marianne Williamson 16, witnessed a brilliant aero form with a distinct disk shape drop below the cloud cover and execute a sharp turn before cruising parallel to a mountain ridge while the group was returning to their residence. All members of the party were awed by the lack of the sound and high speed of the object.

On January 21, 1967 at 2:00 a.m. Susan, Tanya and Marianne, were enjoying a typical teenage pajama party and were doing anything but sleeping, when all three girls simultaneously spotted a peculiar light shimmering through the closed curtains of Susan's bedroom. Without warning, the drapes parted of their own volition and a small triangular object, hovering a few feet from the house, began beaming pinkish light of a painfully brilliant intensity into the bedroom. When the triangle moved to the second window, the curtains repeated their opening act and the intensity of light emanating from the object increased several fold.

At this point the girls became quite frightened and decided to get the hell out of there. Suddenly, all three girls became paralyzed and weak, unable to cry out or do more than whimper helplessly. Not able to move, their terror at this point became so strong that prayer became a viable option. After a few more torturous moments that seemed like an eternity, the light effect dissipated and their freedom of movement was restored, although a weird dizzy sensation continued to haunt the girls for the better part of an hour.

On the 28th things were back to normal when shortly after the dinner hour, two men arrived at the Kushner household. They identified themselves as military investigators and flashed what appeared to be USAF identification. Mrs. Kushner described the ID card as having black printing on a durable white stock. Both men wore tan trench coats, which they kept buttoned from knee to collar. The taller of the two, who, according to the family's testimony, did all the talking, was described, as having blond hair, green eyes, was thin and deeply tanned. The other gentleman was heavyset with dark hair, piercing blue eyes and was also deeply tanned.

The men were very polite but very insistent about one thing; they wanted every shred of information about the girl's experience. Neither parent could explain why they allowed their children to be so intensely grilled by these "government agents." The men moved about the house with apparently total knowledge of the whereabouts of rooms, furniture, objects, etc. Their clothing looked as if it had been purchased 10 minutes before and the bottom of their shoes seemed un-walked on. When the mystery men left, they backed their vehicle out onto the roadway turned off their headlights and powered away down the road. At one point one of the men was seen writing strange symbols in vertical columns, starting from the left, going down one column, up the next, down the third, this on a small booklet. (Typical MIB report of the period).

HC addendum.
Source: Robert A. Goerman,   http://www.worldofthestrange.com/
Type: E

Location: South Ashburnham, Worcester, Massachusetts.
Date: January 25, 1967.
Time: 6:00 p.m.

Shortly after sunset, Betty Andreasson, her parents and her seven children were frightened by a pulsating red-orange light outside their backyard. This was accompanied by a "silent vacuum" and failure of lights in the house. Four entities appeared before Betty in the kitchen, after passing through a closed door. The beings were nearly identical, with large, baldheads, gray skin, large wrap-around eyes with hazy, light gray interiors (later dark pupils were observed), "scar like" mouths, and holes for noses and ears.

They wore sparkly, dark blue uniforms with a lighter blue "Sam Browne" strap. They had bulky hands, possibly gloved, and wore boots. Their leader, 'Quazgaa,' was slightly taller and his suit was darker that the others. The reported height of the entities was 3 ½ and 5 ft, at different times during the encounter. Quazgaa began telepathic communication with Betty in the kitchen; he asked her for some food (and was offered some leftover meat; they declined, asking that it be cooked) and she cooked some meat on the stove. But she determined that their food was "knowledge tried by fire," and they went into the living room (with her) where she handed the leader a Bible. He created several copies and handed them to the crew. He in turn handed her a thin, blue book containing their form of knowledge, which remained in her possession for 9 days.

During these proceedings, the other family members were sitting in the living room in a state of suspended animation. (Her father, who had earlier gone into the kitchen pantry to observe the lights, remained there; it was later suggested that a fifth entity had joined him and, later, remained behind during the "onboard" experience.) However, Betty's daughter remembered and confirmed part of the above testimony. Betty was then "talked into" going on board the entities craft. She was on board an estimated 2 hr. During this time she was led through several rooms, was given a physical exam in which they "tested her for light," inserted a needle in her nostril and navel and scanned her with an eye-like device. (She was then placed in an enclosed seat, which was filled with a soothing liquid, in which she presumably "prepared" for an unusual journey; accompanied by two "guides," fore and aft,) she visited an alien realm where she saw cities, strange bug-eyed creatures, and a vast ocean.

She had a traumatic religious experience, which led her to identify the beings as "angels." Returning from the journey, she was led back to her home by two of the entities, one named 'Joohop;' her family was still in a state of suspended animation. (The daughter later recalled being "baby sat" by the one remaining entity.) The beings, holding spheres of light in their hands, proceeded to put the family to bed, the abductee being the last. The incident is attended by automatic writing, speaking in strange tongues, visions, message transfer and telephone "contact," some of these occurring under hypnosis and during the investigation. Betty was found to have several previous contacts and numerous post 1967 contacts also.

HC addendum.
Source: Ray Fowler, Joe Santangelo, Jules Vaillancourt, David Webb
Fred Youngren and Dr. Herbert Edelstein. Type: G

* * * * * * *

Location: Near Knox City, Missouri.
Date: January 29, 1967.
Time: 10:00 p.m.

Mrs. Enid Campbell saw from a window, what at first she took to be a full moon, but as it moved closer she could see that it was a spherical object, white in color like a frosted light bulb, with a shiny gold horizontal ring around the center in which were numerous round holes. The object came up to within several feet of her window before stopping, and through its semi-transparent material she could see a control panel with a lever on top, and two occupants, one seated at the panel, the other standing. They wore "shiny, silvery wet suits."

She called her sons Gene, 18, and George, 14, who arrived at the window in time to see the object as it rose and moved away. While it hovered nearby, two smaller white luminous spheres approached and entered through an opening, after which the holes in the central ring jetted out red fire. Then the object ascended vertically and disappeared. The snow on the ground under the spot where it hovered was melted; and the area over which the object approached the house failed to grow plants, while the plants elsewhere grew normally.

HC addendum.
Source: Ted Phillips for MUFON. Type: A

Location: Tuscumbia, Missouri.
Date: February 14, 1967.
Time: 7:00 a.m.

Claude Edwards, a 64-year old farmer, saw a gray-green dome shaped object about 15 feet wide in his fields. He thought at first it was a parachute, but as he neared it, he could see that it was resting on a shaft about 18' wide that extended downward from its base. Around the edge of the dome were a number of bright, multicolored lights of oblong shape. Beneath the object were visible several entities less than a meter tall, also gray-green in color, moving about rapidly, with quick moving "lever or arms," very wide-set eyes, and no visible legs. He also noted a protuberance where the nose and mouth would have been.

The witness walked to within 30 feet and threw two stones at the object, which bounced off an invisible wall between him and it. Walking up to within 15 feet, he was able to feel the pressure of this invisible barrier. The surface of the object was seamless, like gray-green silk. By this time the little creatures had disappeared inside the object, and it rocked back and forth several times, and then took off silently, disappearing towards the northeast within seconds.

He further described the creatures as appearing "like a penguin, not human; without a visible neck." The object, "it just looked like a big shell, grayish-green in color. There were still ground traces at the site three months after the encounter. At the site the soil was extremely dehydrated in contrast with the surrounding soil. At the center there was a depression 20mm deep sloping to 30mm in the central area.

HC addendum.
Source: Ted Phillips for APRO and MUFON.   Type: B

Location: Haverhill, Massachusetts.
Date: Spring 1967.
Time: 2:00 a.m.

Hearing a loud whirring noise, Mrs. S woke her husband, who went out and saw a strange object 50 feet in diameter hovering 25 feet above a nearby pond. Shaped like two metallic saucers face to face, and of aluminum like appearance, it had a clear, bubble like canopy on the edge of the upper disc facing him. From elongated holes around the rim, orange flames were issuing. Inside the canopy, illuminated by a greenish light, he could see the silhouettes of two "lobster claw-like" heads.

The witness walked toward it yelling and waving his arms, where upon it moved slowly and silently away; then it began to spin rapidly with a loud whirring sound, tilted at an angle of 30-45 degrees, and took off at a very high speed. He noticed a smell lingering in the air like that from a lighted match.

HC addendum.
Source: Raymond Fowler for NICAP.   Type: A
Comments: Entities with "lobster-like clawed hands" were also reported during the fall of 1973 humanoid wave in the US.

* * * * * * *

Location: El Yunque, Puerto Rico.
Date: Spring 1967.
Time: 10:45 p.m.

Several college students, among them 22-year old Ramon Quiñones, and two teachers had gone camping near the summit of El Yunque. That night they were all sitting around a campfire singing while Ramon played his guitar. Suddenly they all heard a very loud buzzing sound that originated from an unknown source. It lasted 15 minutes. Everything became quiet, and they all resumed their singing. Suddenly they heard footsteps coming from the nearby brush. As the footsteps approached the group, they all stood up and suddenly were able to see a very tall luminous figure that quickly crossed a path in front of them, disappearing into the brush.

Ramon and a teacher named Gonzalez decided to go into the brush and investigate; Ramon took his guitar with him. Soon Gonzalez returned but there was no sign of Ramon. Gonzalez explained that they had become separated in the thick shrubbery. Suddenly as the group stood around looking for Ramon they all saw the strange figure appear again. The figure was described as over 6ft tall, very thin, with long dangling arms that reached to his knees, wearing a tight-fitting bright silvery outfit that gave off a white fluorescent light. The bright light prevented the group from seeing the creature's facial features or the head, which appeared round. The being stood staring at the group for about 15 minutes during which time they all felt paralyzed as if in a trance.

Soon the luminous figure walked slowly backwards and disappeared into the brush. The group regained their ability to move and some of them fled in panic, while others stayed behind looking for Ramon Quiñones. Only his guitar was found propped up against the trunk of a large tree. To this date nothing has been heard of Quiñones. The remaining group was allegedly told by federal authorities not to talk to anyone about the incident, that this was a "common occurrence" in El Yunque.

HC addendum.
Source: Jorge Martin, *Evidencia Ovni #7*.   Type: E or G?
Comments: This case appears to involve a "permanent" abduction.

* * * * * * *

Location: Mexico City, Mexico.
Date: March, 1967.
Time: Midnight.

Maria Cristina Leguizamo said she was listening to the radio when a flying saucer appeared in her backyard. Communicating by telepathy, an "extremely handsome man, with green eyes and silver hair to his shoulders" invited her to take a ride in his craft. She was required to take off her shoes first. The humanoid told her that he came from "the Green Planet" and that "neither Russians nor Americans will ever arrive at the moon." Also, a planet named, 'Hercolubus' exerts "an irresistible force on the planet Earth, attracting it little by little toward the sun."

HC addendum.
Source: Humcat quoting newspaper source. Type: G

* * * * * * *

Location: Near Ponce, Puerto Rico.
Date: March 31, 1967.
Time: Night.

On the evening of March 31, Lester Rosas, acting under a strange compulsion, boarded a bus and took it to the end of the line, which happened to be along a coastal area. He kept walking until he reached a deserted part of the beach. Unsure why he was there, he felt an odd sensation as a man who had shoulder length hair and was dressed in a close fitting garment approached him. The man extended his hand, but when Rosas tried to shake his hand, the stranger withdrew it after a mild pressing of palms.

The stranger spoke in Spanish, and told Rosas that he was from Venus and that his name was 'Laan-Deeka.' He then began to discuss the subject of reincarnation, saying that advanced earthlings who obey nature's laws are permitted to live their next lives on spiritually developed planets. The stranger then led Rosas the other side of a small nearby wall, where they witnessed the materialization of a disc shaped object. A door slide open, and a woman emerged to engage Rosas in a palm-to-palm handshake. "Her hair was long and fair, and she had a fantastic figure; I estimated her measurements at 5'4" and 37-27-35." She introduced herself as Laan Deeka's fiancée.

The couple appeared to be no more than twenty years old, but their manner suggested wiser, older persons. They had high foreheads and slightly slanted eyes, his green, hers blue. There was a musical sound to their voices, a sense of joy in their speech and action. The three then entered the ship and flew off to Venus, which proved to be a paradisiacal world reported by other contactees.

HC addendum.
Source: Jerome Clark, *'Extraordinary Encounters.'* Type: G

Location: Gallipolis Ferry, West Virginia.
Date: April 1, 1967.
Time: 10:00 p.m.

John Keel and Mary Hyre observed a red light circling the woods and fields at treetop height. When it got closer they saw it was a window on a dark object about 15m above the ground. Keel thought he saw a human figure in the window. When Keel flashed a flashlight at the object, it shot straight up, the red light going out.

HC addendum.
Source: John Keel, *'The Mothman Prophecies,'* p. 130.   Type: A

* * * * * * *

Location: Near Gallipolis Ferry, West Virginia.
Date: April 7, 1967.
Time: 10:15 p.m.

Mabel McDaniel, John Keel, and two other women went to a hill, when they spotted the usual reddish glow on a nearby hill. A second one popped up a short distance from the first. Keel flashed his light at them but nothing happened. So he climbed a fence and walked into a field to try to get a closer look. As he crossed the field he suddenly noticed a pale bluish ball of light hovering high in the trees of an orchard behind the nearby farmhouse.

The light moved about from tree to tree as though it were following Keel's movements. He flashed his light at it and it flared with a dazzling brilliance, dimmed, and vanished. The lights on the southern ridge also brightened for a moment and then went out. Coming back to the car, Keel found all three women in a very frightened state. Later they related how they had seen a very tall man in the field, which climbed over a fence then crossed behind their vehicle. Terrified, they locked the doors and ran the windows up.

HC addendum.
Source: John Keel, *'The Mothman Prophecies.'*   Type: C?

Location: San Cataldo, Italy.
Date: April 4, 1967.
Time: 8:00 p.m.

The witness had walked out to his terrace under a light rain and upon opening the terrace door, he was confronted by a hovering metallic disc-shaped object about 80 meters in diameter. In front of the object stood three men wearing tight-fitting overalls. They appeared to have been looking at a caged bird nearby. The men were human-like and from the center of their chests they emitted a green beam of light.

They made an awkward hand gesture towards the witness upon seeing him. The witness watched, unable to move as the three beings entered the object through an opening in the bottom, they went up in a beam of light as if walking up an invisible ladder. The object then departed at high speed.

HC addendum.
Source: Maurizio Vega, Itacat.   Type: B

* * * * * * *

Location: Between Ramstein AFB and Mannheim, Germany.
Date: May, 1967.
Time: Unknown.

A UFO was detected by radar in the vicinity of Ramstein UFSAF Air base in Germany. A couple of interceptors were immediately scrambled. The UFO was chased, but it escaped the fighters. Accidentally and quite unexpectedly for the alien crew, the alien craft was shot down by a surface to air missile from Ramstein AFB, somewhere between Mannheim and Ramstein. Possibly the attention of the alien crew was distracted by the aircrafts and they did not react in time to the missile launch from the ground or have enough time to disable it.

An explosion of an AA-class missile knocked the disk down. An American retrieval team quickly rushed to the scene from Ramstein and found the flat disk-shaped object, about 10 meters in diameter, resembling two flat plates joined together at the rim, the upper plate higher than the lower one. In the lower section the disk had a cylinder shaped central prop or pedestal-like section moving inside and outside the disk, with the encircling band beneath segmented squares. A crew of two aliens was found inside. Both were killed by the explosion and hard impact. They were tall, about 2 meters in height, of the "Nordic" blond type, with long red hair, slanted blue eyes, dressed in tight-fitting silver metallic suits.

The disk was moved in top secret by sea to the USA, and then moved to the S4 base in Nevada at the Nellis range in 1970. The first disk of the very same type was recovered in 1958 in Vietnam; so, using past experience, a team of experts was successful in its examination of the engineering section of the disk. The disk from Vietnam also contained two "Nordic" occupants on board. Both disks were witnessed and drawn by Derek Hennessy (a guard from US Navy Seal Team 6) at the S4 underground base, level 2 in 1987, bays 2 and 3. In February 1993, the disks were moved to a new underground base on the White Sands range, New Mexico, as well as the other disks from S4. These disks belonged to the planet 'TROON' civilization, Tialubba star system.

HC addendum.
Source: Anton Anfalov, Lenura Azizova, also Leonard H. Stringfield and Col. Ret. Philip J. Corso. Type: H

* * * * * * *

Location: Near Marrakech, Morocco.
Date: May, 1967.
Time: 2:00 a.m.

After a full day of work herding sheep and other animals, a Berber named Mohamed was lying in his hut on the carpet trying to get some rest. He had two dogs that slept in an attached enclosure to his hut. At around 2 in the morning, the dogs began to bark which awakened Mohamed. As the dogs continued to bark he got up and decided to investigate the cause of their nervousness. At first he saw nothing abnormal but the dogs continued to bark, running quickly back and forth in the enclosed patio.

Mohamed then went out to check the fields and look around, and still saw nothing unusual. He assumed the dogs had seen a cat or some wild animal. He returned to the court and calmed the dogs. They were silent for a few minutes but once Mohamed returned to his room, they started to bark again. Mohamed then decided to look out the window located in the back of the house, on the opposite side, just for safety measure. Then to his surprise, he saw under the light of the moon in a nearby field, a sort of 'dark mass' which has a slight glint like aged aluminum. The dark mass was the size of the "family Fiat" but nevertheless with a sort of elongated shape, more precisely an oval shape with a sort of dome on top. The object appeared to be resting on the ground on a sort of dark metallic "barrel" about which placed the object actually about 1-meter from the ground. The object was about 5 meters in length and 3 meters in height at its center. He could see no doors or windows. Suddenly Mohamed saw a figure walking towards the object, a character which he likened to creatures spoken of in the 'Koran,' like the Djinn who are said to come from other dimensions and can vanish at will.

The figure or character was the size of a child of 15, lean, and moved on two legs. It had two dangling arms and ahead that appeared to Mohamed to be "enormous." Due to the darkness and the poor lighting he could see no additional details, only a black silhouette which was moving toward the object. If it was wearing any clothing, it was dark and tight-fitting. The figure walked behind the object to its left and disappeared. He walked in a normal pace. Mohamed expected the figure to appear at the other end of the object, but it did not. He had never seen such an object or being, he had no idea what it could be. The dogs meanwhile continued to bark. At this point his wife was awake, but could see nothing, and his children remained sleeping. Mohamed continued to observe and seemed unable to take any action. He remained quiet, waiting to see what would happen next.

Two minutes after the short dark figure had disappeared behind the object, the object began to rise from the round; presumably the figure had entered the object from the opposite side. In the air, the object had a clear oval-shape, the landing platform or "barrel" had disappeared. The object rose to about 10 meters in height, remained motionless for about two or three seconds and then left horizontally with a gradual rise, disappearing north and along the Atlas Mountains towards Ourika. Its speed was relatively fast, disappearing in less than three seconds in the distant night. At no time did Mohamed perceive a sound. Everything took place in perfect calm. He told briefly what he saw to his wife and then went to where the object had landed, but found nothing. The next morning he checked again and found no traces, not even a footprint.

HC addendum.
Source: Gerard Lebat http://www.sciences-fictions-histories.com/blog/ovni-ufo/un-atterrissage-avec-humanoide-pres-de-marrakech.html   Type: C

* * * * * * *

Location: Point Pleasant, West Virginia.
Date: May 5, 1967.
Time: Afternoon.

Mrs. Mary Hyre saw the little man who had visited her in January on the streets of Point Pleasant. When he saw her he ran off and leaped into a black car driven by a very large man.

HC addendum.
Source: John Keel, *'Visitors from Space'* pp. 159.   Type: E?

Location: La Paz, Baja California, Mexico.
Date: May 15, 1967.
Time: 11:00 p.m.

    After an amateur astronomy club meeting, the witness, Benito Hamburgo Valenzuela, returned to his home where there appeared a colossal man at least 9-feet tall, who pulled up a large piece of wood and sat down on it. The man had large blue eyes, red hair, and very large ears; he wore a tight-fitting red coverall like garment with short sleeves, bracelets on both arms, and boots. On his chest was an insignia of white dots, and on his head a white cap that looked nickel-plated. From a wide belt hung a small box with a little antenna.
    He greeted Hamburgo in slightly accented Spanish, introducing himself as; 'Wirkle; chief of the guard,' and answered Benito's questions; anticipating them before the witness actually phrased them. He said he was from a very distant "region" and that they were an advanced race, concerned over the misuse of atomic energy. When he left, he refused to shake hands, explaining that contact with him would aggravate Benito's cardiac condition.

HC addendum.
Source: Mike Culbert and Paul Cerny.   Type: E

* * * * * * *

Location: Mount Misery, Long Island, New York.
Date: May 18, 1967.
Time: 10:30 a.m.

    The day after being instructed by a metallic sounding voice on her phone to go to the small local public library, Jane Paro did as was instructed. The library was deserted except for the librarian, who stuck Jane as being unusual. The woman was dressed in an old fashioned suit like something out of the 1940's with a long skirt, broad shoulders, and flat old looking shoes. She had a dark complexion, with a fine bone structure, and very black eyes and hair.
    When Jane entered, the woman seemed to be expecting her and produced a book instantly from under the desk. Jane sat down at a table and began to look through the book, pausing on page 42. The metallic voice had told her to read that page. Suddenly the print became smaller and smaller, then larger and larger. It changed into a message about contact with earthlings. The print became very small again, and then the normal text reappeared. As soon as Jane left the library she became quite ill.

In early June, she began to see the "librarian" wherever she went. Unable to sleep one night, Jane gout up at the crack of dawn the following morning and went for a walk on an impulse. The dark skinned woman stepped out of an alley and approached her shyly. *"Peter is coming,"* she announced. Jane asked her a question and she repeated, *"Peter is coming very soon."* Next a large black Cadillac came down the street and stopped next to them. It was brand new, very shiny, and polished. The driver was an olive skinned man wearing wraparound sunglasses and dressed in a neat gray suit, apparently of the same material as the woman's clothes.

The rear door opened and a man climbed out with a big grin on his face. He was about five-feet 8 inches tall, with dark skin and Oriental eyes. He had an air of someone very important and was dressed in a well-cut, expensive looking suit of the same gray material that was shiny like silk but was not silk. The stranger said his name was 'Apol.'

HC addendum.
Source: John Keel, *'The Mothman Prophecies.'* Type: E

* * * * * * *

Location: Near Point Pleasant, West Virginia.
Date: May 19, 1967.
Time: 10:30 p.m.

Mrs. Brenda Stone and another woman were driving in the TNT area when they saw the "Mothman" high in a tree off the road; "suddenly this big red light appeared and approached the tree and the form rose up towards it and disappeared. Then the light took off towards the north." Others in Point Pleasant reported UFO sightings that evening.

HC addendum.
Source: John Keel, *'Strange Creatures…'* Athens, *Ohio Messenger*, May 24, 1967. Type: C

* * * * * * *

Location: Michurinsk, Tambov region, Russia.
Date: Summer 1967.
Time: Unknown.

A local schoolboy saw in the sky a cloud in the form of an ellipsis. Within the cloud he saw the figure of a woman wearing a shawl carrying a child in her hands. Local residents resolved that it had been a vision of the Virgin Mary.

HC addendum.
Source: UFOZONE Russia.   Type: E?

* * * * * * *

Location: Oklahoma City, Oklahoma.
Date: Summer 1967.
Time: 2:00 a.m.

    The witness had gone outside to lie down on the grass and look at the star-filled sky, when he noticed three odd looking green lights arranged in an equilateral triangle, hovering high above the area. He began concentrating his thoughts towards the lights, thinking about the possibility of extraterrestrial life. Suddenly one of them shot away from the formation and began moving closer to the witness, the object, which now appeared to be saucer shaped, with its bottom spinning, with red lights on top and green lights on the bottom, hovered briefly above the witness, then landed behind a nearby church.
    Soon, a humanoid figure at least 12-feet tall appeared. The figure was accompanied by an odd looking animal, described as a cross between an ostrich and a buzzard. The giant humanoid was dressed all in black, with arms and legs in proportion to a human. Its head was like a large dome, with no visible facial features.
    The being could apparently read the witness thoughts and answered some of the witness questions by nodding his head. He claimed to be from a planet within our galaxy and that it was looking for a place to raise their "livestock." Soon the being and the strange bird-like animal re-entered the craft, which then shot up to join the other two. Then all three shot out into space and vanished.

HC addendum.
Source: *Heartland UFO Journal* #41.   Type: B

* * * * * * *

Location: Miami, Florida.
Date: Summer 1967.
Time: 3:00 a.m.

    Antonio Martin was fishing at the mouth of the Miami River near an area called Government Cut, when he heard some loud splashing in the water. Suddenly he saw coming out of the water; a huge 8-foot tall hair covered figure. The figure weighted about 400lbs and was covered with thick black hair; it had large eyes and pointy ears, long dangling arms and huge hands and feet.

The figure, dragging his left leg, had no trouble jumping a nearby fence, it stood 10 feet from Martin staring at him, and making a guttural sound. Suddenly the lights of a police car illuminated the figure, which ran and jumped into the water, quickly disappearing from sight. Two police officers with drawn weapons approached the witness and told them that they suspected the creature had come across a nearby canal. They admitted knowledge of the creature apparently having been seen before.

HC addendum.
Source: Virgilio Sanchez Ocejo. Type: E

* * * * * * *

Location: (Undisclosed location) New Brunswick, Canada.
Date: Summer 1967.
Time: Morning.

A man was hunting in the woods and as he aimed his rifle at a buck in the distance he heard whistling. He looked down and went into complete shock. A little man about knee-high walked right across his path only a few feet in front of him. He was wearing old fashioned farmer's clothing, holding an axe or some sort of tool over his shoulder, had a dark tan face, old looking, with a pointed hat.

He didn't look at the witness and didn't say anything, just whistling as he walked by. The witness put down his gun and left the woods for the day. The only thing he could think it could be was a "hobbit." He had heard nothing about little people other than hearing about the Tolkien book.

HC addendum.
Source: http://www.fairygardens.com/sightings Type: E

Location: Fort Lauderdale, Florida.
Date: Summer 1967.
Time: Late afternoon.

Marge Rogers was sitting in her den reading a book on flying saucers when she felt her hair stand up as if from an electrical current. She looked up and saw two men 8ft tall, wearing space suits. "The helmets were like boxes, with a square box on top." The men's eyes appeared to be blue. She heard a deep voice say, *"Tell your people to stop trying to find out about us in space."* The men then disappeared. Since this experience she had "become very psychic."

HC addendum.
Source: Letter to CUFOS. Type: E

* * * * * * *

Location: New York City, New York.
Date: Summer 1967.
Time: Evening.

Max's Kansas City was a famous watering hole for New York's hip crowd. In the summer of 1967, an oddball character wandered into that restaurant noted for its oddball clientele. He was tall and awkward. His chin came to a sharp point and his eyes bulged slightly. He sat down in a booth and gestured to the waitress with his long tapering fingers. *"Something to eat,"* he mumbled. The waitress handed him a menu. He stared at it uncomprehendingly, apparently unable to read. *"Food,"* he said almost pleadingly; *"How about a steak?"* she offered. *"Good."*
She brought him a steak with all the trimmings. He stared at it for a long moment and then picked up his knife and fork, glancing around at the other diners. It was obvious he did not know how to handle the implements. The waitress watched him as he fumbled helplessly. Finally she showed him how to cut the steak and spear it with the fork. He sawed away at the meat. Clearly he really was hungry.
"Where are you from?" she asked gently.
"Not from here."
"Where?"
"Another world," was his incredulous answer.
The waitresses then gathered around and watched the bizarre character as he fumbled with his food.

HC addendum.
Source: John Keel, *'The Mothman Prophecies.'* Type: E

Location: Uyuni, Bolivia.
Date: Early June, 1967.
Time: Afternoon.

An Aimara Indian encountered two strange humanoids about 1 meter in height that wore metallic suits with what resembled a large "H" on the breast area. One of the humanoids, using some type of instrument, proceeded in gutting half of her sheep herd. Both humanoids finally left the area, seemingly propelled with what appeared to have been a rocket-like device attached to their backs.

HC addendum.
Source: Enrique Villagrasa, Bolivia. Type: E
Comments: For some strange reason similar incidents were reported in Bolivia in 1968 and 1969.

* * * * * * *

Location: Morro Branco, Ceara, Brazil.
Date: June, 1967.
Time: 3:00 a.m.

Five men had gone out on a fishing expedition in an isolated area. Late at night while their fishing lines hung down on the water they suddenly heard a low, humming sound. It was so low that it was painful to hear. The men tried to assess where it was coming from, but as suddenly as it had started, it stopped. One of the men went off to discover where it had originated from, but the others decided to stay on quietly where they were, fishing.

After about 5 minutes, the same humming sound was heard again, this time louder and more intense than before. The men soon discovered that it came from behind a hill that stood about 500 meters from the shore, behind them. The men turned around and saw several beams of smoky colored light spreading out in the sky, alternately shining brightly, and dimming. Thoroughly frightened by now the men began collecting their fishing gear as quickly as possible. They picked up their belongings and were ready to leave when something even more terrifying happened.

One of the men, an engineer, who was coming up behind them, suddenly cried out for them to stop. They did and found him pointing his Taurus 38 revolver at them, ordering them to climb the hill above, which the lights were shining. At first they thought he was joking and they started to laugh, but he aimed his gun and started firing, warning them that he would kill them all if they refused to obey him. They noticed that his eyes were wet and bleary, and were shining strangely. They decided to obey.

Shocked they started climbing the hill in the direction of where the lights had appeared. As they stumbled on they heard some unintelligible sounds that seemed to come from nowhere, at very short intervals. Every time they stopped, the engineer cried out; *"We're coming, we're coming!"* The men's heads began to hurt. As they reached the top of the hill they saw a huge object that was hovering at about ten meters above the ground. It was round, phosphorescent, of a light green shade and had fins jutting out from each side of it. It measured about 5 meters from top to bottom.

At the top, a square, slatted hatchway could be seen, studded with funnels, from whence all those multicolored lights appeared. Silvery light covered the ground in all the area occupied by the object. Jutting from the bottom and reaching down to about 30 cm form the ground, a tube (cylinder) about 1 meter in breadth could be seen with a kind of oval shaped door at the lower end. All of a sudden, the men's eyes went out of focus and they found themselves lying on some kind of tables which seemed to be padded with something like foam rubber that was very soft. All the men were lying on similar beds. A voice was heard that apparently came from a reddish-blue lamp on the ceiling, which tinkled and echoed within the men's head.

The voice told them not to be afraid, for nothing would happen to them; to keep calm, for what was occurring to them was for the good of the universe. The room was milky white in color, the walls glass-like and there was a kind of lamp inserted in the ceiling. The walls reflected the general light, which was soft and did not affect their eyes. There were no doors or windows. In one corner of the ceiling, there was a kind of panel filled with little crisscrossed lines in a parallel or slanting position. The powerful voice told the men that they had come from very far and that it would be impossible for them to explain where it was.

The voice then proceeded to ask several questions of the men. At one point a triangular shaped window that opened outwards so the men could breathe better, suddenly appeared. The voice then said that they would not appear to the men since they were very different from humans and there were six of them. They said that there lifespan was similar to 300 Earth years. The voice further explained that they had controlled their engineer friend by using "light waves" and that several of our kind already lived in their planet. The men suddenly woke up around 5:20 a.m. in the field near the hill, not knowing how they had gotten there. Curiously a personal item of each of the men was missing, including the 38-caliber gun from the engineer.

HC addendum.
Source: Irene Granchi, *'UFOs and Abductions in Brazil.'*　　　Type: G

Location: Bjelovar, Croatia (part of Yugoslavia at the time).
Date: June, 1967.
Time: Morning.

The witness Professor Franjo Friedel, was on his way to cut his overgrown brush among some young poplars in his backyard. He had been going there every day for the last week. The poplars had been planted a year and a half ago and they were over three meters tall and their tops were thick with leaves. As he walked deeper into the woods, he thought he saw a figure walking between the trees. To him it appeared to be a person, perhaps a soldier, since the figure appeared to be wearing a helmet and a gray-green suit. Friedel was not surprised since there was an Army installation nearby and the soldiers often drilled in the area.

He had often found dugouts on his property. He then took the "lawnmower" (more like a handheld sickle) off his shoulder and began to cut the brush. Then out of the corner of his eye he saw that the figure he had seen before was now approaching his location. At this point he noticed that whoever it was, it was wearing a very unusual uniform, but he still thought it was soldier wearing a special outfit unknown to him.

The figure approached and said; *"Hoyyek!"* in a loud voice (this is what the witness thought he heard) at the same time a sort of high-voltage current went through Friedel's body, which momentarily stunned the witness as he realized that he was facing an unknown entity (perhaps an extraterrestrial). The witness also realized that the entity had said, *"Peace be with you, do not be afraid!"* The entity stood in front of the witness and again said in his strange language; *"Bhlira ohggy nohm!"* which the witness later learned it meant, *"Time is short."*

The witness felt isolated and unaware of his surroundings, he attempted to answer with a greeting, but his voice was stuck in his throat. The strange entity stood only about 2 meters away from the witness and this time in the witness's language communicated, *"I came to tell you, that everything is all-right with you. If you agree, I want to continue to contact you."* Friedel wanted to tell the intruder that he agreed to his request, but he couldn't utter a word, he felt strong palpitations and pressure in his head in between the temples. He just nodded his head in an affirmative answer.

The entity then said, *"Keep the secret, I will be back! Hoyyek!"* He turned around and walked away taking very quick steps. As the entity walked away, the witness remained in a stunned, confused state. While the entity disappeared from sight, the witness saw in between the vegetation, a bluish gray object in motion that appeared to be rotating. He couldn't see the entity any longer. The object lifted up emitting a strong gust of wind that vigorously agitated all the leaves on the ground. Almost noiselessly, the object ascended vertically, made a sort of jerk and then flew in the direction of the nearby railway, it then gained altitude and disappeared from sight.

Friedel's legs felt weak so he sat down. He sat on the grass for a long time thinking about what he had just experienced. He couldn't understand why he had not been able to move or ask any questions. Suddenly, he heard a voice in his mind that said, *"We are in a safe place now and you shall be at peace."* It was clearly a telepathic message.

He recovered from the shock and got up. He somehow felt 'extraordinary' and as he walked back to his house, he felt that it was a day to 'celebrate.' He walked into the horse stalls and lay on the fresh hay and attempted to recall everything about the encounter. In his mind he repeated the scenes of the encounter. He described the entity as about 125-130cm in height, with a broad and strong body fitted with a dirty green color uniform or suit that appeared to be made out of flexible leather. He could see a round 'box' on the chest area, he could see the entity's chest muscles which resembled that of a woman's breast. However his voice was deep and that of a male, his speech was abrupt and rhythmic, unlike a human voice, and seemed a bit sing-song in nature.

When he departed, the witness saw another similar round box on its back, like the one he saw on its chest. From the box on its back three cables or three tubes protruded out and connected to the helmet. Below the visor Friedel saw a frilled tube which was connected to the round chest box. The peculiar 'box' appeared to be 'transient' in color, like oil on the water. He wore gloves on his hands and contoured boots with very thick soles which possibly made the entity appear taller. The soles appeared flexible when he walked. There appeared to be a glass enclosed hole on his helmet that looked like a camera lens.

He did not see the object as well as he saw the entity, but he described it as disc-shaped, with a sort of tail and rotating. The body of the object seemed to be composed of three different sections. Both, upper and lower section of the object, which seemed to be rotating, with a mid-section that seemed stable, there was a hole in the lower part of the object. There were also a lot of small round windows on the upper section. From the mid-section of the craft there appeared to be some kind of bluish exhaust flowing out. He did not hear any engine noise only the rustling of the trees and leaves. Like a mirror, sunshine reflected on the object's surface. He estimated the size of the object as several average cars put together.

HC addendum.
Source: Matija Matelic, Slovenia, May 18 2011, citing Franjo Friedel's book, *'Lam Arabi.'* Type: C

* * * * * * *

Location: Goleta, California.
Date: June, 1967.
Time: 8:30 p.m.

The two young witnesses were walking along a beachfront area when they became aware of seven three-foot tall beings following them. The beings were humanoid with large round eyes. They wore black jumpsuits with a white "V" pattern down to the waistline. The witnesses then ran to their homes but could see that the beings were still following them. The witnesses then hid behind some bushes until the beings finally apparently left. Both youngsters arrived home and realized that they had lost three hours of time.

HC addendum.
Source: Tom Dongo, *'Alien Tide.'* Type: E or G?
Comments: Unexplored abduction event.

* * * * * * *

Location: Sarandi, Rio Grande do Sul, Brazil.
Date: June, 1967.
Time: 9:00 p.m.

The witness, a local handyman; Dirceu Garcia, had come home from work when about 200 yards from his residence, he saw a luminous ball hovering at about 30ft above the ground and thought that it was what the local inhabitants called "Madre d'Ouro" (Mother of God ghost light). It went down to about 10ft off the ground and stopped, projecting a beam of light downward with a helical movement around its radius and keeping a distance of about 30 or 40 inches from the ground, it dropped two beings to the ground approximately 85 inches tall. Paralyzed by surprise, he was unable to react as the two little men approached and grabbed him by the arms, dragging him towards a hole-like aperture on the hovering craft.

Dirceu could see a third occupant of the craft sitting on a small seat. Soon Dirceu and the two occupants levitated into the object within the beam of light. Inside Dirceu noted that it was as spacious as a large cabin truck, and it did not measure more than 1.5m high and when standing he had to bend (he was 1.64m). The three humanoids had a round face, blue eyes, normal mouths, noses and teeth in proportion to their heights, according to the human standard. They wore gray clothing, with a turtleneck covering the neck area with a belt of the same color; the shoes were a continuation of the clothing.

They spoke to him and spoke among each other in a language he did not understand, but with a pleasant voice. While sitting onboard the craft he felt weak, and the lighting inside the craft which constantly fluctuated, disturbed his vision. After a time that he estimated to have been three hours, he looked out a window and saw darkness and cities with tall buildings and forests darker than he knew. The ship flew into the darkened area.

The crew showed him a panel on which appeared colorful images of people and vehicles that were apparently looking at him. There was only dark in the panel when it was dark outside. Dirceu had the impression that most of the conversation between the little men was about the panel. Upon returning the object descended on the same spot, stopping about three feet off the ground. In the meantime Dirceu had been tied down by one of the little men. The belt came loose on its own accord when the object landed.

Once on the ground, Dirceu watched the craft depart in an oblique flight pattern, disappearing in seconds. At the landing site, Dirceu immediately had to relieve his bladder, which was very full. To his huge surprise he noted that the before evacuating the urine the urethra expelled a hissing gas. This happened for three to four days after the encounter. Since his legs felt weak after he left the object, he sat down on the ground for ten minutes in order to recuperate. He arrived home shortly after 5 a.m. He spent five days in bed, suffering from dysentery and fever. He lost weight and had a headache and weakness for a month.

HC addendum.
Source: *Inforespace* #56. Type: B

Location: Near Mt. Incahuasi, Chile.
Date: June, 1967.
Time: Night.

The main witness, Manuel Munoz Carvajal, a chauffeur who had become sick because of the altitude was returning from a drive when a ball of fire flew by the car. Moments later a light that appeared to be from a truck approached, it shone a brilliant beam on the witness and his companions, hurting their eyes. Soon they passed under a disc shaped object with resembled a walnut, with lights and antennas. A loud noise could be heard. The object followed the vehicle for some time.

Later under hypnosis, Mr. Carvajal was able to recall more details of the event. He remembered getting out of the van and approaching the object, then found himself unable to move and apparently fell asleep. In a dream-like state, he saw two men come out of the object, then woke up again inside the car, while the beings walked around outside. The humanoids were described as having large heads, large protuberant eyes, round faces, and pointed, dog-like ears. They were short and their skin was green. They had broad chests and narrow waists with thin, knee-less legs. Their clothing was skin-tight and one of the beings seemed to be the leader. The witness felt telepathic communication from the humanoids. The next day he reportedly saw two of the beings at the same location on the road.

HC addendum.
Source: *FSR* Vol. 14 #4.   Type: B?

* * * * * * *

Location: Near Veracruz, Mexico.
Date: June, 1967.
Time: Late night.

A vacationing couple traveling along an isolated stretch of road, struck with their vehicle, a huge eight-foot tall furry man like creature with combined human-ape facial features. The driver walked up to the creature that was lying prone on the ground, when it suddenly sprang up and ran into the nearby dense tropical forest. The being was completely covered with reddish hair and had long thin fingers.

HC addendum.
Source: Warren Smith, *'Strange Abominable Snowman.'*   Type: E

Location: Denver City, Texas.
Date: June, 1967.
Time: Night.

The witness, Emily Norris, heard noises and saw lights outside her farmhouse. Looking out the window she saw approximately seven short, gray-colored beings with large slanted eyes that walked around her house peering into the windows and at times attempting to open the front door. After a while the short creatures retreated into the darkness and soon after a large bright circular light became visible on a nearby field. The light suddenly rose up and disappeared at very high speed into the sky.

HC addendum.
Source: KLBK News, Lubbock, Texas. Type: C

* * * * * * *

Location. Kansas City, Kansas.
Date: June, 1967.
Time: Various.

The main witness along with several others were in a sparsely populated area late at night when he observed what he described as a World War II airplane with no lights, suspended in midair. He was driving his 1967 Chevrolet and there were five occupants in the car and all he remembers was the airplane first to the right and then to the left of his car, which emitted a yellowish beam from its rear. He then drove to an area where there were caves used for storage, near the meeting point of two rivers.

Driving along a gravel road he observed an individual facing the road in a green panel van wearing dark black sunglasses. He remembers telling the others how strange this was when a red light came from behind him and a county Sheriff's patrol car and two deputies got out and all the occupants of the witness vehicle got out and were questioned as to why they were out in this area at this time and he told the deputies they were looking out for UFO's and they told him to go home after checking their ID's. The witness thought it was kind of strange that the deputies did not question their story or laugh.

A week later while in his rooming house, the witness went to take a shower on the third floor when a young man with long blond hair and wearing a white outfit and dark sunglasses walked into the restroom and came straight to the shower. As the witness opened the door the stranger grabbed him by his groin, turned and then left. Immediately he got dressed and ran to the lobby to report this to the desk clerk and asked him if he had seen a young man with blond hair wearing dark sunglasses come down and he said no.

At this point another man came downstairs and reported that a similar looking young man had entered the shower but had not touched him. After all this the main witness was examined by doctors and an X-ray clearly showed that an object which the doctors could not identify was lodged near his femur bone. As of two years ago this object is still at the same place according to the witness.

HC addendum.
Source: NUFORC. Type: D?

* * * * * * *

Location: North San Juan, California.
Date: June 1, 1967.
Time: 4:01 p.m.

Two boys, Tony Spruill, 12, and John Bradshaw, 9, said they had seen a UFO come in for a landing in a gravel pit and took three pictures of it, showing something like an inverted cup or bowl on an inverted saucer. A door opened, a ladder unfolded, and a little man 2 to 2.5 feet tall came out and pointed at the boys, who were running away.

They then found themselves standing right next to the man, and were paralyzed. He told them they would not be harmed and escorted them into the object where they saw three more little people, one a female, and a wall with many buttons and blinking lights. They were told that the ufonauts came from Alpha Centauri. The USAF investigator judged the photographs to be fakes.

HC addendum.
Source: Lt. Joseph Kinderman, of Beale AFB for the USAF, also *The Sacramento Bee*, June 10, 12 and 15, 1967, and the *Sacramento Union*, June 16, 1967. Type: G

Location: Itajuba, Minas Gerais, Brazil.
Date: June 7, 1967.
Time: 1:30 a.m.

A disc shaped object with a rectangular protuberance on its underside approached close to an ambulance driven by Geraldo Baqueiro and caused its electrical system to fail. Through a transparent surface of the object, brightly illuminated, the faces of strange beings, resembling bipedal cat-like creatures with cat-like eyes, stared at the stunned witness intently.

HC addendum.
Source: H. B. Aleixo, *FSR* Vol. 14 #6, also Panel Ovni, Brazil.   Type: A

* * * * * * *

Location: Caledonia, Ontario, Canada.
Date: June 13, 1967.
Time: 2:30 a.m.

A night shift worker, Carmen Cuneo, saw two objects in the factory's scrap heap and dump area. A large cigar-shaped object on the ground, 35 feet long by 15 feet thick, and a hovering disc-shaped object about 15 feet in diameter. The smaller object, tilted up at a 45-degree angle, had a row of orange-lighted windows around its periphery. In the larger object were four square windows emitting a pulsating orange light, and from one end of it projected upward a 45 degree angle a boom or rod 15 feet long, bearing a large red light at the end.

Beneath this light moved three small humanoid figures about 3-foot tall, apparently wearing miner's hats with small lights on them, who were picking up and examining small objects on the ground, with quick, jerky movements. After watching for 10 minutes, Cuneo called Marvin Hannigan to see it, but by the time Hannigan arrived, the humanoids were gone. Then the two craft started to rise, very slowly, straight up into the air; after they reached a height of 50 feet, they departed at about 40-45 mph without sound. At the site, branches were broken and the brush charred, and an oily liquid was found on the ground.

HC addendum.
Source: James J. Ferrito and Jeffrey J. Gow for NICAP. Type: C

* * * * * * *

Location: Chimney Rock, Colorado.
Date: Mid-June 1967.
Time: Afternoon

   A month after seeing a strange crescent shaped light over the Great Sand Dunes National Monument and painting a picture of the light, the witness; Mrs. Blundell was visited by a strange character at the Pine Cove Inn. The man was deathly pale, had very dark hair, and wore a dark suit.
   He told Mrs. Blundell that he was not from our universe and could not read but could name the contents of any book in any library. He expressed interest in obtaining the picture of the light, but said he had no money and would return on a later date. The strange visitor then departed in a vehicle with Arizona license plates. He was not seen again.

HC addendum.
Source: *APRG Reporter*, November, 1967. Type: E

* * * * * * *

Location: Cordoba, Argentina.
Date: June 21, 1967.
Time: Daytime?

   Four days prior to a massive wave of UFO sightings in the region, a man dressed in black showed up at the newsroom of Cordoba's *Los Principios* daily, where he delivered a letter addressed to the editor. The letter stated that before the week was out, the 'Southern Cone' would experience a massive fly over, involving hundreds of extraterrestrial craft.
   The day before the sighting began; the newspaper received a phone call stating, *"Attention, it will begin at any moment..."*

HC addendum.
Source: Dr. Rafael Lara. Type: D?

Location: Western Pima County, Arizona.
Date: June 30-July 1, 1967.
Time: Daytime.

On around the above date, a disk-shaped object about nine meters in diameter with a dome on top, crashed for some unknown reason in the desert near the Organ Pipe National Monument; a reservation in the western part of Pima County. The disabled craft was detected and found by the military. The retrieval team was then sent to the crash site. A pre-fabricated hangar was then built around the debris and equipment was brought to the crash site by helicopters and trucks. On July 2, R. T, a Marine with the rank of PFC a trainer in the Canine Corps at Camp Pendleton, San Diego with an Alpha Red (Top Secret) Crypto Clearance, and other marines, were flown in a light cargo transport aircraft to the site, landing on a makeshift strip carved out of the desert. The windows of the aircraft had been blacked out.

At the site, among the cactus and tumbleweed, were tents, a small Quonset hut and what appeared to be a small Pre-Fab hangar. Busy around the structures were men in military fatigues without insignia. Told nothing about the status of the operation he was assigned to a post for guard duty, given orders and told to use only one designated path to the mess hall and latrine. Curious, R. T. decided on the fourth day to see what was so hush-hush and took a different route to the mess tent near the hangar.

When the guard there had his back turned, he peeked inside the hangar and to his shock saw a metallic disk or saucer, about 30ft in diameter. On top was a dome. Around the craft were men at work and tables on which were technical instruments. He also saw a large walk-in refrigerator unit on skids and several empty body bags. If there were bodies, they had already been shipped out or maybe they were in the freezer. R. T's one good glance into the hangar was also his undoing. The guard nearby nabbed him and he was escorted to the headquarters' tent where he faced the officer in command, a Colonel "P" from the USAF medical corps.

Reminded of his security oath he was confined to quarters and sent back to Pendleton for punishment. He told his story 13 years later. In 1980 R. T. was visited by a man dressed in black that lasted for 45 minutes. During the meeting, his dog, a shepherd, behaved uneasily. At one point the stranger in black asked for a glass of water, but when he was approached, he uttered, *"Don't touch me!"* R. T. also noticed that during their conversation about UFOs, the visitor always spoke in third person, using "we" or "they."

According to R. T. the visitor, while describing a UFO incident, suddenly produced from his briefcase a half dozen color photographs. Each showed a small cadavers or parts, not human, in what appeared to be a hospital operating room. The bodies were about 4ft tall. One photo was a close-up of a hand with four fingers, long and slim, with no opposable thumb. Another showed the top of a humanoid head, the flesh cut open and drilled into. Still another showed the upper torso of a chalky white complexion with an incision into its chest, and another showed a body burnt in its suit. But there was one photo that really convinced R.T.; it showed three doctors in the process of dissecting a body on top of a slab with a gutter around its edge.

Later R. T. refused to discuss the subject, because of "threats." The disk from the crash site was later transported to the Yuma Marine Corps base and hidden in a hangar there. Sometime later a military convoy removed the disk in the middle of the night to a more secured and highly secret underground compound on the territory of the Fort Huachuca military reservation in Arizona. Most probably no less than three short humanoid bodies were extracted from the crashed disk and also taken to the underground facility.

HC addendum.
Source: Leonard H. Stringfield, *'UFO Crash/Retrievals: Amassing the evidence Status report III,'* Cincinnati Ohio 1982 and Dr. Anton A. Anfalov PhD. Type: H
Comments: Coincidentally this incident occurred around the same time as the Baja California crash on July 2.

* * * * * * *

Location: Oosterchelde, the Netherlands.
Date: July, 1967.
Time: Night.

Industrialist Stefan Denaerde, was at anchor in his sailboat accompanied by his son, when their radar began to malfunction. Later on he starts to sail towards Burgsluis. At this point they see what they described as "a blue sun" descending from the sky emitting a strident noise. Denaerde then saw a figure that appeared to be injured floating in the water. He jumps in the water and retrieved the body.

At this point the "blue sun" descended over them and Denaerde could see that it was a metallic saucer-shaped craft. A door opened and a staircase was lowered down to the water and a figure was seen standing at the door. Denaerde was suddenly absorbed into the saucer and was confronted by several humanoids about 1.4 meters in height, equipped with astronaut-like uniforms adorned with multiple ornaments. They had a very high face, pointed ears and spoke in a mechanical English voice.

They thanked Denaerde for helping their injured crewmember in the water and told him that they were from a distant planet, which they called 'IARGA,' about 10 light years away. People live there in cylinder-like structures because of the rampant overpopulation. They practice a form of governance similar to communism that holds 'efficiency' as the prime consideration and tell Denaerde that private property does not exist. Their only goal is an "omni spiritual creativity."

HC addendum.
Source: *'Contact from Planet Iarga,'* UFO Geheimnisse.　　　Type: G
Comments: According to Ukrainian researcher Dr. Anfalov and 'Janefarlz' (a reportedly reincarnated alien), planet Iarga is located near the star known on Earth as Epsilon Eridani, which is 10 light years distant from the Earth.

* * * * * * *

Location: Vizcaino Desert, Baja California, Mexico.
Date: July 2, 1967.
Time: Night.

Military intelligence units were called to a remote desert location where a UFO had crashed. Several big trucks went to the scene, including some equipped with what appeared to be special devices. When the special unit arrived at the UFO crash site, a pungent odor permeated the air. The object itself, which was oblong in shape, was broken in two, but apparently landed before exploding. Lying around in several places were bodies of the occupants. They were described as being "hideous."

They were huge, about 9-feet tall, covered with a fine hair, and were a perfect likeness of what has been described as Bigfoot. Their faces were hairless, Mongoloid in appearance, with flat, wide noses. The mouths, which appeared to have been in agony, showed a row of teeth with what looked like stubby fangs. One of the creatures was apparently found alive and when one of the men attempted to give it water, the creature then reached up and grabbed the man's shoulder hard, then gasped and died.

Each of the creatures wore a copper-colored belt with a huge buckle rifted with small buttons. It is said that the belt glowed when activated but the source did not say what it was used for. On the creature's feet were boots resembling sandals but with very thick soles. Apart from these things, the creatures had nothing else on them. The remains of the disc and its occupants was seized by the US military and transported to Yuma Air Base in Arizona, later from there, to an unknown location.

HC addendum.
Source: Bobbie Ann Slate and Peter Guttilla also Anton Anfalov. Type: H

Location: Fox Park, Wyoming.
Date: July, 1967.
Time: Midnight.

The witness' father worked as a lumberjack and they lived at the local timber camp. He was awakened in the night by an 'astronaut' (without the air pack) walking through a solid door into his room to stand at the foot of his bed. The figure never spoke to the witness, and the witness felt unafraid. He wanted the figure to lift his visor to see his face but was afraid if he spoke the figure would go away. The figure stared at the witness for a few minutes/moments.

The witness was too fascinated to look at his clock to break the connection with the intruder. He stood watching him until the intruder heard the witness' mother begin to scream out with her frequent nightmares she had been plagued with all summer. The 'astronaut' then turned to walk back through the same unopened solid door. He laid down back in his bed to return to his sleep thinking he had just had the most unusual dream. His sister and the witness both shared a room but he didn't ever looked at her thinking she was asleep and she wouldn't be interested in his 'dream.'

Yet in 2009, their father was seriously ill and they were traveling back to Missouri where he lived and had been hospitalized they were talking about the story he had been writing. He confessed that the idea of the story had come from this same incident. His sister nearly ran off the road from surprise. She stopped on the side of the road to confess she had seen his 'astronaut' in their room that night. She had watched him stand at the foot of his bed.

HC addendum.
Source: MUFON CMS.   Type: E

* * * * * * *

Location: Cradle Hill, Warminster, England.
Date: July 8, 1967.
Time: Night.

Three people with flashlights (Bob Strong, Sybil Champion, and an anonymous man) discovered a tall man standing at the edge of a wood, clad in a one-piece close fitting garment, shiny "as if made of leatherette;" his face was pale, and on his head he wore a black hood or helmet. He suddenly vanished. A fourth witness, the man's wife, had been very much frightened by seeing this being; she had gone to the copse to investigate a sound like a swarm of bees, and found herself paralyzed when she saw the man.

When she brushed against his clothing it made a crackling sound. Later, recovering in her husband's car, she suddenly started to run back toward the wood again, and had to be dragged back to the car. Then a torpedo shaped red luminous UFO rose with a droning sound, and flew away. The next day, a pear-shaped or crescent impression was found in the grass 650 yards behind the copse as well as large footprints in the copse showing crisscross ridges on the soles.

HC addendum.
Source: Arthur Shuttlewood. Type: C

* * * * * * *

Location: Fairmont Park, Philadelphia, Pennsylvania.
Date: July 15, 1967.
Time: 5:00 a.m.

Charles S, out for a morning's jogging, was doing his roadwork in Fairmont Park when he was joined by two young men who ran along with him. Blond-haired and with eyes set close together, they were wearing mustard colored coveralls, and said nothing to him. After the run, they led him up a trail into a wooded area of the park, where she saw a landed flying saucer, about "one third of a football field" wide, brown on the underside and white on the upper side, resting on four pods.

He was conducted inside, where he found no sign of instrumentation except for several tubes of different shades of yellow, and a computer like machine no bigger than a typewriter. The walls were decorated with photographs of women "who looked Scandinavian, except for the eyes being closer together." Then the craft took off, and "we spent the whole day flying around." The next morning they let him off a the park again, giving him for a souvenir a metal disc, white on one side and black on the other, which he found would levitate 10" at intervals of 123 minutes. No more information.

HC addendum.
Source: Richard Hall from NICAP. Type: G

Location: Near Toledo, Ohio.
Date: July 16, 1967.
Time: 11:00 p.m.

Coming around a bend, Robert Richardson was surprised by a strange object blocking the road ahead. Unable to completely stop in time, he hit it, but not very hard. Immediately on impact, the UFO vanished. Police who accompanied Richardson to the scene could find only his own skid marks as evidence, but on a later visit, Richardson himself found a small lump of metal which he believed might have come from the UFO.

Three days later at 23:00 two men in their twenties appeared at Richardson's house and questioned him for about 10 minutes. They did not identify themselves and Richardson; to his own subsequent surprise; did not ask who they were. They were not unfriendly, gave no warnings and just asked questions. He noted that they left in a black, 1953 Cadillac. The license number, when checked, was found not yet to have been issued.

A week later, Richardson received a visit from two different men, who arrived in a current model Dodge. They wore black suits and were dark complexioned. Although one spoke perfect English, the second had an accent, and Richardson felt there was something vaguely foreign about them. At first they seemed to be trying to persuade him that he had not hit anything at all, but then they asked for the piece of metal. When he told them it had gone to the Aerial Phenomenon Research Organization (APRO) for analysis, they threatened; *"If you want your wife to stay as pretty as she is, then you'd better get the metal back."*

HC addendum.
Source: http://messageboard.cinescape.com/phenomenamagazine
Comments: Typical and classic MIB encounter of the period.   Type: E

* * * * * * *

Location: Mendota, California.
Date: July 20, 1967.
Time: Night.

The witness remembers the night that a misfired Russian missile was to pass over California, that his mother, ever practical, herded the family outside. When they asked why, she simply said, *"If it crashes here, we'll see it die together."* While looking for the missile, they heard the radio tell them, step by step where the missile was. When it was close to them, his mom had them look towards the north, and sure enough they were relieved when it passed over.

Later that night they were all still looking up at the night sky when someone pointed out something to them in the sky that there were three cigar-shaped UFOs. They thought they were blimps first, but they could tell they had nothing above them. They moved over to the dark side of their home to get a better look. They had no fear, just wonderment. The crafts made sharp turns and were quiet. The front and back ends were shaped like a helicopter window, but larger. There were windows around the entire crafts. They saw people looking out and moving about the ships. They could not see any details because all the windows were green. They were amazed that no-one else apparently saw them.

HC addendum.
Source: http://mufoncms.com/ Type: A

* * * * * * *

Location: Pamlico County, North Carolina.
Date: July 21, 1967.
Time: Afternoon.

14-year old Ronnie Hill was playing in the garden when he noticed a strange odor in the air. His eyes began to tear. He then saw a spherical object about three meters in diameter descending from the sky and landing on a field nearby. Thinking that nobody would believe him, he ran inside his home and obtained a small Kodak camera. Once outside he saw a small figure emerging from behind the object.
The figure was about 1.25 meters in height. It wore a tight-fitting silvery suit and it carried a black object in its hand, which the figure inserted into the ground, he then returned to the object, which took off into the sky at high speed. The odor was described as resembling propane gas. Hill also noticed a total lack of sound during the encounter. A controversial photograph of the humanoid was taken.

HC addendum.
Source: John Keel. Type: B

Location: Between Sydney and Bell, New South Wales, Australia.
Date: August, 1967.
Time: 11:00 p.m.

Mr. David Flood was traveling from Sydney towards Bell on his way to Lithgow, when at about 11pm he saw a "great egg-shaped craft, yellow glowing and emitting bright silvery rays of light from large floodlights at both ends of the craft as it descended to hover close to the ground." He could see a long narrow window and the craft was lit from within, so that he could see "five people," head and shoulders only, watching him. Below this was an oddly shaped door. It opened and he could see a humanoid, a dark figure outlined inside the glow. It seemed to float to the ground. The craft descended to a couple of meters above the road and his car suddenly "died" and he became petrified, unable to move, seated in his car barely 30 meters away.

He was terrified and frozen as the figure approached him. Then as the being stood in front of the car, he found he was able to move again and the car also "came alive" again, the headlights came on and lit up the figure, who was about 2 meters in height. He had a greenish egg-shaped head, two longish narrow white eyes and a small mouth. Flood was able to see that the being wore dark colored boots, light brownish skin-tight trousers and a black shirt-like garment that covered him from wrists to neck. He carried a strange dark metallic tool-like object in his left hand and Flood noticed a wide silvery belt with long narrow metallic decorative objects. However, as the being stood watching him, David frantically turned the car around and put his foot hard on the pedal; speeding back the way he had come. "I returned the next day with two mates and we searched about the road area but found no trace of anything that might have indicated space beings had landed there."

HC addendum.
Source: Rex Gilroy, *the Temple of Nim* Newsletter, Nov, 2009. Type: B

* * * * * * * *

Location: Caracas, Venezuela.
Date: August 7, 1967.
Time: Afternoon.

Dr. Luis Sanchez Vegas, a well-known doctor in Caracas, was confronted in his office by a little humanoid being less than 4-feet tall, who requested a physical examination. Speaking perfect Spanish, he told the doctor not to be surprised at his high temperature, as he was not from Earth. He had a large, round head with large eyes extending to the sides of his head, no ears, a slit-like mouth, and only 10 teeth.

He told Dr. Sanchez that on his planet reproduction was different from that on Earth, and that he did not know his parents. The strange humanoid called himself 'Astrum.' His lung capacity was above normal, and his pulse was incredibly slow. In order to confirm his extraterrestrial origin the strange humanoid levitated a pencil in front of several astonished people and then simply disappeared in plain sight of the witnesses. After the visit Dr. Sanchez suffered a heart attack.

HC addendum.
Source: Carlos Castillo. Type: E

* * * * * * *

Location: Westport, Washington.
Date: August 15, 1967.
Time: 9:00 p.m.

Standing 100 feet away at the other side of the top of the hill behind Kilahanna, campground the witness observed a gold spacecraft land on the dunes, one third of a mile from the coastline. It was near silent when it landed 120 yards from his view. He was looking down on a small grade at the landed craft. It was 100% shiny 24k gold in color. It landed gracefully. The landing gear popped straight out like thin legs. The witness just stared at it for about 30 seconds wondering what to do. Just then a door opened on the opposite side from his view.

An alien dressed in matching 24k gold spacesuit came out of what looked like a ramp. It just flew straight through the air about 20 miles an hour to a nearby fir tree branch. The witness could see it close now and was frightened and shaking. The figure was standing 100 feet from the witness up in the tree about 20 feet above the ground. It looked like a human body in a gold space suit. It was 5 foot 8 inches tall, with a round helmet which you could not see inside. It was holding what looked like a machine gun with a ½ thick cable attached to it. Everything was 100% shiny gold.

The witness just stood motionless and very scared. He watched the figure stand there as if on guard duty, it was turning its head looking back down the hill to the south of the space craft. It was 100 feet northwest of it. The frightened witness does not think the alien noticed him as it looked down the dunes. The witness then ran as fast as he could into the woods, down the hill and into the campground. He told a friend who went to the location a few minutes later but did not see anything.

HC addendum.
Source: HBCC UFO Research – http://www.hbccufo.org Type: B

Location: Sedlescombe, Hastings, Sussex, England.
Date: August 17, 1967-September 23, 1967.
Time: After midnight.

The witness, Edwin, a retired military figure and scientist specializing in audiology reported that between the above dates he had no fewer than nine visits by aliens. On the first occasion he met them while out walking with his dogs and invited them in. On later occasions they simply turned up in the house, always in the early hours after midnight. They communicated with each other by whistles and twittering noises but at no point spoke to Edwin, except by gestures. The object from which they emerged was conical and resting on three legs.

At no time did he see it land and in later visits the beings prevented him from going out to look at it. They literally carried him back into his house as indication that they did not wish him to watch them depart. The entities themselves were exceptionally thin and only just over five feet tall. Their skin was described as "gray like parchment" and they seemed to have no body hair at all. He had ample time to study them closely as they stayed for an hour or so at a time, once watching TV with him. (!) Their lips were almost invisible and their ears just a ring inset into the head. Their hands felt like "withered leaves" and had only three fingers and a thumb. They wore tight-fitting wetsuits with balaclava helmets and always came into the house in pairs.

During their visits to his home, Edwin claims that they took samples of many things, being particularly interested in fruit. They even had sips of whisky and showed great distaste. On their penultimate visit they reputedly stayed in the garden taking samples of shrubs and bushes. Another time they motioned to him that they wanted to take his dog with them. He refused but Edwin placated them by offering two china model dogs instead. They took these. His only attempt to real communication was when he drew a sketch of the solar system and asked them to mark it. They noted a spot outside the orbits of all the planets, which he took to mean they were from another star system.

On their ninth visit Edwin decided to defy their ban on watching their departure. He went out after they had left and noted a blue glow coming from beneath the object. It did not take off as he expected but simply disappeared on the spot. This was the last time he saw them. However before they left they had given him two gifts. One was a few seeds, which they told him to plant. He did so and something resembling a flowering cactus with a single thick and spike-less stump grew from the spot.

It was long dead before he reported the case to investigators. The second gift was tiny bits of crystal that superficially resembled uncut diamonds. Thinking they were indeed diamonds he had them examined by a London diamond merchant, but the result was that they were "probably quartz."

HC addendum.
Source: Jenny Randles, *'Mind Monsters, Alien Contacts and Abductions: The Real Story from the Other Side.'*

* * * * * * *

Location: Near Chambersburg, Pennsylvania.
Date: August 19, 1967.
Time: 9:45 p.m.

    Miss Lonnie Jo H. was driving home with her boyfriend, Bill B of Philadelphia, when he shouted to her that he had seen a UFO in a field. She turned the car around and drove back and they both saw a brightly white luminous object in the field.
    Then they heard a noise from the fencerow beside the road, and saw there a little humanoid figure whose sight terrified the girl. There was "something strange about his hands," and he was wearing luminous clothing that was "formed in blocks" (like a quilt). She was too frightened to recall the features of his face; she drove off as fast as she could. There was interference with the car radio during the encounter.

HC addendum.
Source: George Cook for NICAP.   Type: C

* * * * * * *

Location: Near Joyceville, Ontario, Canada.
Date: August 23, 1967.
Time: 4:00 a.m.

    Stanley Moxon, a salesman, was in his car 40 miles southwest of Smith Falls on Highway 15 near Glen Grove Road north of Kingston, when he saw a huge glowing object giving off a brilliant green light as it descended from the sky. At treetop height it moved down the Highway ahead of the witnesses' car and went around a bend in the road. Minutes later Stanley rounded the same bend and saw an inverted soup bowl sitting on three legs in a field 200 yards away from the road. Stanley pulled up and switched off the cars' lights. Stanley watched three small human-like creatures that were collecting bits of soil and plants.
    The little humanoids were three feet tall and wore white coveralls with bubble-type helmets on their heads. After a few minutes Stanley switched on the headlights to high-beam to get a better look. Stanley beamed the headlights at them and they scurried into their disc-shaped craft and ascended noiselessly but rapidly into the sky. The craft went

straight up at tremendous speed. Then Stanley went to the police who had received calls about a strange green light in the sky. The police and Stanley went back to the site. There were burn marks on the ground and three indentations from something very heavy that had been pressed into the ground.

HC addendum.
Source: Local Police and APRO.   Type: B

* * * * * * *

Location: Kolmarden, Ostergotland, Sweden.
Date: August 23, 1967.
Time: 11:00 p.m.

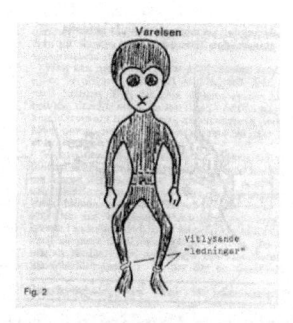

Fig. 2

In the neighborhood of Kolmarden a 15-year old boy and his girlfriend of the same age were out strolling on a road adjacent to an industrial lot, when they noticed a red light over the wood coming from the south and descending close to the ground. No details were visible behind this light. They felt trapped as though someone was watching them and quickly left the scene, taking a short cut across a field. As they got nearer home, however, curiosity got the better of them and they went back onto the road.

They then saw the light move away to the east. The couple now reached an empty and padlocked area cabin, around which, to their surprise, were strange light phenomena, both inside and outside. The former consisted of small yellow lights floating around one of the rooms, the latter a sort of cone of light moving up from the ground on the outer wall facing the road. They could also hear sounds like thumps on a plank. While the youngsters were still taking this in, the red light appeared again from the west, moving on a curved trajectory towards the north at treetop height.

This red light changed to white before apparently landing in a cornfield and going out. The couple then ran back to the boy's house, but finding it unoccupied went to his sister's house nearby.

Just as they arrived there, a luminosity suddenly appeared 3m above the ground. It seemed like a large torch which uttered a curious whistling sound. At the same time they heard fast, gentle steps coming from a brook. The couple walked forward, at which a figure jumped, almost flew, out of the bushes, and then stood completely still not more than 10m away. It was a being 1.3m tall dressed in some sort of dark clothing, standing with its head bent down and arms close to the body. It was difficult to make out details in the poor light, and the girl, thinking it was a friend playing a trick, stepped forward.

As she did so the figure raised its head and arms in a jerky unsteady fashion. The boy then realized it was something inhuman and dragged his girlfriend back. They both now saw that the being was carrying a box with a sort of projection which was directed towards them. A sort of gleaming light played at the top of this projection.

As they stood rooted to the spot in panic, they could see that the creature had an oversized head, covered on top with a dark hood, which went down in a "V" between eyes, which were large, dark and had a horrible penetrating expression. The place where the mouth should have been was an X-shaped marking. The arms and legs were very thin, the latter being bandy. As far as they could tell the creature wore a sort of blue-black overall, with a kind of belt at the waist.

Around its ankle joints, encircling each joint, was something resembling a cable 2m thick which flashed for an instant. The creature looked paradoxically both "tough" and unsteady. The couple then got themselves quickly admitted to the house. The boy's sisters confirmed how shaken the couple were, as did his mother when she arrived.

The next day, traces were found in the form of unusually damaged apples, strange footprints, 25 cm long, very deep and showing three toes. On the night of the 24/25 one of the sisters heard sounds outside the house and a light from a flashlight shone in through the window, footsteps were heard and two shutters were found dislodged from the window.

HC addendum.
Source: K. Gosta Rehn for APRO and Sven Schalin.   Type: C

Location: Wodonga, Victoria, Australia.
Date: August 24, 1967.
Time: 5:00 p.m.

While riding his motorcycle from Sydney to Melbourne, Ron Hydes was blinded by a light above him so brilliant that he was forced to stop. He then saw, 100 feet away, a metallic object 25-30 feet in diameter, shaped like two saucers put together but separated by a band of metal 9-12" deep. The underside of the object was dark gray, the upper half like polished chrome; it bore a small dome of aluminum like appearance, surmounted by a small flat-topped bell 12" deep.

Hyde's attention was diverted momentarily, and when he looked back he saw two figures about 5-foot tall standing by the UFO, wearing close fitting silvery coveralls that covered hands and feet. On their heads they wore opaque "fishbowl" type helmets. One of the figures took two steps forward and beckoned to the witness, but Hydes jumped onto his machine, in fear, and took off at 100 mph. However, the UFO, giving off a pink glow, followed him. When he stopped again he saw it tilt up at a 45-degree, the glow turning a bright red, and shot up into the air at tremendous speed, disappearing in only seconds. The entire episode had lasted approximately 5 minutes.

HC addendum.
Source: N. Thornhill and Peter Norris. Type: C

* * * * * * *

Location: Maquetia Airport, Venezuela.
Date: August 26, 1967.
Time: 2:00 a.m.

Marine Private Esteban Cova was just leaving the hangar at Maquetia Airport when he was accosted by a small being about 3-feet tall and covered with a sort of wiry hair. The little man had a very large head, bulging eyes, and made a deep whistling sound that gave the witness a prickling sensation throughout his body. He then spoke, in Spanish, asking Cova, *"Won't you come with us? We need one more."* Cova fainted.

HC addendum.
Source: *APRO Bulletin* Sep/Oct, 1967. Type: E

Location: Near Maturin, Venezuela.
Date: August 26, 1967.
Time: Morning.

Driving on the highway to Maturin, Mr. Saki Macharechi saw what appeared to be a large bird flying overhead. It landed near a bridge and he took it at first to be a heron. On approaching closer (within 9 feet), he saw that it was a little human like figure and not a heron. Frightened, he stepped on the gas and drove away.

HC addendum.
Source: *APRO Bulletin* Sep/Oct, 1967.   Type: E

* * * * * * *

Location: Warminster, England.
Date: August 27, 1967.
Time: Late night.

After arriving home in the early hours, Arthur Shuttlewood was lying in bed when he had a vision of a "very special person." Arthur only describes him as having long hair flowing gently down to white robed shoulders and parted in the center from the crown and a rich copper beech red color, face and eyes; "glorious eyes," truly out of this world; violet blue glowing lamps, beautiful and blazing a mute appeal, unlined skin of a soft pink, great majesty and strength, a noble spirit in the set of the high yet broad forehead, slightly jutting outward over finely chiseled features. A brilliant light was shining around him, illuminating the room.

HC addendum.
Source: *'50 Years of UFOs,'* By John and Anne Spencer.   Type: E

* * * * * * *

Location: Cussac, Cantal, France.
Date: August 29, 1967.
Time: 10:30 a.m.

13-year old Francois Delpeuch and his younger sister, Anne Marie, 9, tending the cows, saw four figures 3.5 to 4-feet tall on the other side of the road, near a 6-foot spherical object of dazzling brilliance that was resting on the ground. On looking closer they saw that the beings were completely black; either naked or wearing skin-tight black coveralls.

They had pointed heads, which were also black. One was picking something up off the ground. Another had a bright object, like a mirror. On becoming aware of the children, they rose up vertically, one after the other and plunged head first into the top of the sphere, which then rose on a spiral with a whistling noise. It left a smell of sulfur behind it.

HC addendum.
Source: Joel Mesnard and Claude Pavy for GEPA.   Type: B

* * * * * * *

Location: Cradle Hill, Warminster, England.
Date: August 29, 1967.
Time: Night.

A cone shaped UFO was seen by 25 witnesses to land 1000 yards from the copse of Cradle Hill; Arthur Shuttlewood went toward it, finding that bright beams of light were shooting out from a conical and revolving rim. 300 yards from the UFO, he spoke to a being (he gave no details, except that the meeting was "reassuring.") The spaceship "blacked out" after 6 minutes. As he walked back, Shuttlewood heard above his head something like a gigantic bird flapping its wings, and felt a downdraft of wind.

HC addendum.
Source: Arthur Shuttlewood.   Type: C

* * * * * * *

Location: Near Point Pleasant, West Virginia.
Date: Fall 1967.
Time: Late afternoon.

A family was on their way to a private event in Point Pleasant and was southbound on the highway by the Ohio River on the West Virginia side. It was a long ride and their young son was getting restless when he suddenly caught sight of something from the corner of his eye. On the side of the road, in a thin stretch of woods between the highway and the river was what at first appeared to the witness to be a "bum." He was wearing a brown flannel shirt and grubby, baggy brown pants and a brown hunting hat with ear flaps down. He was running alongside their car. The witness checked the speedometer and they were moving at 35mph. The witness kept looking at the figure as it was running alongside the car, then he turned and looked at the witness. It looked like he was wearing old-style welding goggles or old-style motorcycle goggles. They were brown-framed circles with bright red lenses.

    He kept up with the car for several hundred yards until a wide bend in the road moved them apart and the witness lost sight of him. About two seconds later, his brothers started yelling, *"The man, he is flying! The guy is flying!"* It didn't appear to be the same guy this one was in a silver suit with wings. He held his arms up by his chest, the witness didn't know how he was controlling his flight. He shot straight up out of the woods, then leveled out and headed towards the east. He had red eyes, but not like the running guy seen originally. The flying figure's eyes were glowing very brightly. He flew behind a hill and disappeared from sight.

HC addendum.
Source: Witness firsthand account in *Phantoms & Monsters* blog.
Type: E

* * * * * * *

Location: Point Isabel, Ohio.
Date: Fall 1967.
Time: Night.

    Perry Adams, 15, heard a metallic kind of noise outside his home and, with his father and brother in law, went outside with a flashlight to investigate. About 50 feet away, "we saw it, a monster; rising up…it was walking toward us." It was 10-feet tall and four feet across the shoulders, with long arms, and of a light tan color. It had pointed ears, short horns, large glowing eyes, and large teeth.

    It wore no clothing and seemed hairy. The men retreated indoors where Adams and his brother in law armed themselves with a .22 rifle. Outside, on seeing the creature again, they fired three shots at it, hitting it at least once. The being screamed, and then "changed into a white colored mist or cloud" that dissipated. No trace of its presence could be found in the morning.

HC addendum.
Source: Leonard Stringfield. Type: E

Location: Utica, New York.
Date: Fall 1967.
Time: 8:00 p.m.

A mother and daughter were in their home when they noticed three perpendicular red lights off toward the horizon; they thought briefly that these must be some previously unnoticed radio tower, until the lights pivoted and assumed a horizontal position. The object began to move and went directly behind their house (maybe only ten feet away and at ground level). It looked like a football, and the daughter thought she saw a shadowy form moving behind one of the lighted areas.

The mother took several pictures of it. The negatives never returned, and half of the pictures were not sent back. The few that arrived gradually frittered away through the years and none may still exist. "About the same time that we saw the big UFO, we had visitors of two gentlemen. They were in very dark outfits and hats, and they were dark skinned, and they came and talked to my mother."

The mother and daughter were puzzled that the men seemed to arrive without a car on a rainy day. "They told my mother not to say anything to anyone. And she was a very stubborn lady, but they somehow silenced her." She said, *"Then I won't say anything."* And they were gone, and still no sign of any transportation that they used.

HC addendum.
Source: Michael D. Swords, *'Grassroots UFOs.'*   Type: A & E
Comments: Did the MIB threaten the main witness with somehow harming her daughter?

* * * * * * *

Location: Near Carlisle, England.
Date: Autumn 1967.
Time: 1:30 a.m.-2:00 a.m.

The members of the band, *The Moody Blues,* composed of Graeme Edge, Denny Laine, Mike Pinder, Ray Thomas and Clint Warwick, were returning to London after a concert. According to Graeme; contrary to the reputation of musicians for consuming alcohol and other substances after a show, all the "Moody Blues" personnel were completely sober and straight. The road crew had, as usual, taken the equipment into the truck, and the band members were following along by car. Around about 1:30am—2:00am they were driving south on the A6, when a bright light appeared and flashed past them. Everyone became highly excited as to what the light might be, with the usual nervous jokey references to "UFOs."

However, Edge was convinced it was probably an aircraft warning light on top of a radio mast, apparently moving because of the motion of the car. However, the light returned from the opposite direction, and he suggested stopping the car for a proper look. He was still convinced of a logical terrestrial explanation. As the car halted, they all saw the light again to the left-hand side of them. It went backwards and forwards, and then actually *over* the car before settling in a field near the road, but on the opposite side of the dual carriageway. As they scrambled out of the car, half scared, half fascinated, they all noted an odd stillness around them. No road traffic came, in either direction, and there were none of the usual nocturnal animal rustlings or bird noises. It was quite uncanny and they were mesmerized as if in a dream.

They could see the object in the opposite field; it was shaped like a fat cigar with a low protrusion on top, with seven dull red lights on it. The upper half of the object appeared metallic, whereas the lower half was red, and pulsed from left to right. The lower half was a bright red on the left and a duller red to the right, and did not seem to be metallic like the upper half. Suddenly all five of them were gripped simultaneously with dread and panic. They rushed back into the car, which started perfectly, and drove off. As they looked back, they could see the object pulsing away in the field. Graeme Edge feels that something may have happened that night. He doesn't recall any "missing time" but as is typical of touring musicians, no-one bothered to check what time they arrived home. In those days the "Moodies" were a Rock/Pop band, but after this experience they tended to write and release all kinds of "cosmic" albums, such as *'Days of Future Past.'*

A couple of years later Graeme was asked mockingly, *"What did the aliens look like?"* In answer he drew a sketch of what is now considered a typical small-bodied large-headed entity. In those days; as far as is known; no such entities had been drawn by any witnesses in any book published at that time, and anyway, Graeme never read any literature on the subject. He said the sketch seemed "to come from inside" (referring to his mind) and that, at the time it seemed like a fun thing to do.

HC addendum.
Source: Pete Willsher, *FSR* 1991.   Type: G?

Location: Caracas, Venezuela.
Date: September 3, 1967.
Time: Afternoon.

Miss Paula Valdez, an aspiring actor, came home from work early with a headache. Laying down in her room, she was suddenly aware of someone else nearby, when she heard a kind of whistling noise. At the side of her bed was a small man, leaning toward her; the being had a large head and prominent eyes, and said to her, in Spanish, *"I want you to come with us so that you will know other worlds."*
Miss Valdez began screaming at the top of her lungs and the little man fled through the window. By the time her family arrived, he had departed.

HC addendum.
Source: Horacio Gonzalez Ganteaume for APRO.   Type: E

* * * * * * *

Location: Pedra da Baleia, Minas Gerais, Brazil.
Date: September 14, 1967.
Time: 9:00 a.m.

A 16-year old youth, Fabio Jose Dinis, noticed a brown mushroom shaped object (dome supported by a short central pillar from its flat bottom), 60 feet in diameter, in the middle of a football field. It had round portholes around the edge and flashing red, yellow, and blue lights from the underside of the dome. When he approached, a glass like screen dropped from the edge of the dome to the ground, and at the same time an opening appeared at the base of the central column.
Two men nearly 7 feet tall, emerged from this opening and addressed him in Portuguese; *"Don't run away; come back!"* While the one entity made a complete turn, around the column, the other again addressed the youth, saying; *"Appear here tomorrow, or we will take your family."* Then they re-entered the object and the transparent curtain was retracted and the UFO, rotating, rose slowly in a vertical ascent. The beings were dressed from head to foot in green, tight fitting "diver's suits" leaving only part of the face visible. Their skin appeared greenish, with two large round eyes set far apart, surmounted by triangular eyebrows; the nose and mouth were hidden by the helmet (of one piece with rest of the outfit), from which a thin tube ran downward, through the legs and to the back. One of the entities carried in his arm a large cylindrical implement.
Later, at the site, a small quantity of scorched granular material with an unpleasant odor was found and analyses showed it to be comprised of

iron, aluminum, magnesium, and silica. The youth went back to the site the next day, as instructed, with the investigators, but the UFO failed to appear.

HC addendum.
Source: Dr. Hulvio B. Alexio. Type: B

* * * * * * *

Location: Near Langley, British Columbia, Canada.
Date: September 17, 1967.
Time: 2:00 a.m.

In a wooded area an anonymous witness observed an eight-foot tall humanoid, apparently pink colored and covered with scaly skin. No other information.

HC addendum.
Source: John Brent Musgrave, *'UFO Occupants and Critters.'* Type: E

* * * * * * *

Location: Near San Feliu de Codines Barcelona, Spain.
Date: End of September, 1967.
Time: 9:30 p.m.

Mauricio Weisenthal and his fiancée, Rosa Maria Font, were about 4km, from San Feliu de Codines, driving to Barcelona, when they saw in the headlights of their car, a humanoid being about 2-feet tall, with a protuberant stomach and buttocks, with a bright green skin, short thick legs, and long arms. They had to swerve to avoid hitting it and were shocked by its appearance.

HC addendum.
Source: Joan Crexells. Type: E

Location: Reseda, California.
Date: October, 1967.
Time: Night.

The witness was abducted out of her home by several humanoids, described as having wrinkled grayish skin with huge dark eyes and large baldheads. The beings wore tight-fitting uniforms. The witness described the inside of the object as having gray walls and a rounded ceiling.

The beings apparently attempted to perform some type of procedure on the witness's brain and she apparently fought back. Later she experienced additional bedroom visitations by small balls of light that would paralyze her and communicate with her telepathically.

HC addendum.
Source: Preston Dennett, *UFO Encounters* Vol. 2 #4.   Type: G

* * * * * * *

Location: Belfast, Northern Ireland.
Date: October 6, 1967.
Time: Night.

Eugene Browne (involved in a previous encounter) was walking home from a jazz club when he saw a craft in the sky. A yellow light came from it, which danced around him making him feel dizzy and lose consciousness. He awoke on a table in a windowless, oblong room, lit by a blue light from the floor. Metal bands attached to an apparatus at the side strapped him down. Four men and a woman surrounded him; they had a bluish aura. The tallest, dressed in a dark one-piece suit, said, *"At last, someone who will do,"* and released him.

The woman had long blond hair, high cheekbones and was very fair with freckled complexion. He had sex with her and she told him they were "from another galaxy" and were experimenting to get human seed. Afterwards he was tied up and told it would not be long before he was returned. He blacked out, recovering in a field about a mile from the original location. He saw an object, which took off with a whistle as its tripod landing-gear retracted.

HC addendum.
Source: Peter Rogerson.   Type: G

Location: Lakewood, Colorado.
Date: October 10, 1967.
Time: 12:45 a.m.

Norman C, driving home, was flagged down by a man with a forked goatee, well over 6-feet tall wearing a jacket with four gold bars on each shoulder. The man talked to the witness without moving his mouth, presumably by telepathy. He asked where the North Star was, and what the date was; in response to the answer, he replied, *"In your primitive time."* He asked what the witness had in his mouth; on being told it was a cigarette, he replied, *"Oh, one of your... vices."* He asked about the car and called it; *"your primitive mode of transportation."*

When the witness asked who he was and where he was from, the man replied, *"I cannot tell you now, but my colleagues and I will return."* Then the man walked about four feet away and vanished. Norman then heard a noise, looked up and saw hovering overhead; a red object the size of a football field. With a whining noise it went straight up, joined two more objects, and disappeared at tremendous speed.

HC addendum.
Source: Lt. Col A P Webb Air Force and Dr. Leo Sprinkle for APRO.
Type: C

* * * * * * *

Location: Santa Ana, California.
Date: October 11, 1967.
Time: Evening.

Two years after taking the now famous UFO photographs, Rex Heflin received another group of strange visitors. They appeared at his home at dusk dressed in Air Force uniforms. Because of his earlier experience, Heflin inspected their credentials carefully and wrote down their names and other information. They questioned him about the photos and asked him if he knew anything about the Bermuda Triangle.

During the questioning, the witness says he noted a car parked in the street with indistinct lettering on the front door. In the back seat he could see a figure and violet (not blue) glow, which the witness attributed to instrument dials. He believed he was being photographed or recorded. In the meantime his FM multiplex radio was playing in the living room and during the questioning it made several loud audible pops. Dr. James E McDonald and other investigators later tried to check out the identity of these visitors. They drew a complete blank. Despite their credentials and uniforms, these men were apparently imposters.

HC addendum.
Source: John A. Keel, *'Our Haunted Planet.'*   Type: E
Comments: Classic MIB Report.

* * * * * * *

Location: Jungle area near border, North Vietnam.
Date: October 12, 1967.
Time: 1:45 a.m.

    The main witness was at the time a team leader on a LRRP unit (Long Range Recon Patrol) which consisted of a team of six men. He was out with his team in the IV Corps in a jungle area and after humping through the boonies all day had set up an NDP (Night Defensive Perimeter). The men took turns sleeping and keeping watch. At about 1:45 a.m. the witness heard movement ahead. Another man (Levin) heard it also, they woke up the other four men and they all readied themselves for the upcoming contact. Suddenly they saw what appeared to be an "alien."
    The witness described it as resembling the modern gray-human hybrid with a long face and large black eyes. It gave off an eerie glow. One of the men named 'Boltach' raised his weapon and fired. He hit the being in the head with a short controlled burst. A brilliant blue syrupy fluid splattered the trees behind the alien. Just then, they saw a dull light in the sky. They had a device called a "Starlight Scope," which only special operations teams had. It was a lot like night vision. The main witness focused it on the light in the sky and at that moment two more lights appeared. They formed the shape of a perfect triangle. The light at the top circled the two below in a figure 8 and zipped off. The remaining two seemed to collide and both zip off in the same direction as the first.
    That night two other LRRP teams in their AO (area of operations) reported in the same activities. The men called their headquarters and were informed that there was radio trouble and would be offline for the rest of the night. The linked up with the other two teams for security reasons and shared their encounter with them. Four of the other men with the main witness that night were later killed in various engagements in the war. Only he and Levin are still around.

HC addendum.
Source: NUFORC.   Type: C or H?

Location: White Rocks, Utah.
Date: October 12, 1967.
Time: 3:00 a.m.

In the midst of a mini wave of UFO sightings in the Uintah Basin, in northeast Utah, during the night of October 11-12, Jay Anderson, of White Rocks, observed a strange figure standing in a doorway of his home. Dressed in a metallic looking suit, and giving off a luminous glow, the figure turned and walked out after being discovered.

HC addendum.
Source: Joseph Junior Hicks and Frank Salisbury.　　　　　Type: D

* * * * * * *

Location: Milan, Italy.
Date: October 13, 1967.
Time: Unknown.

　　Andreina Zatti was walking along the Via Amedeo on her way to visit a friend when a man about 35 years of age with very strange physical characteristics approached her. His skin was a pale bluish-green color and he was dressed entirely in black with dark goggle-like glasses. He stood staring at Andreina with his hands to his knees. Apparently this produced a painful sensation in Andreina, who immediately thought that the stranger was an extraterrestrial. At this point she received a telepathic message from the stranger confirming his extraterrestrial origins. Andreina felt paralyzed as the stranger disappeared.
　　Later that same month while Andreina attended a soccer game, she noticed a strange gray, dirigible-shaped craft that appeared to be hiding behind some clouds. She suddenly found herself inside the object where a tall man dressed in blue with a belt, a gold collar and bracelet confronted her. The man had long, shoulder-length black hair, and his skin was pale blue in color. The humanoid touched a button on his chest and Andreina suddenly found herself back in the field, not knowing how she got there.

HC addendum.
Source: CUN Milano and Archivio S.U.F.　　　　　Type: E & G

Location: Duncan, Oklahoma.
Date: October 21, 1967.
Time: 10:00 p.m.

Four teenaged boys, including Ivan Ritter and Jerry Bennett, were driving east of Duncan on Route 7 when they saw three little men in the car's headlights. When the driver turned the beam on high, the three beings "flew off the road and disappeared." They were about 4-feet tall with shiny blue-green skin, or tight coveralls. Their faces were human but their ears were very large. There was a 20-foot drop off on either side of the highway at the site, making normal egress off the highway difficult. At the site the next day, Ritter and Bennett found an unusual footprint in the mud of a creek bed 100 yards from the road.

HC addendum.
Source: Lt Elmer McGill and Detective Pleasant Foster for Local Police.
Type: E

* * * * * * *

Location: Hunter Liggett Military Reservation, California.
Date: October 24, 1967.
Time: Evening.

George W. Ritter and three other soldiers were on guard duty when they all observed an orange fluorescent oval shaped craft approach slowly, leaving a tail behind it. A hatch opened on the bottom of the craft and five small drones dropped out of it. They formed into a V formation and began hovering above the witnesses. As the men looked up mesmerized, Ritter began hearing a "blip-blip" like sound like sonar. All four felt paralyzed at this point.

Suddenly Ritter's next recollection was of being lifted up into one of the objects. He then found himself lying down with a gray colored humanoid looking down on him. The other three soldiers were nowhere in sight. The being had large black oval shaped eyes and did not appear to be wearing any clothing. He saw three other smaller similar creatures that appeared to be assistants. He heard a voice in his head telling him that he was not going to be hurt.

Inside the object there was a constant weird misty light, resembling a black light. He was then given a shot in the thigh near the groin area and then one of the beings came up to his left side and somehow put his whole hand, inside the upper left side of the witness's chest. After an undetermined amount of time he was taken into another room where he saw a bright ball of light that emanated energy and love towards Ritter and communicated telepathically. Ritter was told that in the near future "something wonderful was going to happen." His next recollection was of standing on the ground looking up, but the objects are gone. The other men reported the incident to military authorities. As a result Ritter spent two months in a military mental hospital.

HC addendum.
Source: Linda Moulton Howe. Type: G

* * * * * * *

Location: Santa Adelita, Sao Paolo, Brazil.
Date: October 29, 1967.
Time: 11:00 p.m.

Mr. P, 51, was driving home after a clandestine love escapade. The moon was shining, in its fourth quarter. When he came to the top of a ridge, he saw, 200ft away, hovering 4ft above the ground, an aluminum colored plate shaped object with a convexity on its bottom side, about 30ft in diameter. He arrived within 30-50ft of it and stopped (or the car motor spontaneously stopped); he then saw that it was "full of lights," red and of other colors, which alternately lighted and went out.

Standing near the saucer was a robustly built man about 5-½ft tall, dressed in a light colored garment (the witness could not specify the color, being color blind.) This person walked in front of the witness and from a flashlight like object turned on a very bright white beam of light. The witness thought someone was waylaying him connected with his amorous adventure. He half opened the car door, rested his .22 revolver on it, and fired six shots at the person. (He was a good shot with this revolver.) Then he no longer saw him.

The saucer began to oscillate, and he heard a sound like a cowbell. Then the UFO flew away on an oblique course.

HC addendum.
Source: Dr. Walter Buhler. Type: C

Location: Melfort, Saskatchewan, Canada.
Date: October 30, 1967.
Time: 9:00 p.m.

Approaching his home, Donald Marshall saw a light beyond it. Upon getting a closer look, he found a rectangular lighted panel about 4 feet high and 16 feet long, 12 feet off the ground, which looked like a large window in an object whose shape was not clearly seen, but perhaps 50 feet long.

When he was 200 feet away a bright spotlight came on, and he saw three small humanoid figures, the size of ten-year old children, coming from the machine. They moved very fast and were clothed in green uniforms, and wore some type of headgear. They disappeared into the darkness and the craft took off slowly, at about 5 mph. It moved at first (breaking some trees) into a gully, where it remained another three or four minutes. The total time during which Marshall observed the object was 18-19 minutes.

HC addendum.
Source: R. Meizeka, *Saskatchewan UFO Bulletin.*   Type: C

* * * * * * *

Location: Dupuy, West Abitibi, Quebec, Canada.
Date: November 8, 1967.
Time: 2:20 p.m.

The witness Gilles L., involved in an abduction event in 1960 was again summoned telepathically to an area near his barn and again was confronted by the same hovering red 'intelligent' sphere. However this time, a huge object suddenly appeared before him. Losing all will and control, he walked towards the object. Soon a sort of beam of light enveloped him and he was drawn into the object. Strange he felt no fear this time. He found himself lying on a sort of bench with three beings standing around him; the same avian (bird-like) beings he encountered before.

Suddenly an object like a 'cap' descended over him and an unknown device resembling a rod emerged from the object and the witness felt severe pain on the right side of his head. At this point he apparently became unconscious. Later he woke up still inside the alien's vessel. Below and above him were what to him resembled 'prisms' and before him on a wall he saw the same unknown symbols he had seen before. Suddenly the meaning of the same symbols appeared in his head, apparently as a result of the beings doing. It is as if they had wanted him to remember this time. After that he fell unconscious again. He woke up lying on the grass on his side, feeling very cold. The time was 16:20.

According to this witness, in 1939, his father had seen a similar red sphere, but there are no additional details available. Also Gilles states that these beings are capable of changing their molecules so that they can walk through solid doors or walls without leaving any traces, completely disregarding our law of physics. In a recent letter to investigators, Gilles claims to have been abducted in 1971 but gave no details.

HC addendum.
Source: Annie Theriault, investigator AQU insolite08@hotmail.com
Type: G

* * * * * * *

Location: Manaus, Amazonas, Brazil.
Date: November 8, 1967.
Time: Night.

A creature described by police as a "mini skirted" vampire reportedly terrorize locals on a beach. Several people who were attacked described the creature as a blond haired woman with sharp and pointed teeth, wearing a mini skirt and black stockings. Two small round marks were said to have been found near the jugular vein of a child that was bitten.

HC addendum.
Source: Jacques Bergier for INFO.   Type: E

* * * * * * *

Location: Alexania, Goias, Brazil.
Date: November 28, 1967.
Time: 2:18 a.m.

Farmer Wilson Gusmao (involved in other encounters) was suddenly awakened by a telepathic voice that called his name. He got up from bed and upon raising the curtain on the window he noticed a huge bright light resting on the ground about 100 meters from the house. Immediately he attempted to wake his wife but to no avail "she seemed dead" according to Gusmao, he also attempted to awake his brother in law but with the same results.

Walking over the living room he could now clearly see a landed object encased in a bright blue glow that was about 5 meters in diameter. He left a written note to his wife telling her that he was going to check a landed "spacecraft" and grabbing a flashlight walked outside. It was also raining very heavily as Wilson approached to within 3 meters from the object, at this point a bright beam of light from the object struck Wilson around the waist area, this caused him to levitate closer to the object completely paralyzing him.

A door now opened and Wilson could clearly see inside the craft. He could see four humanoids, all dressed in tight-fitting coveralls. They wore a belt with a large buckle that had what appeared to be "piano keys" on it. The beings started at Wilson intently. Wilson somehow felt inferior as the humanoids observed him. He described them as human-like, with long blond hair. Their skin appeared porcelain-like, as they had never been exposed to any sunlight. The leader of the group apparently conversed with Wilson and gave him several messages dealing with the nuclear armaments on Earth. He was to have later contacts along with members of the Brazilian defense establishment including General Uchoa.

HC addendum.
Source: *'Revista Brasileira de Ovnis.'* Type: B

* * * * * * *

Location: Near Americana, Brazil.
Date: November 28, 1967.
Time: 2:30 a.m.

An unidentified Brazilian highway patrolman saw an immense object, "as high as a 15 story building, apparently made of aluminum and with enormous rivets on it," come down to hover 50 yards from the ground. It carried searchlights too bright to look at and made a loud humming sound that made the patrolman's head ache. His police car would not start, and its lights went out, as well as the lights in the police booth; they came back on as soon as the object departed.

Two nights later, the UFO returned, stopping 100 feet up, 50 yards away from him. From its underside descended a sort of open elevator, in which he could see two men dressed like frogmen in skin-tight clothing, wearing wide belts with lights on them. One of them spoke to the patrolman, telling him to put his gun away and not to be afraid, saying that they would be coming back again. Then the object immediately took off. The officer was unable to move during the encounter; "His legs would not obey his will." The object apparently did not return, as promised by the humanoid.

HC addendum.
Source: Methodios Kalkaslief and Dr. Max Berezavsky. Type: B

Location: Pamir Mountains, Tajikistan.
Date: Winter 1967.
Time: Unknown.

Border guards of the Kevran unit saw a hairy "snowman." They reported their observation to their superior, Kuzkov, the officer in charge of the unit. He did not, at first pay any attention to it. The soldiers of the next watch again saw a creature and reported the face. Subsequently, the duty officer accompanied the soldiers to the spot and personally observed the creature. Kuzkov then informed his superior officer, a colonel in Khorog; a settlement on the Tajikistan-Afghanistan border.

News eventually reached the Central Asia Command where in February 1968, a high ranking officer gave the order, *"Catch him or, if that isn't possible, eliminate him!"* Thereupon, the border guards shot the creature and took it to the border post. The body was stored in a woodshed. A subsequent article disclosed that the body was taken to Moscow in great secrecy. (It was also later established that the body of a "Snowman" was found by a shepherd in the Pamir Mountains in the autumn of 1968, but only pieces of the fur and teeth were recovered for study by scientists.)

HC addendum.
Source: Gurov, Boris, *'Snowman against the USSR,'* August, 2001.
Type: H?

* * * * * * *

Location: Barcelona, Spain.
Date: December 3, 1967.
Time: Unknown.

A woman reported seeing a strange bipedal, cactus-like humanoid with four limbs, leaving deep footprints. The witness no longer wants to discuss the incident. No other information.

HC addendum.
Source: Antonio Ribera. Type: E

Location: Near Ashland, Nebraska.
Date: December 3, 1967.
Time: 2:30 a.m.

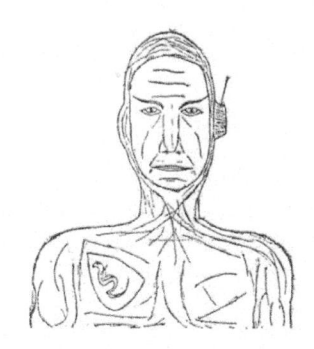

As patrolman Herbert Schirmer's police car approached the junction of Routes 6 and 6-63, the witness saw a row of blinking red lights, which proved to be on a football shaped object about 25 feet long, with a Saturn-like rim. Almost immediately, the object began to rise with a sound like a pulsating siren. At the police station, he made out a report, recording a time lapse of some 20 minutes. A few days later, a Geiger counter showed significant levels of radioactivity at the site. Schirmer took a polygraph test about the same time, which he passed.

Under hypnosis, Schirmer disclosed further details. As he drove toward the UFO, his engine stalled and his lights went out. He reached for his gun and a beam of light from the object paralyzed him. He then saw a white, blurred figure 4-5 feet tall, emerge from the object and approach the car, which had been displaced from the highway from up a slight grade well off the road. By telepathy, he was told that the craft was from another galaxy and its occupants were here "to prevent Earth people from destroying the Earth."

A few months later, under still another hypnotic regression, still more information was forthcoming. He had been conducted inside the object by the figure who approached the car. The details of the occupants were now more detailed; they wore tight fitting pale-gray uniforms, and only their faces were visible; their skin was a pale gray white color, with wide set eyes like a cat's, a slit like mouth and rudimentary nose. They wore boots and gloves and had an emblem in the shape of a winged serpent on the left side of their chest. Additional information was disclosed to Schirmer onboard the object;

- The humanoids "borrowed" electricity from our electric lines.
- They have bases at the poles and on nearby planets.
- They are able to monitor all our communications systems.

- They desire their presence to be known, but not clearly or in detail.
- Their vessels are protected by force fields that are erected around the objects.
- They operate from large "mother-ships" based in nearby space.

Note: On December 25; between Ashland and Lincoln, Nebraska, Gary Lambert, a student from Omaha, was driving home at Christmas when he saw a dimly outlined object with a row of lights hovering over an underpass. The sighting precipitated a number of vivid dreams, in which he believed he had somehow been "contacted" by the beings aboard the object.

HC addendum.
Source: Dr. Roy Craig, Dr. Fred Ahrens, Dr. Leo Sprinkle, Ralph and Judy Blum, Eric Norman and Loring Williams. Type: G

* * * * * * *

Location: Pierre Buffiere, Haute-Vienne, France.
Date: December 6, 1967.
Time: 6:00 a.m.

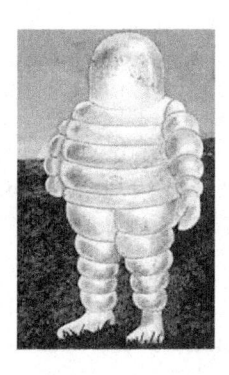

Mr. and Mrs. Pealon were in car when they saw a being about 1.1m in height, wearing an outfit resembling that of the "Michelin" man; the head was like a globe. The figure slid down the embankment near the road, apparently floating in mid-air. He held his hand up twice before disappearing.

HC addendum.
Source: LDLN #195. Type: E

Location: Near Adelphi, Maryland.
Date: December 10, 1967.
Time: 1:15 a.m.

College student Tom Monteleone was driving alone outside of Washington DC. As he was crossing the then partially completed cutoff on Interstate 70, he saw a large object on the road directly ahead. At first he thought it was a tractor-trailer jackknifed across the road. Then he realized it was a bone-white reflective object shaped like an egg and standing on four legs. As he pulled to a stop a few feet from the object he could make out two figures standing next to the craft. One of them walked to his car with a broad grin on his face. He was about 5-feet, ten inches tall, wore light blue coveralls, thick soled boots and he had a ruddy suntanned complexion with large eyes.

The grin remained fixed on his face throughout the episode. *"Do not be afraid of me,"* he said several times in an audible voice. His name, he said, was 'Vadig.' He spoke with the witness for several minutes, asking ordinary questions. Finally he said pointedly, *"I'll see you in time,"* and walked back to the object. A small door opened and a metal ladder folded down. A hand reached out and helped Vadig aboard, and then the object rose silently into the air and disappeared.

HC addendum.
Source: John Keel, *'The Mothman Prophecies.'* Type: B

* * * * * * *

Location: Near Bilcala, Queensland, Australia.
Date: Late December, 1967.
Time: 8:00 p.m.

Silvo Milno was driving near Ballentyne's Lookout, from Gladstone, when he noticed three men in silvery uniforms standing in the road, 100 yards below the lookout. He claimed to have hit one of the men, after which he turned around and drove back to report the incident. The car bore the mark of an impact, although it was first suspected that he had driven into a post.

An hour after the above, a car was seen with five occupants, two girls and three men. The car stopped and the three men were seen to have silver suits; the girls left the car, running toward Gladstone, apparently terrified. Report was made to Bilcala police, who investigated, and sustained a flat tire in the area. They apparently found nothing. Mr. S Dale, a Bilcala ambulance driver, took a sick man to Rockhampton Hospital.

The patient told the driver of an overturned car on the Galliope Range. It was noted that a number of small men in silver uniforms emerged and put the car right side up.

HC addendum.
Source: Keith Basterfield. Type: E?

1968

Location: Nellis Air Force Base, Nevada.
Date: 1968.
Time: Unknown.

Military personnel reported watching a large object hovering above the base for three consecutive days. Three small objects were seen departing the larger craft and one landed on the base grounds. A Colonel accompanied by an armed security detachment was sent to meet the landed craft. While waiting outside, the men watched a short stocky humanoid disembark from the craft.

A green beam of light was then aimed at the Colonel from inside the object causing him to become paralyzed. Orders were then issued to fire on the object and humanoid but all weapons mysteriously jammed. The object and humanoid eventually departed into the larger hovering craft. No other information.

HC addendum.
Source: Len Stringfield, *'UFO Ohio Yearbook,'* 1979.   Type: B
Comments: Interesting report. There has been several reports of alleged contacts in American military bases between aliens and military personnel.

Location: Between Conchali and Santiago, Chile.
Date: 1968.
Time: Unknown.

Agronomist Roberto Iglesias reported hearing a sound resembling the buzzing of helicopter blades, but softer, and at the same time a bright light began illuminating his backyard and an oval-shaped object similar to a top, descended to the ground. Once the object landed, the noises stopped. Soon two human-like figures emerged from the craft. They wore tight-fitting diver's suits that emitted bright flashes of light and walked towards the window where Iglesias stood watching stunned. Moments later the two humanoid figures made several hand gestures to Iglesias indicating that he should step out, but Iglesias chose to remain inside. Then in perfect Spanish the humanoids told Iglesias;

"We have come to invite you on a space journey, do you want to come with us?"

The question further stunned Iglesias and he immediately remembered Einstein's theory of relativity and also thought that if he accepted the invitation he would be used for experiments, he wondered what would happen to his wife and children if he didn't return.

A lot of thoughts crossed his mind. His answer was cordial, *"I thank you for choosing me among millions of other humans that live on Earth. But I am a family man, responsible for my wife and children and would cause them worry if I am gone."* The two humanoids then nodded slightly, apparently agreeing with Iglesias's statement and walked back to their craft, which immediately took off. An area of scorched grass remained on the ground after the incident.

HC addendum.
Source: Jorge Luis Anfruns, *'Ovnis Extraterrestres y otros en Chile.'*
Comments: Translated by Albert S. Rosales.　　　　　　　Type: C?

* * * * * * *

Location: Merida, Yucatan, Mexico.
Date: 1968.
Time: 4:00 p.m.

The main witness, Maricela Soto Ortega (involved in other encounters) was at the time living in a house on 68 Street on the corner of Central de Autobuses de Oriente (Central Bus Station). As she sat on her bed and her husband washed dishes in the kitchen, a strange luminous beam of light suddenly entered the room through the window. Inside the window she could see several 'child-like' figures. The figures or humanoids wore silvery outfits and approached Maricela slowly until they were only about half a meter from her. They were speaking among themselves in a strange language, according to Maricela and their lips did not move as they 'spoke.' They were apparently using telepathy.

At this point Maricela told her husband that there were "extraterrestrials" in the bedroom, but he answered, *"That's not true, they are angels, start praying."* Maricela further described the humanoids as having blue eyes, lacking eyebrows or eyelashes, and small noses and mouths, they had no hair on their heads. Maricela sat on her bed not knowing what to do and a bit afraid she called out to her dog, a German shepherd, so he could chase them out. However as her dog approached the strange figures one of them pulled out a strange "pistol-like implement" which he pointed at the animal. Seconds later a green beam of light shot out of the "pistol" and struck the dog; which fell to the floor prostrate. Maricela thought her dog was dead and began to cry.

She watched as the humanoids seemed to inspect her house and walked by her husband who now seemed to be paralyzed like a statue; apparently in a trance-like state. He later told Maricela that he could not remember the event. Soon after the humanoids left, Maricela took her dog to several veterinarians who could not determine what was wrong with the dog. Sadly the dog had to be put to sleep eventually. Maricela claims that soon after the incident she visited several local media outlets but was ignored.

HC addendum.
Source: http://sipse.com/milenio/extraterrestres-la-secuestraron-dos-veces-24387.html Translated by Albert S. Rosales.   Type: E

* * * * * * *

Location: Savsjon, Varmland, Sweden.
Date: 1968.
Time: Evening.

Lyyli Nilsson had been out fishing with her 11 year old daughter. The girl left her and went home alone. As the child came to a ridge she saw two persons wearing overall like outfits and a bit further up a brownish bell shaped object. A while later her mother passed the same place and saw the men who talked between themselves in an unknown language.

Hiding about 40 meters from them, she saw that they were of a Nordic type and wore silvery overall like outfits. Their craft stood a bit further up on the ridge. When she came home her daughter confirmed Mrs. Nilsson observation.

HC addendum.
Source: Sven Olof Svensson.   Type: C

Location: Trans-Caucasus region, Russia, USSR.
Date: 1968.
Time: Evening.

E. F., a young geologist with a prospecting party in a mountainous rocky area was working near the foothills when he suddenly encountered an unknown "apparatus" the size of a mini-van standing on the surface of the earth. The object had a slit-like opening on its hull. The witness approached the object thinking that maybe it was a brand new experimental Soviet vehicle. As he neared the object he heard strange voices coming from inside the object, through the slit-like opening. He tried to look into the opening but a powerful jolt of energy threw him back, away from the craft, he then blacked out.

He returned to consciousness many hours later under a light rain and was still unable to move. He tried to move his paralyzed body, rocking slightly from side to side. It appeared to be already morning. Gradually the witness on all fours was able to move toward the base camp. From time to time he was able to rise, grabbing on to tree branches, and he would rest for a few minutes and then continue on.

Finally as it got dark the witness reached his camp. There he received stunning news; apparently he had been gone for 2 days, indicating a possible abduction and memory loss. After the incident E.F. began to radically change. The usual interests in life were excluded by a desire to know the foundations of the Universe, astronomy, physics and the existence of other spiritual realms. E. F. obtained paranormal extrasensory capabilities and at times was able to predict the future. He began to see strange humanoid figures around him when no one else was able to see them. His colleagues could not understand him and gradually began to ignore him.

HC addendum.
Source: Dr. Vladimir G. Azhazha PhD, 'Careful, Flying Saucers,' Moscow, 2008. Type: A G or F?
Comments: Obviously an unexplored abduction event with far reaching consequences.

Location: Danvers, Massachusetts.
Date: 1968.
Time: Late evening.

At the same time that his cousin; Gail Wilkins, watched a gigantic cylindrical shaped object while driving along Linebrook Road, Jeffrey Morgan Foss (involved in other encounters), was taken aboard an object that was apparently launched from the large cigar-shaped mothership. Onboard the craft, he remembered that several female and male "grays" were kind and gentle to him. The male being reflected tenderness by placing his hand on Foss while the female was helping Foss to remember about their mutual love for waterfalls. (?)

He was shown a simple test tube with yellow and red blood cells; genetics/incubation technology, self-sustaining deep voyage artificial environment production technology, and microscopic liquid chips. Then they escorted him through a curved corridor running between the inner drum shaped central control room and the outer edge of the disc. Just 15 feet or so around the curved corridor to the left was a room on the right which was very dark without room or control lights. There was a "homeworld head" there that examined Foss closely and then reflected approval to the male and female grays about the project which in this case was Foss himself. He noticed, as his eyes adjusted to the dark, bumps all over the being's head. At first he thought it was a disease but then he saw they were laid out in a perfect pattern. Then he saw a hair-thin line on his forehead. He was wearing a skin-tight cap with perfectly matched the gray of his skin bearing sensors. Upon telepathic inquiry, it was revealed they were for (wireless) multitask fleet communications.

HC addendum.
Source: Jeffrey Morgan Foss liastar@usermail.com   Type: G

* * * * * * *

Location: River Amur, Primorskiy Kray region, Far East, Russia.
Date: 1968.
Time: Night.

Because of the tense relations between the USSR and China at the time, Soviet KGB frontier troops intensified their patrols in the territories of the Russian Far East which bordered the People's Republic of China. One night the crew of a Soviet patrol boat on the River Amur spotted a suspicious object flying in from the Chinese bank of the Amur. When the strange object came closer, the men on the boat realized that the object resembled a winged human figure. The wings were visibly flapping in the air as the entity flew overhead.

At the moment that the winged figure crossed the frontier into Russia, the frontier guards opened fire with their automatic weapons. The flying entity stopped moving its wings and glided down sharply to the nearby taiga and dense pine forest. The crew of the patrol boat radioed headquarters about the incident and the order was given to find the object or creature whatever it was. The KGB frontier guards suspected that the figure was probably a Chinese spy, wearing some kind of flying apparatus or equipment. However a thorough search which included dogs conducted by the frontier guards proved fruitless. The mysterious flying man had disappeared.

HC addendum.
Source: Polina Belova in, *Mir Uvlecheniy* newspaper, Kiev, Ukraine.
Type: E

* * * * * * *

Location: Tacoma, Washington.
Date: 1968.
Time: Night.

Vera Jones should have been in bed, but instead she sat in her kitchen, looking out the window. She had a problem; a husband who drank and mistreated her. Out near the street light she was amazed to see what looked like three large bubbles float down. She hurried outside and was watching when a big round black object with bright, beautiful, red lights came in over the church across the street. Vera rushed back into her house and peered out a window. Three light-skinned tall men, wearing skin-tight diver's suits, were standing near the window. They had handsome faces and spoke in very pleasant, masculine English. The method of communication was mind to mind and not vocal. Here is what Mrs. Jones said happened next.

"The spacemen asked me if I wanted to go for a ride. They said they were from Saturn. They said they had been watching me for some time and that I was a goddess. Then they got mean and said they were going to take my kids away from me. I asked them how they could do such a thing. Then I blew up at them and they went away." In the following days the witness began to hear the spacemen's voices in her front room. They seemed to be discussing her husband's treatment of her.

Once she heard what sounded like swords clashing. She heard them talking about her as she took a bath. At night in bed she felt like something was making love to her but could not see anything. Distraught and full of fear for her children and herself, she went to a nearby fire station, and began to tell the men there about what was happening to her. They soon called the police, and it was not long before she found herself in the local hospital for the insane.

HC addendum.
Source: Don Worley, '*Earthlink*,' spring 1980. Type: E & F
Comments: Did the unfortunate witness meet 'negative' entities that caused her to become paranoid and delusional?

* * * * * * *

Location: Near Vladivostok, Primorsky Kray region, Russia.
Date: 1968.
Time: Night.

At a very isolated region of Northern Siberia a taiga hunter was brought into one of the villages suffering from severe wounds. He had deep facial lacerations and on his hands, and his clothing was torn to shreds, he lost one of his eyes. While at the small medical facility in the village he was flown by helicopter to a better equipped hospital in a larger city. While recovering he told a most amazing story.

According to the unidentified hunter he was in a very isolated area and had come up to a ridge and there during the evening he sought a place where he could stay for the night. Passing by a large rock he noticed a small cave, it was cold and windy so he immediately sought refuge in the cave. His immediate plans including building a small fire in order to warm up, the cave entrance was narrow, so wearing his bulky clothing he barely squeezed through the crevice. However the cave was surprisingly long and narrow, but suddenly expanded by three meters as he found himself in a sort of 'hall' five meters wide.

The far end of the cave was lost in deep darkness as the cave was only illuminated by a weak ray of light from a small torch he carried. The hunter decided to go out and gather branches so he could build his fire; he left behind his gun and small backpack. Collecting twigs and brushwood he returned and built his fire. After warming up he decided to go out again and explore the nearby wood, however later as he returned to the cave he noticed that at the end of the 'hall' something dark stirred. He immediately ran for his rifle but suddenly there was a loud shrilling scream and something attacked him.

As he stood by the fire defending himself he clearly saw the sort of creature that he was fighting against, but only for a moment. He was able to describe a dark man-like creature with huge wings with an approximate wingspan of about 2 meters. The creature had a human head covered with hair but there was no hair on its face. He saw huge eyes and almost no discernible mouth or nose. The creature suddenly glided towards him emitting an incessant wailing howl and suddenly tearing claws were grabbing his face and arms.

As the hunter fell, severely wounded, the strange creature jumped out of the cave. The unfortunate hunter did not notice any legs but noticed that the body was short and forked below. After the creature left, the injured hunter treated his wounds with alcohol and bandaged them as best he could, but he could not completely stop the bleeding. He grabbed his weapon and sat by the fire afraid to go out. An hour later he heard a noise at the entrance of the cave and he fired a shot towards the crevice. He heard a shrill cry and the flapping of wings. As soon as dawn broke the injured hunter left the cave and stumbled towards the closest village. He apparently lost consciousness near the village and was later found by other hunters. He had also lost two fingers on his right hand.

HC addendum.
Source: *Gentry*, 1993, #3, Russia. Type: E

* * * * * * *

Location: Derinkuyu, Turkey.
Date: 1968.
Time: Late night.

Archaeologists exploring burial chambers, tunnels, and catacomb-cities (several of which are linked together at the lower levels) had reached a depth of 900 feet when they were suddenly attacked by a group of 7ft tall albino hairy creatures. One team member was killed and another was hospitalized for several months, and all had serious wounds.

HC addendum.
Source: Raymond Bond, *UFO Annual* 1980 and Kurt Braun, *Beyond Reality* December, 1968. Type: E?
Comments: There is no additional detail on this intriguing case however I can recall another case also in Turkey where a witness was killed by a huge hairy humanoid that apparently was dropped off by a UFO (1964 Koyulhaisar). This case appears to describe a colony of hairy humanoids living underground. Other cases are on record.

Location: Ovsjannikovo, Tselinskiy area, Altay region, Russia.
Date: 1968.
Time: Late night.

Together with her younger sister, Korobkova Tatyana Nikolaevna saw in the darkness the silhouette of a strange figure highlighted by light, wearing loose-fitting overalls with long sleeves. The luminous figure contrasted with the dark sky in the background. A luminous area was also seen in the bottom of the figure which made several movements. Residents of the nearby village of Popovichi saw a bright light in the sky.

HC addendum.
Source: Korobkov Vladimir Vasilevich, Barnaul, and Mikhail Gershtein
Type: E

* * * * * * *

Location: Otoco, Potosi, Bolivia.
Date: Early 1968.
Time: 6:00 p.m.

Valentina Flores was bringing in her llamas when she discovered that her sheep pen was covered with a net made of some plastic like material. Inside the pen was a helmeted being, 3.5ft tall, who was engaged in the killing of her sheep by a tubular instrument having a hook on the end of it. Mrs. Flores threw stones at the being, whereupon he walked over to an instrument resembling a radio and, moving a wheel on it, quickly absorbed all the netting.

The farm woman approached the pen with a cudgel, upon which the being threw his instrument at her several times; it returned to him like a boomerang, after inflicting superficial cuts on her arms. The entity picked up the machine, which had absorbed the net, as well as a bag containing sheep entrails, and put them into a rucksack on his back. Two legs emerged from the rucksack and extended down to the ground, at which time the entity rose straight up into the air with an "extraordinary" sound, and vanished. 34 sheep were found dead and from every one, "certain small portions of the digestive organs were missing."

HC addendum.
Source: Col. R. Ayala and son, and Oscar A Galindez.   Type: E
Comments: Very important and intriguing case actually describing some sort of humanoid performing mutilations on animals. This incident occurred well before the start of the Chupacabra craze and before the 1972-1980 worldwide animal mutilations.

Location: Torres, Rio Grande Do Sul, Brazil.
Date: January 25, 1968.
Time: 11:00 p.m.

Axel Aberg Cobo, a Professor of Human Relations and Journalism, was walking along the beach when a silver colored, luminous object emerged from the ocean 25 yards away, and he felt as though paralyzed. Shortly after, two "men" over 6ft tall, "who looked as though they were made of crystal," walked up to him stiffly, without bending their knees. He felt as if they were communicating with him telepathically.

They greeted him by touching shoulders, and one of the beings, which had introduced himself as 'Rubinako,' said to him, *"Krebs, Navis, Karsicujo, Krero."* Cobo noted these words down, writing with a ballpoint pen on his bare arms and legs. Then they told him they would meet him again in Mar Del Plata, Argentina. He had a vague recollection that the craft took off vertically.

HC addendum.
Source: *FSR* Vol. 14 #6.   Type: G?
Comments: Possibly an unexplored abduction event. I believe the witness had further contacts with the aliens.

* * * * * * *

Location: Near Adelphi, Maryland.
Date: February, 1968.
Time: Night.

After work Sunday, a friend dropped off Tom Monteleone at home. As the friend pulled away, a large black car with its lights out glided out of the shadows and halted at the curb. The entity called 'Vadig' then called out to the witness from the car. Another man was in the car, Monteleone later recalled only that he wore a gray coat, had black hair, and never spoke. The witness got into the car. The car was a very old Buick, but was very well kept, it looked brand new, and it even smelled brand new. They drove for about 30 minutes to a remote spot on a back road.

When the witness got out of the car he was astonished to see an egg-shaped object waiting for them. Inside the object he was put into a circular room containing nothing but a couple of bucket seats and a gray TV screen. Vadig and his companion disappeared into another part of the craft. After a few minutes the TV screen came alive, the object shuddered, and the witness watched the image of the earth receding to a tiny speck on the screen. Three or four hours passed. It seemed like hours before another planet appeared on the screen, it grew larger, and then the craft landed with a thump. The young witness found himself in a place no too unlike the Earth. He and Vadig got into a wheel-less vehicle that traveled along a kind of through.

"This is Lanulos," Vadig announced with pride in his voice. Their vehicle traveled through a large city with low, flat buildings and signs written in some kind of Oriental looking characters. The people, male and female, were all nude. After the tour, they returned to the egg-shaped craft and took off again. The witness sat alone in the same circular room watching the television screen for hours. Finally they arrived back on Earth at the same place from which they had left. The witness, Vadig, and the silent man returned to the old Buick and drove for about 30 minutes until they reached his apartment house. "I'll see you in time," Vadig declared as the car drove off. To the witness amazement the whole trip, including the 30-minute rides to and from the planet, had taken less than two hours.

HC addendum.
Source: John Keel, *'The Mothman Prophecies.'* Type: G

* * * * * * *

Location: Honolulu, Hawaii.
Date: Spring 1968.
Time: 5:00 a.m.

Robert D. Miles who was living onboard a forty seven foot trimaran was docked at Honolulu's Alawi Yacht Harbor. On that early morning he had gotten up early and made some coffee and was lying on his bunk worrying about current events in his life. Suddenly he experienced a dazzling array of shimmering light followed by an intense tingling of energy, which filled the entire stateroom and engulfed him. His entire body began to vibrate as a beautiful woman materialized in the walkway right next to his bed. His first reaction was, believing that he was dreaming or hallucinating. But the woman spoke to him and took his hand. In a matter of moments he came to understand that the woman was real and much more alive than him. The energy aura that she emanated made his entire being vibrate at a level that could only be described as ecstasy.

He asked, *"Why have you come to visit me?"* She replied, *"Myself and others like me are friends, and we want you to come to a very important briefing."* Moments after agreeing to go with her, an unparalleled series of events occurred. First he was teleported to New York City. He then boarded a saucer-like spacecraft and was transported to an extraterrestrial location for the briefing. The extraterrestrials orchestrated the briefing to give him and about fifty other guests a glimpse of Earth's history. They also showed them a dramatic and vivid view of humankind's potential destiny.

After the briefing, he was asked to undertake a mission. He agreed to publish a story about his experience and to place an ad in a major newspaper, saying simply, if you have the spirit of adventure and are willing to work, come sail with us. Upon returning to the sailboat he realized that only 33 minutes had passed. However from his personal perspective, it seemed like many unhurried hours had been spent with these incredible beings. To this day he remains convinced that the series of events were real and not a dream or delusion.

HC addendum.
Source: http://ufoexperiences.blogspot.com and Robert D. Miles.
www.safespaceproject.com   Type: G

* * * * * * *

Location: Point Pleasant, West Virginia.
Date: March, 1968.
Time: 1:00 a.m.

The witness was coming back home from work late one night when he noticed something whisk across his windshield. At first he thought it was a bird, but was not sure. When he looked over on the side of the road, he saw a very tall man-like figure. Just then, a flash of light came from the being and it was gone. One month later, his right ear (the ear closest to the flash) went deaf for no apparent reason and still is.

HC addendum.
Source: Cryptozoology.com   Type: E
Comments: Appears to be one of the last Mothman reports from the area. The flash of light is intriguing.

* * * * * * *

Location: Embarcacion, Salta, Argentina.
Date: March, 1968.
Time: Afternoon.

A girl playing in an empty field was suddenly confronted by a strange female entity she described as being "the virgin." Witnesses reported that the girl stood transfixed staring at a point for more than an hour.

HC addendum.
Source: Proyecto CATENT, Argentina.   Type: E

Location: Valparaiso, Chile.
Date: March 4, 1968.
Time: 1:45 a.m.

Ricardo Antonio Castillo was resting in his home on Eloy Alfaro Street when he suddenly watched a brilliant elongated craft descend towards the ground nearby. At the same time the object emitted a strong roaring sound. Two tall humanoids, wearing tight fitting white-silvery clothing exited the object. Both appeared to be wearing some sort of 'mask' that covered their faces. The beings approach Castillo and a telepathic exchange ensued:
Entities: *"We will cure your eyesight but it will be bad for you."*
Castillo: *"I don't understand, why."*
Entities: *"You will carry the message. The inhabitants of Earth are very close minded."*
Castillo then asked the entities if they would take him to their ship and was told that they will return for him. After this enigmatic exchange, the entities returned to their craft and it left. Antonio Castillo needed prescription eyeglasses but after this experience he never had to use them again. This fact was corroborated by attended eye doctors or physicians.

HC addendum.
Source: Jorge Luis Anfruns, *'Extraterrestres en Chile.'*　　　　Type: B

* * * * * * *

Location: (Undisclosed location) Mekong River, Vietnam.
Date: March 16, 1968.
Time: 11:20 p.m.

The main witness who was on vessel security watch on this night and another crewman had both previously seen fireballs crossing over the river. So, on this night he decided to wave his flashlight at it. It crossed to the center of the river, always to the same spot, where they anchored their gravel barges. It sat there for about 10 minutes, just a ball of fire, soon the fire dissipated and the witness saw a disc-shaped object about 30 meters in diameter with a dome on top and a smaller dome on the bottom.

The color of the object was silver metallic and it had rotating amber and white lights with a small greenish light on the bottom. It hovered for about two minutes and then started moving towards their vessel (a US Army 65ft harbor tug). The disc then turned off its lights and stopped at approximately 10 feet from where the main witness was standing. For some reason he felt no fear. There was absolutely no noise as the upper dome started to shift, revealing a window-like opening which covered a quarter of the dome. An eerie green light illuminated the inside of the craft. Suddenly an occupant peered from the side of the window, then two more appeared, just looking at the witness. He wavedd at them and they wave back.

This went on for about five minutes or so. The occupants were pointing at his uniform and rifle, so he put the rifle down. He described the humanoids as about 3.5ft in height, with bluish-green skin, large eyes; not almond shaped but round with bright green pupils, slender bodies with four digits on each hand. They resembled small children, with small ears, nose and mouth which never opened. They appeared to be using hand language and were pointing at different items. The witness was trying to communicate but didn't know how. So he gestured to them that he was going to get another crewmember from below, so he went below and woke the skipper.

The skipper didn't know what the witness was trying to tell him so he came topside and the disk had moved around the rear of the vessel, and the skipper was about to "chew him out" when the disc moved forward. At this point the skipper began screaming and began grabbing for the rifle. The witness fought with skipper, preventing him from shooting at the disc and kept yelling at the occupants of the disc to get "out of range." Just as soon as the disc moved away from the vessel, the skipper started calming down. The disc then moved up the river and suddenly disappeared at high speed.

HC addendum.
Source: MUFON CMS. Type: A

* * * * * * *

Location: Fos-su-Mer, Arles, France.
Date: March 29, 1968.
Time: 1:15 a.m.

An unidentified 22-year-old mechanic, on a motorbike between Fos-sur-Mer and Port Saint Louis, observed a UFO, descend, and land near a power transformer. An opening appeared in the base from which was emitted a bright white light. Then a human appearing entity emerged and descended to the ground on a kind of ramp. He wore a sort of security guard's outfit with a "rolled collar." The suit was light colored and brilliant, woven of heavy stitches. The man's hair was white-blond or white, and cut in a crew-cut.

He examined the ground around him and then noticed the witness, whom he watched for a moment before re-entering the object. The UFO took off gently with a gust of cool air.

HC addendum.
Source: Joel Mesnard and Jean Marie Bigorne. Type: B
Comments: Clear case describing a human-like occupant, this time with a crew cut instead of long blond hair.

* * * * * * *

Location: Near Selah, Washington.
Date: Between April 28 and May 6, 1968.
Time: Night.

A woman who owns several hundred acres of orchards in the Selah-Yakima area, and who resides elsewhere except during the smudging season, related the following information to an APRO member, which involved members of her smudging crews. According to the informant, many members of the crew had seen strange objects in the air for eight days. These consisted of reddish and yellowish lights moving slowly or hovering near the orchards. On one occasion a very large object which disgorged five smaller objects was seen, and the smaller objects, upon taking to the air disappeared in different directions at very high speed.

On the same night that the large object was observed, a 16-year old member of one of the crews was en route to another part of the orchard by car. He was just coming to work and was unaware of the sighting which had taken place earlier. As he passed through a wooded area, his attention was arrested by a light off to his left. He stopped the car for a better look and was astonished to see three "beings" emerge from the trees. He estimated the distance from the beings to himself to be about 600 feet and they were coming toward him.

The closer they got, he realized that they were very small; 4 feet tall or less. He described them as being dressed in orange-colored clothing of a shiny texture. He said they were human-like in appearance and he recalls seeing what he thought were ears but the other facial features were indistinct. There was no hair or other covering on the heads. The boy was badly frightened and wondered why they were approaching and what they intended to do. He began to panic, and thinking of nothing else to do, he honked the horn of the car as loud and as long as he could. At this point two other similar beings of the same size emerged from the right side of the road and came toward the car.

At this juncture, another young man; also a member of the smudging crew, heard the sounds of the car horn and ran up the road to investigate. He came up to the other's car and opened the door and found the young man virtually at the point of collapse. He thought the car's occupant was dying because he gave no response and seemed almost unconscious. After being revived, the principal in this case was taken back to the ranch house and he stated that the beings had approached to within about 25 feet of the car when they suddenly turned around and walked back toward the left of his car and disappeared among the trees. They did not "glide" as is reported in some landing cases, nor did they run; they simply walked away.

On the morning after the incident the lady who owns the orchards went with the two boys to the area where the beings were seen. At the place where the beings turned back, a fence (a mesh "hog fence") was strung across that area. At this spot and surrounding it were six imprints in the soil which resembled footprints but were 8 inches long, had a narrow heel, no instep and a "paddle-shaped" foot. There was also an area which appeared to have been dug up. Also during the eight day period during which many phenomena were seen, was the manifestation of an all-encompassing blue light which would suddenly illuminate a large area of several acres and just as suddenly disappear. Those who reported this phenomenon said it was so bright they could see every twig and every detail of the landscape. Nothing was seen in the sky or on the ground to account for the light.

HC addendum.
Source: *APRO Bulletin*, May-June, 1968. Type: E

* * * * * * *

Location: Between Fargo and Kindred, North Dakota.
Date: May 5, 1968.
Time: 1:45 a.m.

Jerome Clark and three other young men had gone to a site where a "ghost light" was reported to be seen, and had chased it fruitlessly in their car. When it re-appeared a few minutes later, against its red orange light they could see the silhouette of a huge figure that was gliding toward them. They took off in the car, but when they looked again from a side road, the silhouetted figure was still visible, and still moving towards them. This time they drove several miles before stopping.

HC addendum.
Source: Jerome Clark, *FSR* Vol. 15 #6. Type: E

Location: La Florida, Argentina.
Date: May 22, 1968.
Time: 3:00 a.m.

Mr. T. Banescu was returning home when he observed a luminous sphere coming down rapidly from the sky. It landed about 300 meters away. Shortly afterwards he heard footsteps behind him, but noticed nothing strange about then. When he got to the house he encountered a creature no more than 39" tall, with big ears and of luminous green coloring. He had his arms crossed, and was rocking his body slightly, back and forth. When Mr. Banescu in desperation, tried to open the door of his house, he found that the individual had disappeared.

HC addendum.
Source: Carlos Banchs. Type: C?

* * * * * * *

Location: Near Flagstaff, Arizona.
Date: Summer 1968.
Time: Evening.

    The witness and her daughter were driving across the Mojave Desert, about two hours outside of Flagstaff. The daughter began to shout that she saw a spaceship in the sky. The sky was unusually cloudy, and she looked to where her daughter was pointing and saw first two and then three lights moving rapidly in the sky, turning at ninety degree angles, pulsating an disappearing, etc. She decided to pull off the road onto a dirt trail she saw on the right, leading into the desert. They were away from the road lights, but she thought she could still see them at a distance.
    They watched the sky together, when suddenly in the front of the car there appeared a huge, dark and glowing object with a partial row of lights in the middle. The next thing she remembers was her breath being knocked out of her as she somehow went through the windshield of the car. She remembers looking back for an instant and the car was completely empty of herself and her daughter, and she was stepping into an opening in a vehicle. She couldn't see her daughter and she asked in terror about her. *"She's going to be all right,"* was what she heard in the center of her mind, and she was strangely soothed and unusually happy.
    The beings were tall, about six and a half feet, and seemed to be robed in a fabric that emitted a type of light periodically, during movement. Their skin was silvery and their eyes were round and a violet-blue that sometimes streamed out on her with a feeling of love or long lost family; it was almost like a homecoming. Their eyes were closer to the surface of their faces than humans,' and the nose wasn't well defined. Their mouths

were fascinating. Sometimes it seemed that they weren't dressed at all, and the body definition wasn't sexually differentiated.

She was standing with two of them and noticing that they had no hair, but there was something like fabric that was crumpled and folded behind their backs. They seemed to be smiling, without moving their mouths. As soon as she thought "hair," one of them seemed to produce beautiful reddish gold hair all over its head. This frightened her. The room she was looking into was about twenty five feet wide and semicircular. It was rather dark, and filled with TV screens running the full wall area, stacked upon one another three and sometimes four rows high. All sorts of pictures appeared on the screens, and strange symbols, and terrains she'd never seen. Under the screens was a type of built-in-desk, curving all along the wall.

In the middle of the room was a long table with three or four chairs that were movable. There were three beings in the chairs, two of them facing the screens and moving around, while another one at the desk area stood from time to time, moving things around. They did not look up. They seemed to be of the same slender body type as the two that stood with her, but were not quite so tall. Those two seemed to be laughing all the time and sometimes there was a sound like wind. They kept saying, *"Welcome, welcome!"* in her mind, and laughing. They then told her some strange things about human origins and alien intervention on the planet Earth at various times in the past and future. Then they started speaking to her about her individual history.

There was a whole generation of beings that came to Earth in the far past and took up Earth life. They were from the family of "Ranm." That root family was their name root also, but either that planet wasn't in existence anymore, or it was now inaccessible. They said that was why the old god names were as they were on Earth; Rama, Brahma, Ra in Egypt and Abraham, etc, in order that humans might remember. But so much confusion set in that the names became designations for gods, heroes, and that wasn't the point at all. Rather it indicated the name form of the origin of them and some of us, being from other star systems. Then they began telling her, her name in their tongue, 'Shalisha Li Ekimu Ranm,' and kept saying it in her head until she got it right. They said those words meant much more, and could be found in Earth literature. There was such love flowing through them, as they helped her with the name and the earth lineages that went back to the stars. This communication wasn't exactly like 'words' but were rather images or sound pictures that moved between them.

Then they took her through a gray, curved corridor to the right of the entrance where she'd come in. She can remember not being able to walk, and then walking with ease. They came to a room at the end and to the left of the corridor. This room contained the ship's driving mechanism. In front of her was a huge crystal, perhaps three feet across in the middle.

It looked like two pyramids placed base to base, although at times it seemed multifaceted and totally brilliant and jewel-like. The crystal seemed suspended in the air, and around it was a matrix of wires or tubes connected into a solid type of material concealing the ends of the tubes in a dark smooth mass, so that the entire thing rose about four feet from the floor. They told her to put her mind into the crystal, and as she did she'd be able to learn how to fly the ship. (!)

One of them telepathically told her how to do it, she tried and failed, but they kept coaxing her and she could hear them smiling, *"Go on, you can do it!"* Finally she got it right and they began to move out, first above the Earth and then through the angular pattern of space that was also time. She asked why she had to do this, and they only said, *"So that you can remember flying and piloting when necessary,"* and then there was laughter. After the initial information was placed in the crystal and wire matrix, nothing more was necessary, but they stood there anyway until they said, *"Time to return to Earth."* Frantically, she panicked and asked about her daughter and was soothed again by them saying she was okay.

Then they said they were sorry, but didn't say why, and then there was great love. As they moved to the exit place, they said her name again several times, and something about "soul lineage." She was reluctant to go, but the next thing she knew she had gone through the car windshield again, and found herself hanging out of the window gasping for air; she began to cry and was covered with sweat. Her daughter was in the backseat crying. Her daughter told her never to touch her again, and that she knew who she was and she hated her. She tried to calm her and asked what had happened to her, and she shouted, *"I'll never tell you! Leave me alone!"* After the incident, the witness hair began to fall out and her mouth started bleeding, and she was exhausted.

HC addendum.
Source: Whitley and Anne Strieber, *'The Communion Letters.'*
Type: G

* * * * * * *

Location: Taranto, Italy.
Date: June, 1968.
Time: 00:20 a.m.

While walking along the Ceglie Messapica Road the witness, A. C. noticed at about 100 meters away a very strong luminosity blue-violet in color, about 10 meters in diameter and apparently hovering about 20/30 cm from the ground. Approaching the object he noticed that within the light he could see an illuminated disc-shaped craft. Through an opening he could see two humanoid figures about 1.2 meters in height, wearing tight-fitting dark coveralls and helmets moving about, apparently operating some instruments.

Moments later one of the humanoids turned around and stared directly at the witness who felt afraid and turned to run to his car. As he ran away he "heard" a voice in his head telling him; *"Do not be afraid, we are a peaceful people,"* he fled without seeing the object leave. The next morning upon returning to the site, he found a depressed section on the ground of about 10 meters in diameter and about 30 cm in depth. He also found a strange looking irregular-shaped silvery stone, which he kept. Analysis proved to be made out of "normal" Earth minerals.

HC addendum.
Source: CISU Puglia. Translated by Albert S. Rosales.	Type: A

* * * * * * *

Location: Jay, Florida.
Date: June, 1968.
Time: Late night.

The main witness was sleeping with her young daughter, who was suffering from an inoperable cancerous brain tumor, when she suddenly awoke to see three cloaked beings that were standing at the foot of their bed. They were apparently communicating with each other but not with the witness. When the witness attempted to reach over to touch her daughter she realized that she was unable to move. All she could do was move her eyes.

The beings then came over to the side of her bed and a very peaceful feeling came over her, the being that was directly opposite to the witness right shoulder, bent over and touched her daughter, and everything went quiet and the witness' memory ended at this point.

The next day her daughter experienced a massive nosebleed, she apparently expelled a very large blood clot from her nose, almost gagging her. A few moments later the witness took her daughter for a new CT scan. Soon she was surprised to learn her daughter's tumor was completely gone apparently removed by a laser, according to her doctor. Her daughter is now cancer free.

HC addendum.
Source: NUFORC.	Type: E
Comments: Another apparent cure claim.

Location: Near Buenos Aires, Argentina.
Date: June 4, 1968.
Time: 1:00 a.m.

Walking home after midnight, artist Benjamin Solari Parravicini, was suddenly confronted by a fair-skinned man with eyes "so light in color that he looked as if blind," who addressed him in an unintelligible guttural language. Looking upward, the witness saw only 50 yards away; a hovering aerial craft, with no lights.

He became dizzy, and when he recovered, he found himself inside the machine, with three other persons. One of these, very handsome, was questioning Parravicini in an alien language, which he was able to understand telepathically. They told him that they would take him once around the Earth, and he observed Japan, France, and Chile before being returned to the same street corner. Since this experience, the alien beings have contacted Parravicini several times.

HC addendum.
Source: Gordon Creighton, *FSR* Vol. 14 #5, citing *La Razon*, June 4, 1968, and Correio do Povo, June 11, 1968.   Type: G

* * * * * * *

Location: Near Celano, Abruzzi, Italy.
Date: June 14, 1968.
Time: 6:00 p.m.

At the same time that an asteroid named "Icarus" came very close to the Earth, strange events were reported in northern Italy. A hysterical woman phoned the police station reporting that three huge, disc-shaped objects were hovering outside of town, the objects glowed a pale red. Lt. Germonde took the call. Minutes later, other witnesses reported seeing "spinning discs" the size of houses slowly descend to the ground in a wooded area near the town. But soon it really got weirder. Germonde received a call from a bar-restaurant owner reporting "huge birds with tiny wings and with faces like humans."

According to the witness there were four or five huge birds flying towards Celano. The strange creatures were described as 3-feet in height and flying upright, as if they were men being propelled above the ground by some unknown force. No wings were visible; only a blur above their shoulders, like the wings of a hummingbird. Whatever kept them flying was small and moving very fast. The creatures reportedly flew at a height of only a few feet above the ground. They appeared to have trouble moving in heavily wooded areas. Their faces were reported to have been human like, which contained a blank look. The next day, Arturo Gerraci, on his way home and drunk, stumbled on a bird-like corpse in the woods. Running all the way back to the tavern howling that he came across the "corpse of a winged monster" in the woods.

First reluctant to follow him to the woods, some men did go to the spot and recovered the body of a strange creature. A Dr. Respighi examined the corpse and described it as, "A creature of about 3-feet in height, weighing approximately 41 pounds, having arms and legs formed roughly the same as those of a normal human, that is to say with fingers, opposing thumb, and toes, complete with joint structure. A wing like appendage attached roughly halfway between shoulder and neck on each side of the head. It was made up of tiny, thin, but extremely strong pieces of cartilage, apparently capable of moving very rapidly."

The creature had no eyes. In their place was a cluster of tiny, filament like antenna, protected by a tissue thin membrane of skin. It had also gill like apertures capable of oxygen intake. Incredibly as the body was being examined, it was decomposing at an incredibly rapid rate. The tissue seemed to dry up and crumble into powdery flakes. Respighi had the corpse put in a freezer, hoping to preserve it, until colleagues could arrive and examine it. By the time they arrived, even on the ice, the corpse decomposed to a grayish white powder.

HC addendum.
Source: Richardo Salvador, *The Ohio Sky Watcher*, quoting Roger Veillith.   Type: D & H?

* * * * * * *

Location: Poopo, Oruro, Bolivia.
Date: June 19, 1968.
Time: Night.

Romulo Velazquez, 25, a miner, saw a UFO land, from which emerged a strange being, tall and thin, to which the witness felt drawn "as if by a magnet." When he got close, the humanoid took hold of his right wrist, which he then felt paralyzed and lost consciousness.

Neighbors, including police officers, saw the UFO maneuvering for some minutes over Poopo at a low altitude, illuminating the village "like daylight." Emitting blue rays, it rose and disappeared. Velazquez was found paralyzed on one side by a stroke, caused by cerebral hemorrhage. At the landing site was a wide area of burnt grass.

HC addendum.
Source: *FSR* Vol. 14 #5.   Type: B

Location: Bulnes, Chillan, Chile.
Date: June 20, 1968.
Time: Various.

A strange creature said to be a mixture between a human and an animal, about 2 and a half meters in height and with wing-like protrusions coming out of each arm has been reported by several locals in the area. The strange creature's torso and head was described as totally white in color.

Many local farmers panicked and the sight of the creature. Locals organized search groups in order to locate the strange beasts but there were reports that some of the cars filled with the 'vigilantes' were repelled backwards at least 10 meters by some unseen and inexplicable force as they traveled through the area where the creature had been seen.

HC addendum.
Source: Cesar Parra, *'Guia Magica de Santiago'* quoting Agencia EFE news service, June 24. Type: E

* * * * * * *

Location: Avellaneda, Buenos Aires, Argentina.
Date: June 20, 1968.
Time: Unknown.

Eustaqui Zogorwski, 63, a Polish immigrant, claimed that on the above date he was drugged by a man who drove up to his house in Avellaneda in a black car. When he came to, he found himself in "a hallucination world, where giant beings were dwelling in an aerial city." Two of these beings, over 2 meters tall, conducted Mr. Zogorwski to a tower in the center of the city, seemingly suspended in space; he was seated at a table around which sat 12 similar giants.

They took his arms and he began to "trace signs automatically." He believed that they had "brain washed" him. He was finally released between the towns of Brinkmann and Cotagaita, in Cordoba, where the mysterious man in the black car picked him up and delivered him to his home.

HC addendum.
Source: Humcat quoting, Newspaper source. Type: G

Location: Near Las Vegas, Nevada.
Date: June 23, 1968.
Time: 8:00 p.m.

The witness was driving from Las Vegas when he saw a round saucer-shaped object land on a dirt road not too far away from the road. The witness drove up the dirt road to the craft, which had landed on three leg-like protrusions. Soon three bearded men, very human in appearance disembark from the object. They approached the witness that had by now exited his vehicle and expressed curiosity as to his long hair.

The witness explained that he just wanted to wear it like that and was not into drugs or anything. They seemed to appreciate that. They then told him that they came from a world with no cities where its inhabitants were born in the wilderness. They told him that cities were a danger to their society. They called themselves "Dodonians." The witness shook hands with the men and they boarded the craft, which quickly left the area.

HC addendum.
Source: NUFORC. Type: B

* * * * * * *

Location: Laguna Paiva, Santa Fe, Argentina.
Date: June 24, 1968.
Time: 1:10 a.m.

The witness, Mrs. Dora Egger de Torrez was sleeping with her husband when she was suddenly awakened by a strong buzzing sound that was hurting her ears. When she looked around she noticed on the corner of the bedroom an oval-shaped light and inside of it two human-like figures, one tall, about 2 meters in height and the second only about 50 or 70cm in height. Both wore tight-fitting metallic brown diving suits and helmets with plastic-visors that covered their faces.

The shorter creature seemed to move its hands and walked towards the witness who suddenly felt a sort of burning sensation in her body. The shorter figure appeared to have noticed and retreated backwards. The taller figures at times walked around the shorter humanoid at times showing his back. When the witness attempted to wake her husband the shorter figure again approached and she felt paralyzed, and could not move her hand, which seemed to bump against something invisible. She is not sure how long the observation lasted.

The humanoids seemed to have communicated with her and she felt that they had told her they would return someday. However she did not hear any words being spoken and did not noticed their lips moving.

Finally the oval shaped light its occupants seemed to suddenly shrink in size until vanishing from sight along with the loud buzzing sound. Only at that moment was Dora able to wake her husband punching him really hard on the stomach. He found his wife in an extremely excited state, repeating the phrase, "they will return."

Dora later found a strange blister on the top of her mouth that remained there for several days. A neighbor that visited the location noticed a strong odor resembling that of burning electrical wire, which appeared to be stronger on the corner where the humanoids had originally appeared.

HC addendum.
Source: Dr. Oscar A Galindez, *FSR* Vol. 27 #1.   Type: E

* * * * * * *

Location: Cerro De Las Rosas, Cordoba, Argentina.
Date: June 27, 1968.
Time: 5:30 p.m.

Three children, Hugo Cesar Messina, Oscar Crespo, and a third boy whose name has been kept confidential, were bicycling when they were surprised by the appearance of a silvery colored object, which had on its lower part a kind of helix, where lights of white and sky-blue were revolving. The UFO remained hovering about 20 meters up and 50 meters away from the boys.

On the upper part of the object appeared a couple, a man, and a woman, floating in the air. They were of enormous stature, with long white hair, and wore luminous close fitting garments. Holding hands, they began to go down slowly, disappearing into the object without any door opening. The luminous helix began to rotate at greater speed, and the UFO went away at great speed.

HC addendum.
Source: Carlos Banchs.   Type: B

Location: Borrego Sink, near Borrego Springs, California.
Date: July, 1968.
Time: Morning.

    Treasure hunter, Harold Lancaster was prospecting in the Borrego Sink when he saw a "sandman." He was camped up on a mesa one morning when he saw a 'man' walking in the desert. The figure came closer, and he thought it was another prospector. Then he picked up his binoculars and saw the strangest sight in his life. "It was a real giant ape-man," Lancaster said. He had heard about the screaming giant ape-man up in Tuolumne County that frightened people for a couple of years. As the 'sandman' drew closer, Lancaster became worried. "That thing was big. I was no match for it," he reported. He had a .22 pistol on his hip but it would have been like shooting at a gorilla with a pea shooter.
    He was afraid the beast might get too close. So he fired a couple of rounds into the air. The sandman jumped a good three feet off the ground when the sounds of the shots reached him. He turned his head, looked toward Lancaster and then took off running in the other direction. Lancaster later admitted that he was afraid to shoot the strange beast. "They should be protected. They're a form of human, a primitive species. It would be murder to kill one. They should be studied."

HC addendum.
Source: http://thechurchofufology.blogspot.com/   Type: E

* * * * * * *

Location: Grodner Pass, Dolomite Mountains, Italy.
Date: July, 1968.
Time: 1:00 a.m.

    The witness, Walter Rizzi, had been working with a Bolzano firm, as their representative for all Southern Tyrol. Since he had been born in the Dolomite Mountains himself (in Campitello di Fassa) it had always given him great pleasure to travel around in this region, and thus it came about that he had his UFO experience, one night in July of that year. He had spent the evening in the company of a Dutch girl who was holidaying at St. Kassian in the Gader Valley. He said goodbye to her at midnight and decided to go via the Grodner Pass and the Stella Pass to Campitello, where his aunt managed a Sporthotel.

The weather that night was not very good. The sky was overcast with very thick, heavy clouds, and only rarely did he catch a glimpse of any stars. At times the road went through banks of mist which enveloped the mountains, so that he had to drive very slowly and stop to take his bearings repeatedly. Several times he had been within meters of driving off the road and over the edge so finally he decided that, at the first favorable opportunity, he would pull up and park beside the road and try to get a little sleep.

After going over the Grodner Pass he came to a spot where there was a heap of sand beside the road, and he decided to stop near there. He lowered his seat so as to recline. It was about one o'clock and he was very tired and badly in need of sleep. Then suddenly he found himself awake again, and he smelt a strong odor as though from something burning. At once he thought his Fiat 600 must be on fire, or maybe he had a short circuit somewhere in the wiring. He jumped out of the car quickly and with his flashlight made a checkup but found everything in perfect order.

As he was walking around the car he caught sight of a light, about 500 meters or so it seemed, further on downhill, on the other side of the road, shining through the mist. It looked like the light from the terrace of some hotel, and this made him wonder, for he knew very well indeed there were no hotels whatsoever in that area, and no houses either, the whole place being quite uninhabited. He knew the whole area like the inside of his trouser pockets, as he must have been through there a good thousand times in his life. Then the bank of mist parted, and he saw an enormous thing there with a very queer white light. His heart started to beat madly, and simultaneously he recalled his meeting with a strange hermit during his time in the Italian Army in 1942.

At the time of the meeting he was serving as an interpreter between the Italian and German Air Forces, and was stationed at the Gadurra airfield on the Greek Island of Rhodes. The civilian population of Rhodes was suffering extreme privation at the time, and almost daily a little Greek girl about ten years old came to Walter to beg for a piece of bread. He enjoyed a good deal of freedom in his job, for he was always with the senior officers, and in actual fact they did not have any control over him, as one time he would be at the German headquarters and at another time with the Italians.

Consequently he had quite a lot of free time, and he was able to fix it for the little girl with the angel face to have some good food from the Mess. One day he asked her whether she took all the food home, and how many brothers and sisters there were in the family. She explained that she had only her parents and that she gave half the food to a Holy Man who had been living in the mountains for more than a hundred years and never came down into the valley, and she said she was the only person permitted to take food to him and talk to him.

It took him many weeks before he could persuade her to take him to the see the Holy Man, and when he first set eyes on him he was struck by his thinness. His skin was all wrinkled like a shrunken apple, he was almost stark naked with very long hair and beard, and his eyes were pitch black and shining. He did not extend his hand to Walter in greeting, but did it by raising his hand in the air. His look went right through the witness and he said to him, *"Esi kala"* meaning; *"You are good."* And so it came to pass that Walter spent a lot of time with the old hermit, sometimes for even as much as two or three days in a row. In order to absent himself for so long without anyone going to look for him, he would go the Italian Headquarters and tell them he had to go over with the Germans who needed him and then would tell the Germans the same thing about the Italians.

The hermit told him he was over a hundred years old, and he taught him how to read the most important signs from the palm of the hand, and how to tell a person's character from his face, and he also taught him a prayer in magical ancient Greek, words which had always to be pronounced at precisely the same time of the day and in trance. This was, he explained, good for purifying the spirit and for achieving a positive influence in the Cosmic Magnetic Field. Once a month the old hermit retired into isolation and remained immobile like a statue for two days.

He told Rizzi that he was able to travel through the Universe, and there were countless numbers of planets far distant from our solar system and inhabited by completely different creatures. He prophesized that Rizzi would one day meet beings from the Cosmos and that they would provide him with the assurance and the certainty of the existence of life throughout the Universe. Rizzi asked him to tell him more about his future, and he said that the "voice of your conscience is already seeking for the Light, and that all he needed to do was to carry on along the same path." He told him that once he had attained perfect concentration in the prayer that he had taught him, he would be able to give me a sign of his presence, and this would be simply by means of a powerful odor. Finally after many years, Rizzi did manage, every three or four months or so, to reach such concentration that, wherever he might be, he would receive a strong smell of roses and lilies of the valley.

Returning to the matter of the enormous object, Rizzi was instantly convinced that the moment had now come that had been foretold by the old hermit. The ground sloped away down from the side of the road and as it was very dark, he had to take his flashlight. Treading with great care, he made his way down to the level area where the huge object was standing, and as he got closer, he could see it more and more clearly.

There was now another break in the belt of mist and his heart started beating madly. He could feel the veins in his neck greatly swollen, but he had no fear, he was merely terribly excited.

The object was wonderfully beautiful, silvery in color, and about 80 meters in diameter, standing on three legs about two meters long and about two meters thick at the bottom. The UFO was bathed in a fleecy white light, and the burning smell that had awakened Rizzi was intense and overwhelming. When he got to a distance of about three meters from the object, he felt himself suddenly halted, blocked with a sensation that his body weighed 1,000 kilos. He could not move another inch and found that great effort was needed to breathe. The transparent cupola on the top of the craft now lit up brightly and he saw two beings in it that were looking down at him.

On the right hand side of the machine there was a robot, about 2 and a half meters high, and with three legs and four arms. It was holding the outside of the craft and making it rotate. From the center of the craft came a beam of light about 2 meters wide; alternating between violet and orange in color. And from within this beam of light he saw coming down out of the craft, a being dressed in a tight-fitting suit and with a glass helmet over his head. This being was about 1.6m in height. He came right up to Rizzi, until he was no more than one meter from him and raised the right hand in greeting just like the old hermit had done. The being had very beautiful eyes, which gave Rizzi a strange and very sweet sensation. He felt himself as free and as light as a feather. At the same time he also felt quite calm and he gazed at the humanoid eagerly. He was very similar to a human. The glass helmet started at his shoulders and encompassed the entire head.

In Italian, Rizzi asked the humanoid where he came from, and no sooner had he said it, than he already had the answer inside his brain, as though he had always known it. The planet from which he had come is far distant from our Galaxy, and is ten times the size of our Earth and has two Suns, one large and one smaller. Their day is far longer than ours. One third of it is less bright than the rest, and their night itself is very brief. The vegetation there resembles Earth. There are very high mountains, and immensely tall trees. They have two icy poles as we do, and desolate rocky zones. They also have animals that resemble ours but of different structures and sizes.

Then the thought came to Rizzi to ask them how they lived, and what they eat, and straight away he had the answer. The being's mouth had moved slightly, but Rizzi heard no voice, and he believes the being used telepathy. The alien told Rizzi that they did not work, everything being automatic. They are all equal, and each has whatever he wants. There are also ape-like creatures there that perform certain work tasks, planting fruit and vegetables and reaping the crops, and so on. After Rizzi had studied the alien very thoroughly from head to toe, the alien made him understand that this type of structure was the one best suited for life on his particular planet. The upper part of his head was wider than ours, because their brain is twice the size of our brain, and they make use of the whole of it.

Merely by means of thought and by the emanation of waves of energy they are able to do things that we cannot even imagine. As his head and neck were completely visible under the glass helmet, Rizzi was able to examine him closely. His hair was quite short, and of the shade of a light-colored beaver; resembling fur. His eyes were beautiful, set further apart than ours and slanting slightly upwards at the outer corners and shaped rather like cat's eyes. The area of the eye that is white in humans was chestnut color on the alien. The pupils themselves resembled ours, but their color was green, with blue reflections.

In the center of their pupils there was a black spot which from time to time changed shape and became long and narrow. The alien's nose was very small, also like a cat. His lips were small and thin, when he laughed no individual teeth were visible, but simply two very white uniform rows. The alien told Rizzi that they had no use for teeth, since they were not flesh eaters. The alien said that we, on the other hand have the body-structure of animals. Their food is fruit, vegetables and seed grain. Furthermore they possess devices which store up energy, and there is no sickness among them. The being's skin was smooth and of clear olive-green shade, looking as though made of rubber, there was not a single wrinkle to be seen on his neck. Rizzi felt the urge to ask him why he had an olive-green skin and he told him that the color which he was now seeing was not the true one "because their system of the magnetic content of the color was not the same as with them." Rizzi did not understand this. (?)

His shoulders were very broad and he had a very slim middle part to his body. Rizzi also had a look at his feet and arms. They were a little bit different from ours. The part of the leg running from the back-quarters of the body to the knee was considerably longer than the part below the knee, and it seemed to Rizzi furthermore that the feet were somewhat shaped like that of a horse's hoof. The upper part of the arm was also longer than the lower part. Rizzi did not have a good view of the hands and had the impression that the alien was wearing gloves. His fingers must have been very long. He told Rizzi that their organism was less complicated than ours. They have only one digestive tract, and lack all the entrails that humans have. But their heart and lungs were very highly developed, since they required a great deal of oxygen to nourish the brain and to purify the fluid which flows in their veins and which, has a composition different from our blood. Furthermore they possess very powerful muscles, required as a result of the great atmospheric pressure on their planet.

In fact when he came down from his machine, he came toward Rizzi using a hopping gait, just like the astronauts who landed on the Moon. This being due to the fact that our atmospheric pressure is much less, and also to the fact that their composition is different from ours. Rizzi was still fascinated by the being's beautiful eyes and wanted to ask whether he was a man or a woman. His eyes glowed more brightly for an instant and he smiled, and he gave Rizzi to understand that he was neither, and that when they desired to propagate themselves they do not couple as animals do.

Since he was only a meter distant from the being, he tried twice to touch him, but was instantly prevented. Meanwhile the robot was still at work on the other side of the object. It was like a ring, sticking out to a distance of two meters and two meters high. It frequently bent down towards the ground and its central part became sharp-pointed while one half moved towards one side and the other half towards the other side. Rizzi was about to ask the being whether that part of the robot that formed a sharp point was for the purpose of splitting meteorites flying at tremendous speeds against their ship. The being laughed again and made Rizzi understand that they preferred to disintegrate or 'displace' them. He said that the outer ring was used by them only when they sought to enter the atmospheres of other planets for the purpose of being able to remain there for a certain length of time. He added that in the depths of space they travel in their mother ship, which remained outside the Earth's magnetic field.

Their mother ship is propelled by a different sort of energy. It is of the same shape of their smaller craft, but is far, far bigger; Rizzi thinks the alien said that it had a diameter of five 'kilometers.' The mother ship carries many more of the smaller craft, and it also has a very small type of unmanned craft (or drone) which is sent out to gather information. These are operated by a particular sort of magnetic drive. When not in an atmosphere these small drones are subject to no particular speed limit, and they suffer no effects from attraction or temperatures, etc. The alien said that aboard the mother-ship, hundreds of their type of beings are living just as they do on their home planet.

He said that they fly along 'neutral channels' which exist in the intermediate stretches of space. This is done in order to avoid being drawn into the magnetic fields of other planets or encountering meteorites or 'dead planets.' Rizzi asked what sort of defensive weapons they had, to which the alien replied that they can disintegrate anything, even at great distances. He motioned Rizzi to pick up a stone that was lying about two meters from him. Rizzi picked it up and was told to attempt to throw the stone; which weighed about a kilogram; at the cupola of the UFO. Rizzi swung himself around twice to develop a better throwing speed and hurled the stone with all his strength at the cupola whereupon a whitish-lilac colored beam of light shot out from it and the stone exploded with a dull report and Rizzi did not even see a single fragment fall to the ground.

Rizzi then asked why they were not willing to help us with their technology and remain on our planet and also how long it would be before we had their kind of technology. The alien made Rizzi understand that, firstly, they are not allowed to interfere in the development of another planet, and that the time they spend in our solar system makes them age far too rapidly. Secondly, he said that we would never reach their level of evolution, since the crust of our planet is far too variable and that in the near future there will be a displacement of the poles. In the process of adjustment to this Polar Shift, an enormous crack would develop in the surface of our planet and this would entail an upheaval on the Earth that would destroy 80% of all living things here, leaving the survivors to carry on, on a habitable strip of the planet.

At this point Rizzi asked the alien if he believed in God, he seemed a bit surprised at the question, but made Rizzi understand with a cosmic turn of phrase that 'everything' is God; we, nature, the planets, rocks, grass; in fact everything that exists. Rizzi also asked them how they die and to what age do they live, the alien replied that they die when the cosmic energy within them runs out and that they live about a hundred times longer than we do, reckoning on the basis of our planetary time cycle.

Meanwhile the robot had stopped working. It became smaller, the cylinder grew narrower and moved towards the center of the UFO, where an orange light came on, and it went into the craft as though floating. Consequently, Rizzi understood that they were leaving. Then the other being in the cupola signaled to Rizzi in salutation. He did not have a very clear view of him, but he looked the same as the one standing beside him.

During the whole time that Rizzi had been talking with the being, the object had been enveloped in a fleecy white light which threw no shadows and did not hurt the eyes. He now asked the being whether he could give him something of theirs. He said no, since it would be harmful to Rizzi. Rizzi was so fascinated with this being that he asked him whether he could take him with them, saying that it would be all the same to him whether or not he ever returned. Then he was overcome by a great wave of emotion at the mere thought that he would not see them again and he started to weep. He even knelt down and begged the alien to be taken with them, he tried to put his arms around him but every time he did so he was stopped.

The alien then motioned to Rizzi to stand up, his eyes then glowed with a strange light which sent a feeling of warmth right through Rizzi's body. The alien made Rizzi understand that he was very brave and that he had been lucky on two counts, firstly if he had gone as much as one meter closer to their craft he would have been disintegrated. But as they had been controlling the ring, their magnetic field had not been permitted to extend beyond the diameter of the craft. Secondly, he had been lucky to see them at such close quarters and to be able to talk to them. But that neither he nor any being from this Earth can be with them, and even less, travel with them in their spacecraft.

The alien then raised his arm in a greeting, just like in the beginning of the encounter and Rizzi was flung far away from the object by a powerful force, while the being, returning to the machine, disappeared into the brightly lit ring. Up in the cupola the other being waved to Rizzi with his long arms. The white light of the object was now growing dimmer, and meanwhile this force which he had just mentioned had continued to push him away until he was at a distance of some 300 meters or so, where he found that he once more was able to move freely. The light from the cupola had now turned to violet. The outside of the craft was violet also, with transitions now and then to orange.

At this point the machine was making a noise like a circular saw being started up. It began to move, and rose to about two or three meters or so above the ground, and Rizzi watched the three legs, one after the other, being retracted. The violet light was now growing steadily whiter, until at last it was totally white. Then he heard for a moment a sharp whistle that he felt was going to blow his head off. The object then started to dip from side to side, as though bidding him goodbye, and slowly it rose to a height of about 300 meters or so. Then in the twinkling of an eye, it shot straight up into the sky at a terrifying speed and was gone.

Rizzi, tears running down his face was overcome with despair. The air seemed warm, and he touched the ground and it felt tepid also. The mist had now cleared, it was quite dark and the sky was full of stars. Twenty days after the event, he drove back to the spot where the UFO had stood, in order to take photographs of the marks left by the weight of the craft. (These marks can still be seen today). One thing that astounded him greatly was that near where the opening was in the craft, from which the light was beamed out, the grass had grown to be three times as long as the rest of the grass around.

After the event, Rizzi found that his watch was losing as much as two hours in a day, he eventually had to discard it. For a month he felt very tired the whole time and lost a lot of his hair. He cured himself with fresh honey, coffee, egg-yolk and brandy; a preparation that he had learned from his grandmother. He also took garlic pills thrice a day.

HC addendum.
Source: Walter Rizzi and Gordon Creighton in *Flying Saucer Review* 1980. Type: B

Location: Monte Britton, El Yunque, Puerto Rico.
Date: July, 1968.
Time: 4:00 p.m.

Freddie Anderson and several of his friends were hiking down the slope of the mountain following a stream when they came upon a strange creature standing in the middle of the water, very close to state road 191. The creature stood only 12 feet away from the group and it was described as about six-feet tall, very thin, with long thin arms. Its hands reached the knees and were long with extremely long fingers. It appeared to be naked and was green in color.

It had a large elongated head that ended in a point. Its body was completely covered by a layer of very thin hair. It also had two large protruding eyes; a small thin mouth and appeared to have no ears. The stunned witnesses apparently went into a trance like state and suddenly woke up to realize that it was already nighttime and that the creature was gone. They had no recollection as to what happened during the missing hours.

HC addendum.
Source: Jorge Martin, *Evidencia Ovni* #8.   Type: E?

* * * * * * *

Location: Near Las Cruces, New Mexico.
Date: July, 1968.
Time: 11:30 p.m.

Kenneth and Cosette Willoughby were returning from visiting friends in Anthony and were driving north of Las Cruces when they came upon a strange 'thing' squatting right in the middle of the highway, devouring something which they guessed had been killed by a car. The beast was much too big to be a dog and it looked like an ape, covered with long black wavy dusty-looking fur. As soon as the thing noticed their headlights, it jumped up and disappeared into the darkness in a flash.

A friend, Mildred Sanders who lived a few miles north of where they saw the creature reported that for quite a while they have been bothered at night by what she thought was a prowler. It sounded to her as if something or someone would come around at night and rake a stick across the lower part of her window screens. One night whatever it was almost tore the screen door off the kitchen. It worried her so much that her husband hooked up lights outside to light up the whole yard outside to light up the whole yard and he put the switch right by her bed. The next time she heard the window scraping sounds she snapped on the lights but didn't get to a window quick enough to see anything. However from out toward the highway and out of the lighted area came deep guttural animal sounds.

The next time she heard the window scraping, she snapped on the lights and moved fast to the kitchen window. The first thing she saw was moving very quickly. It looked like a bear running on its hind legs. The second figure didn't move so fast and she had a good view of it in the lighted area. It looked like a man running on all fours yet not a man for it had shaggy tan fur. She also reported that farmers nearby were missing a lot of their calves and blaming the losses on wild dogs.

HC addendum.
Source: Letter from Cosette Willoughby, *Fate,* June 1971.   Type: E

* * * * * * *

Location: Sierra Chica, Buenos Aires, Argentina.
Date: July 2, 1968.
Time: 11:25 a.m.

Oscar M. Iriart, 15, was riding his horse on his father's 22 hectare farm near Sierra Chica when, by a wire fence, he saw two individuals gesturing him to approach. Riding over to them, he saw they were about his own height (1.7m) with short white hair and red shirts. They gazed at him with deep set unblinking eyes. Oscar then realized that their legs were transparent, as he could see the grass through them. The strangers told him they would take him to their world, but not now as they had a heavy load. They then showed him, standing in a muddy drainage ditch, an elliptical machine on three landing legs, one behind the other two.

The machine was 2 meters long 60 cm. high, the legs were 50 cm. high. The conversation seemed to be taking place in Spanish as Oscar understood it perfectly. One of the beings gave him an envelope on which a message was scribbled and told him to dip it into a muddy puddle. He did this and found that his hands and the message remained perfectly dry. Scribbled in bad handwriting and misspelt Spanish was the message *"You are going to know the world."* The beings then climbed on to the top of the machine, lifted the top and got in. As soon as the top was closed again the machine took off with great speed, accompanied by flashes of light. Almost instantaneously it became a tiny dot in the sky and was gone.

Feeling that he just awoken from a dream, Oscar ran over to his horse, only to find that it and his dog were both paralyzed. As soon as they could move he rode for the house 800m away. There he made an impression on everyone with his excited condition and bulging eyes. He returned to the spot with neighbors. There they found three holes 12 cm deep, forming a perfect isosceles triangle, base 2 cm, sides 1.58 cm.

That night at 23:15 the local police officer, Sgt. Raul Coronel and four friends (butcher Carlos Marinangelli, his brother Jose Luis (a prison administrative officer) mechanic Hugo Rodriguez and Walter Vacarro went to the site to investigate, with the intention of proving the story was a hoax. They had just arrived when Carlos saw a light zigzagging towards them across the meadow, only a few meters above the ground. It came towards them so low that they were forced to duck and Raul would have shot it with his revolver had not Carlos restrained him. The object carried on its zigzag course, gathered speed, climbed straight up and vanished.

HC addendum.
Source: Gordon Creighton, *FSR* Vol. 14 #5 citing 'La Razon,' July 1968.
Type: B

* * * * * * *

Location: Cofico, Salta, Argentina.
Date: July 2, 1968.
Time: 8:15 p.m.

In an area near the local sports club, several persons reported seeing a strange sight. Among the witnesses, was Corina Robles who stated that upon going outside to her garden, she spotted in the sky; a huge disc-shaped object which emitted a powerful beam of light. Afraid, she ran into the house to get her mother. Once outside again, the girl now encountered at the same spot where the disc had hovered, a huge robot-like figure no less than three meters in height.

The entity seemed to float in mid-air and then departed, slowly flying above the ground until it disappeared behind some hills. Apparently this strange entity was also seen by a 14-year old boy named Francisco Emilio Sola around the same area. Sola had been watching the movements of the disc-shaped object near a hill called "Veinte de Febrero" (20th of

February) when suddenly he saw a huge luminous figure about 2.5m in height, floating in the air that quickly disappeared behind the hill.

Other witnesses included Silvia Rosa Olmos, and two stonemasons reported a similar encounter earlier that day on another nearby hill. That same night three police officers reported a UFO above the suburb of 'Barrio El Portezuelo.'

HC addendum.
Source: *FSR* Vol. 14 #5, also http://ufologie.net quoting CEFAI. Type: C

* * * * * * *

Location: Near Hushtosyrt, Kabardino-Balkaria Republic, Russia.
Date: July 6-7, 1968.
Time: 3:00 a.m.

In a mountain settlement, the witness; Victor Petrovich Kostrykin, was laying out on a haystack on one of the numerous pastures in the area. There wasn't anybody else around. Around 3:00 a.m. he suddenly saw an unusually bright vertically falling "meteorite." Then the brightness diminished. The object descended, trailing a smoky effusion at a very close proximity to the witness, coming down in a spiraling movement. He instantly came to a sitting position amazed and waited for an imminent explosion, but there was only silence. Close to him was a small wooded area and from that place he sensed something watching him and he was instilled with an overwhelming feeling of terror.

He looked behind him and saw a humanoid figure in flames standing still, unmoving. Immediately he fell out of the haystack and ran as fast as his legs would carry him. "I thought it was a 'Yeti,' an Abominable Snowman." He thought in his fevered condition that the Yeti had been torched by our technology and was now in his pain and going to revenge himself upon him. In his headlong rush he had forgotten ten firecrackers he had taken with him, in order to scare off any wild animals. In his panic and confusion he came to a dead halt. His ability to move deserted him; he had no control over his limbs. Every hair on his body stood on end. He was completely free of any pain, but broke into a cold sweat, his heart thumped like a beating drum and his conscious mind was clear.

He was soon gripped by a feeling of "suspended animation" and his oppressive fear dissipated. His previous feelings gave way to a wonderful sense of lightness filling his whole being. He then heard a voice calling him. Behind the hill he saw disc-shaped object of immense proportions that could not be of Earth construction. It was bright and glowing; it had a circle of portholes around its center which emitted a bright light. On drawing closer to the object he realized that they were not portholes.

They were in fact round mouths of tubes. There were no portholes in the earthly sense of the word. Every tube along the whole radius of the craft pierced deep into the bowels of the object. Like spokes from the rim of a bicycle wheel, they ran to the hub. The light coming from the tubes was a soft milky hue. This strange light circled the body of the object as if under the influence of a magnetic field. It gave the impression of being cocooned in a sea of light.

He was met by an alien of very similar appearance to a human being, except in some small details. There were a few tongues of flame running across his silver coverall, which later disappeared. This silver figure had five digit hands and other limbs of similar proportions to humans. He was of slightly higher than average height. Later they explained that a man being in their close presence will perceive them to be of regular human dimensions. Their real height is 5-6 meters. They can compress dimension or extend it. The color of their uniform was light and around their heads and legs there was a luminescence.

The figures were slim, thin with normal proportions; their movement was staid, slow and sublime. They didn't like when anyone spoke loudly, or waved their hands. They stopped the witness numerous times asking; *"Speak or be quiet but don't wave your hands."* By gesture he was invited into the spacecraft. He crossed the threshold (where beyond stops all of Earth's powers). It was warm inside, warmer than on the pastures at that time, his footsteps were muffled. The light inside the craft was soft, not like electrical or our daylight. There were no sharp strong shadows. The light was warming soft-milky, falling from above. He couldn't remember seeing any bulbs or lamps. Near the wall there was a control desk with colored glimmering buttons. All furniture or aggregates went in or out of the walls or floor. There weren't any curtains or slide valves on the walls, but walls can move apart and a screen appear.

Inside he saw additional figures. There were five of them in the craft. They looked identical like twins and dressed the same. Their heads were large and oval in shape. Their faces were handsome and had something special on their features. Somehow he perceived the feeling that they looked through him and knew his every thought. There wasn't any hostility or curiosity from their side. The most particular thing was their large wraparound eyes; it seemed that they could see all around them. There was something on their heads that looked like a skull cap made of "gold and stones." From the side it looked like a field cap. Later he was told that it was a "brain phone" for long distance talks-thoughts transmissions.

Soon he noticed that there weren't any buttons or zippers on the coveralls and all of them were dressed in silver coveralls and thick soled shoes. Their hair was gray and short, and their faces young without wrinkles. The witness presented himself as a native Caucasian. He was told that in the Caucasus there were only four native nations, that all others were either mixed or brought there. The aliens spoke by using telepathically using perfect modern Russian. They spoke very politely and respectfully. Their voices were young, different in timber and directions. They didn't open their mouths when they communicated.

Among themselves they used a language unknown to the witness; he could remember one word that sounded like; *"Taila-Laila."* They invited him to sit on an armchair and told him in Russian, *"We are now on our way to the mountain,"* pointing in the direction of Mount Elbrus. As he sat on the armchair, two extraterrestrials looking like twins came up to him. One of them had long black gloves on his hands. He noticed that they had long thin fingers and was impressed by the quality of the gloves, which were absolutely black in color. They then took his left hand, turned it edgewise, pulled the thumb aside and took a piece of skin between first finger and thumb using a strange device. It was quite fast without any pain or blood.

The witness was curious as to what kind of gloves they were wearing, guessing they were for some medical purpose when suddenly the hand in the black glove with all five fingers began to sink into his thorax. With wide opened eyes he watched this unusual (spectacular) performance. Only when the fingers touched his heart that he felt a strong pain and screamed, the black gloved hand immediately retracted leaving no traces of blood on his chest. Apparently the witness was healed from an old heart condition. He was eventually returned to the same location where he was originally picked up.

HC addendum.
Source: X-Libri UFO Russia, quoting *Komsomol Truth* July 18, 2003.
Type: G
Comments: Peculiar contactee like report from the old Soviet Union. There is probably more information on it, but I have not been able to find it as of yet.

Location: Manduria, Taranto, Italy.
Date: July 6, 1968.
Time: 11:20 p.m.

Driving on a road between San Pancrazio and Manduria, the main witness was in the car with his sister and nephew when they were struck by a powerful beam of light that was apparently in the middle of the road. Thinking that it was another approaching motorist with high headlights, the driver blinked his headlights at the supposedly oncoming vehicle several times, but got no response.

So he slowed down and as he approached the light source, the driver and his sister saw standing on the roadside two very tall beings, approximately 2-meters in height, they were wearing a sort of green suit and a helmet, with a sort of luminescent plate in one arm. The stunned witnesses also noticed that the two figures had very large eyes. Terrified the driver quickly sped away from the area.

HC addendum.
Source: UFO Center Taranto, quoting Courier of the day July-9-1968.
Type: E

* * * * * * *

Location: Cerro De La Gloria, Mendoza, Argentina.
Date: July 9, 1968.
Time: Night.

The police agent Arsenio Romero, of the fifth district of that city, was on duty in Cerro De La Gloria when he saw an intense light on the platform. He went up to it to find out what it was and then observed a round object which was emitting blue and red lights. Two little beings wearing two bright antennas on their heads came out of the UFO.

When Romero started to point his pistol at them, the entities turned on him a sort of luminous ray that immobilized him, causing him to fall down in a faint. Thus he was found on the ground and was taken to the said police headquarters. He was hospitalized, suffering a nervous breakdown.

HC addendum.
Source: Dr. Carlos Banchs.   Type: B

Location: La Plata, Buenos Aires, Argentina.
Date: July 9, 1968.
Time: 2:30 a.m.

Estela and Silvia Boquin, 15 and 10 years of age respectively, were suddenly awoken by a loud buzzing sound. As they woke up they saw at a close distance from them a man about 2m in height, with long blond hair and large blue staring eyes, who was apparently attempting to communicate with them using unintelligible language. His legs and arms were extremely long and he had pointy ears. The stranger wore a shiny one-piece diver's outfit and was encased in a sort of greenish 'capsule,' which rotated and emitted red and violet lights.

HC addendum.
Source: *FSR* Vol. 16 #1, citing *Gente y Actualidad*, Nr. 157.   Type: E?

* * * * * * *

Location: Near Rivesville, West Virginia.
Date: Mid July, 1968.
Time: Evening.

Jennings H. Frederick had been hunting unsuccessfully for woodchuck and as the sun was setting, he decided to return home. Near his father's property line he stopped under some maple trees. He removed the arrow from his 45-lb. bow and transferred both to his left hand to rest his arm. As he paused he heard a high-pitched jabbering, much like that of a tape recording running at exaggerated speed. He believed he could understand the words, but he may have experienced telepathic communication.

"You need not fear me. I wish to communicate. I come as a friend. We know of you all. I come in peace. I wish medical assistance. I need your help!"

Stunned and puzzled, he reached with his right arm for a handkerchief in his hip pocked to wipe perspiration. He winced. At first he thought his hand had become entangled in a wild berry briar and he quickly withdrew his arm. Attached to his wrist was what looked like a thin, flexible right hand and arm, of a green color like a plant, and the size of a quarter coin in diameter. The hand, which terminated with three fingers about seven inches long, and with needle-like tips and suction cups, grasped his arm more tightly and punctured a blood vessel. He heard a suction sound and knew blood was being drawn.

Frederick turned to see a terrifying being with semi-human facial features, though there the resemblance ended. Its slanting eyes were yellow and it had pointed ears. Its body reminded him of the stalk of some huge ungainly plant, though it had remarkable physical power, coupled with the hypnotic effect the sing-song message imparted. He cried out in pain from the incisions and fright.

Suddenly the eyes changed from yellow to red and seemed to rotate, and spinning orange circles emerged from them. His pain immediately ceased as the eyes created what obviously was a hypnotic effect, and he froze in his tracks, though his terror had also vanished. Frederick isn't sure, but he believes the "transfusion" lasted only about a minute, after which the creature suddenly released him, turned and ran up the hill in great leaping jumps, covering 25 feet or more in each leap, like a modern day "Spring-heeled Jack." He estimated the height of the leaps by noting it cleared a five-foot fence with about three feet to spare. At the hilltop it vanished into the woods.

The pain in his arm returned as he stared in the direction of the creature's spectacular exit. Then he heard a humming and whistling sound coming from the woods, as if the saucer the creature may have arrived in was taking off. He stumbled to his home and washed the wounded arm and put a bandage on it. Though the wound convinced him that he was sane and had actually experienced the horror, he doubted that anybody else would believe him. So he told his family he had been scratched by a briar and didn't see a doctor for fear of disclosure.

HC addendum.
Source: Gray Barker. Type: E

Location: Cluj-Napoca, Romania.
Date: July 20, 1968.
Time: 11:00 a.m.

A man out on a hiking trip in the area was scanning some fields with a pair of binoculars when he noticed four bizarre looking humanoids in a field. The humanoids were walking around, apparently inspecting the area, except for one that looked to be lying prone on the ground. These human-like figures appeared to be naked or topless as if sunning themselves on a beach.

As he watched, five minutes later a large gray balloon shaped object appeared above some trees. It was flying in a west-east direction and appeared to be about 25 meters in diameter. At one point the object ejected a small sphere that descended in a vertical parabolic trajectory disappearing behind the trees. Soon four bell-parachute shaped objects appeared and descended over each of the humanoids covering them completely, each of the humanoids raised their arms as if waiting to be covered by the objects.

The parachute-like objects then disappeared along with the humanoids. The witness described the humanoids as about 1.40 meters in height, of a robust build with short muscular legs and over-developed calves. Their skin was dark reddish in color and their hair was dark and swarthy. Their heads and faces were peculiar since they had dog or canine-like characteristics.

HC addendum.
Source: Calin Turcu, Romania. Type: E or B

* * * * * * *

Location: St. Bruno, Quebec, Canada.
Date: July 22, 1968.
Time: Evening.

Six young girls, ages 7 to 13, reportedly saw a figure they described as "The Virgin Mary." The apparition appeared before them hovering in the air; four of the girls merely saw the figure, whereas two, heard a voice they described as "soft and slow." It advised them to pray and promised to return on October 7.

HC addendum.
Source: John A. Keel, 'Operation Trojan Horse.' Type: E?

Location: Tapalque, near Olavarria, Buenos Aires, Argentina.
Date: July 25, 1968.
Time: 2:05 a.m.

Armed with sub-machineguns, a corporal and several soldiers drove to the spot in a jeep to where a UFO emitting multicolored flashes and making a droning sound, was apparently about to land. It settled and three beings more than 6ft tall wearing silvery uniforms, emerged and advanced with slow, steady steps toward the soldiers.

The corporal fired a burst of submachine gun fire at them, upon which the beings lifted up their hands to show a small luminous ball, whereupon all the witnesses were overcome by a strange lassitude and were incapable of using their guns. However one of the men, a Corporal Menendez managed to fire five shots without any apparent effect on the humanoids. Only after the figures re-entered the UFO and it had taken off with a zigzag motion did the soldiers recover their faculties.

HC addendum.
Source: *FSR* Vol. 14 #6, citing newspaper source. Type: B
Comments: Other sources site the date as July 19, 1968.

* * * * * * *

Location: La Plaine Des Cafres, Reunion Island.
Date: July 31, 1968.
Time: 9:00 a.m.

Luce Fontaine, 31, a local farmer, was in a small clearing in the middle of a forest of acacia trees and was bending down and picking some grass for his rabbits when he suddenly saw a sort of ova-shaped cabin in the clearing. It was 25 meters from him, and as though suspended at a height of four or five meters from the ground. The extremities of it were dark blue, the center part lighter, more transparent rather like the windscreen of a Peugeot 404. Above and below it had what looked like two feet of shining metal.

In the center of the cabin were two individuals with their backs towards him. The one on the left turned right around and so faced him. He was small, about 90 cm in height, enveloped from head to feet in a sort of one-piece overall a bit like the suit worn by the "Michelin man." The one on the right simply turned his head around towards him, but all the same he had time to catch a glimpse of his face, which was partly masked by a sort of helmet. Then both turned their backs to him, and there was a flash, as strong as the electric arc of a welding torch. Everything went white around him. A powerful heat was given off and as if were a sort of blast of wind, and a few seconds later there was nothing there anymore.

Then Fontaine approached the spot over which the object had been. There were no marks. The object had a diameter of 4 or 5 meters and was about 2 ½ meters measured through from top to bottom. It was of a bluish color, with white on the upper and lower parts. He told his wife all about it and then the Gendarmerie and everyone believed him. The Gendarmerie enquiry was conducted by Captain Maljean of St. Pierre and Captain Legros of the Service de la Protection Civile. They went to the site with instruments for detecting radioactivity. A surprise awaited them. They found a certain degree of radioactivity in a radius of from 5-6 meters from the presumed scene of the near-landing, and also even on the clothing worn that day by Fontaine.

HC addendum.
Source: Local police, Gordon Creighton *FSR* Vol. 15 #1.   Type: A

* * * * * * *

Location: Vancouver, British Columbia, Canada.
Date: August, 1968.
Time: Late afternoon.

The main witness (involved in other encounters) and some friends were playing with bb-guns on the grounds of the Shaughnessy Golf course when they saw a small metallic "flying saucer" on the ground. The main witness went up to it, to show off to his friends and actually played "bongos" on it. The object was as big as a VW beetle (but round). He then walked to one side to get a better view of the silver object and saw a small "non-human man" next to it. The figure was very pale, almost blue in color and was wearing a white suit with a blue sash around his waist and looked like "the man from the Glad television commercials."

The witness said, *"My name is Kim"* and put his right hand on his heart. The creature responded by holding his palms upward and made a sound, but he didn't seem to "have a tongue." At one point he put out his right arm and nodded for the witness to do the same thing with his left, and he was allowed to compare his hand with the alien's and except for the pallor they were very similar. At this point he heard a voice in his head that spoke the words, *"Would you like to pray?"* And he bowed and put his arms pointing down with palms towards the witness.

He was a bit embarrassed and to get a laugh from his friends who were literally "stunned," he made a gesture towards this BB gun in his right pocket. The alien seemed to sense this and the witness had to apologize for this and explained that it was only a bb-gun and was not real, the alien seemed to understand. The witness said a few more things and then waved at the alien and the alien waved back. The witness then rejoined his friends and they left the area.

HC addendum.
Source: http://www.ufobc.ca/sightings/   Type: C

* * * * * * *

Location: Mojave Desert, California.
Date: August, 1968.
Time: Evening.

    While riding bikes and listening to the CB radio in the high desert area one evening the main witness heard a commotion on a nearby hill and heard someone yell, *"flying saucer!"* Going up to look he noticed an aircraft down on the other side of the hill about 60 to 100 yards away. The object was sort of rounded. Its base was larger than its rounded top and it was sitting on three or four legs, which all had round feet. A door was opened; like a chopper door that folds out and down.
    The underside of the craft was lighted with a beige diffuse light. The door was open facing the witness and there was a yellowish light inside. There were three men outside doing something. One seemed to notice the witness. The men all looked to be in their twenties, had short blond hair and were dressed in what appeared to be a gray, silvery jumpsuit. After some minutes the men got back inside the object, the door closed in a normal manner, and it started an easy vertical takeoff. There was no noise as the object rose to about 40ft up, turned off its bottom light and blue and red lights came on. The takeoff seemed to change the local air pressure considerably. The craft then shot away slowly into the night and vanished.

HC addendum.
Source: UFORCE Case Studies.   Type: B

* * * * * * *

Location: Near Brasilia, Brazil.
Date: August, 1968.
Time: Night.

    A group of individuals, under the leadership of General Alfredo Moacyr Uchoa, had taken up residence at the plantation of Wilson Da Silva, near the capital; several sightings were recorded and photographs taken. After five months of observations and as predicted by Da Silva, who had been in telepathic communication with the aliens, a brightly illuminated disc came down at the designated spot on his property, hovering 4ft above the ground. The party of observers took photographs.

As Da Silva left the group and walked toward the landing site, he saw a door open in the object and a normal sized man, wearing a blue coverall with a wide belt, descended. Upon his return to the group, Da Silva could remember nothing except the message he had received, which was, *"We are peaceful. Your atomic experiments are causing an imbalance in our world."* The craft shot up into the sky while he was returning to the group. Additional contacts were claimed subsequently, into 1969.

HC addendum.
Source: General Uchoa and Gordon Creighton, *FSR* Case Histories #12.
Type: B

* * * * * * *

Location: Brooksville, Florida.
Date: August 6, 1968.
Time: Afternoon.

Obeying an inner urge, John Reeves went to the woods and there encountered two men in silver space suits with helmets under their arms. They took him to their spaceship, where he met six others, including a beautiful young girl in a brown jumpsuit named 'Detzee.' On takeoff he blacked out from acceleration and came to two hours later.

After a six-hour trip in total they landed on the moon, where he found the air breathable, though thin. They also flew over the "dark side," where he noticed 18 people along the banks of a stream. He was returned to earth 48 hours after being taken aboard, but could remember only one day's experiences. He was promised a later trip to the humanoid's home planet.

HC addendum.
Source: Jim Twithy for the *Tampa Tribune*.   Type: G

Location: Buff Ledge, Lake Champlain, Vermont.
Date: August 7, 1968.
Time: Sunset.

During their tenure as summer camp employees, Michael Lapp, a sixteen year old maintenance man and 19-year old water ski instructor Janet Cornell were relaxing at a boat dock on a slack day. On this particular August afternoon, the swim team had a made a trip to Burlington to compete in a meet, and the camp was virtually deserted. Late in the afternoon, the two friends were enjoying the view of the sun setting over the water, when a bright light appeared in the darkening sky. Michael thought they were being treated to a beautiful close up view of the planet Venus.

All of a sudden, the glowing light began to move downward, and ever closer to Michael and Janet. The object, at first a round glow, now began to flatten out as it approached even closer. Michael shouted, *"Wow, Venus is falling!"* As the two steadfastly watched the light, three smaller lights seemed to drop from the larger one, which quickly moved up and disappeared from sight. The three smaller objects moved over the lake. They were obviously under intelligent control. The objects put on a type of show for Michael and Janet, doing zigzag maneuvers, loops, and then descended like falling leaves. The three objects now moved even closer to the two baffled teenagers.

After forming a triangle, two of the objects pulled back. Michael would later recall a sound "like a thousand tuning forks" when the two left, leaving a single craft behind. The lone UFO passed over Michael and Janet, and then shot upward and momentarily disappeared. It very soon reappeared, tilted to one side, and dropped into the lake. A couple of minutes seemed to pass before the object reemerged from the water, and began gliding straight toward them. The object was now close enough to see a transparent dome occupied by two child-like creatures, Michael would describe the beings as having elongated necks, big heads, and no hair. Their eyes were also large, and extended around the side of their heads.

Michael began to sense a kind of communication with the two beings. Watching them intently, Michael slapped his knee, and to his surprise, one of the occupants mimicked his movement. The craft now moved overhead, and shot a beam directly at Michael and Janet. Grabbing Janet's shoulder, Michael pulled both of them on their backs on the dock. Frightened by being kidnapped, Michael remembers screaming, *"We don't want to go!"* The light from the beam was so bright that Michael recalls being able to see the bones in his hand. The two teenagers both related that the beam had a "liquid" feeling to it, and gave them the sense of floating.

Their next conscious thoughts would be that of staring at the object again from the dock. The sky was now totally black and Michael wondered how long he had been in this one spot. Looking at Janet, Michael could see that she was in a trancelike state, drowsy and disoriented. The UFO now moved upward into the black sky, flashed its light beam repeatedly and then vanished from sight. Strangely, Michael and Janet did not discuss what had happened to them. After summer camp they both went their separate ways.

Years later under regressive hypnosis, Michael vividly recalled his experiences that August night of 1968. He remembered how the beam of light lifted him into the craft's interior, how he entered a bigger craft, and how he saw Janet lying on a table being examined. The small beings shone a light into her eyes, scraped her skin, and took fluids from her body. Michael recalled that the aliens were very similar to each other. They had large eyes, a mouth without lips, no ears, and two small openings for a nose. He also described the beings as having three pointed, web-like digits for fingers, and their bodies felt "damp and clammy."

The aliens related to Michael that their mission was to "make life like ours in other places." Janet also underwent the regression. She recalled feeling cold on the examining table, with something "pulling her hair, and pinching her neck." Other camp employees reported seeing UFOs over the lake around the same time.

HC addendum.
Source: Walter N. Webb, *Mufon Journal #241*.   Type: G

* * * * * * *

Location: Canuelas, Buenos Aires, Argentina.
Date: August 8, 1968.
Time: 2:00 a.m.

Miguel Bitschko was sleeping in his home when he suddenly woke up surrounded by a bright light coming from outside. Going out he was surprised to see a huge disc-shaped object on the ground in a nearby field. The object had a dome on top on which a revolving red light appeared. As he stared at the object in disbelief, a door opened on the craft and a ladder then descended to the ground.

Soon a huge, humanoid figure over two meters in height emerged from the object. The figure wore a shiny metallic close-fitting outfit. At the same time the object was emitting a loud humming sound. The giant being began walking towards the witness, who remained paralyzed with fear. The figure suddenly stopped and then walked back to the object and entered it. The craft then climbed up vertically at high speed and disappeared from sight.

HC addendum.
Source: Fabio Picasso. Type: B

* * * * * * *

Location: Nasielsko/Chrcynna, Poland.
Date: August 13, 1968.
Time: Before noon.

17-year old local Andrzej Domaa, was picking mushrooms in a nearby forest. As usual he planned to collect mushrooms and sell them during Sunday's fete. When he entered the forest he was surprised at the abnormal silence around him. Anxious he rushed towards the fence of a local military garrison (OPK) but when he turned his head he spotted a strange woman standing about a dozen meters from him. From the waist up she looked quite normal but the rest of her body from the waist down was dwarfish in appearance. She was dressed in a tight-fitting uniform without buttons or zippers. Only her face was visible. She had neither lashes nor eyebrows.

Her eyes were big, slanted and devoid of white. Despite of the unusual appearance of the eyes, these emanated a kind of "softness." Her nose was tiny and her mouth resembled a small horizontal hole, she was about 160cm in height. For some time both Andrzej and the strange woman stared at each other and then she came closer and began to draw geometrical symbols on the ground. Then unexpectedly he fell asleep. In a "dream" he saw himself lying in something like a laboratory table. He was then placed inside some kind of device and then tubes were connected to him and he then levitated up in the air. The strange woman stood on the floor. Allegedly he then had sex with the alien woman.

He later woke up on a field in the same location in which he had observed a strange "stain" on the sun's surface. It was midday. He thought that he had hallucinated but then found strange footprints pressed on the soil. The footprints led to within the forest. When he went into the forest he found his bag. He claims that after the encounter he changed as a young man. He became more sensitive, and claims he was able to help the elderly. There was controversy related to this case as the witness claims that he had "children" with the extraterrestrial woman.

HC addendum.
Source: woe_vp@pl.com Type: G?

Location: Sierra De Almos, Tivissa, Terragona, Spain
Date: August 16, 1968.
Time: 6:00 a.m.

A farmer named Sebastian Mateu, walking toward a light, found a very luminous hemispherical object hovering 3ft above the ground. On the far side of it he saw, about 100 yards away and hurrying toward it, two creatures resembling octopus, about 3ft high, with "4 or 5 legs," very light in color and "thoroughly disgusting." The UFO left a large area of burnt grass, and "watches stopped three times at the site."

HC addendum.
Source: Julio Roca Muntanola, *FSR* Special Bulletin #4   Type: C

* * * * * * *

Location: Near Townsville, Queensland, Australia.
Date: August 25, 1968.
Time: 2:00 a.m.

Mr. and Mrs. Hector Davis were asleep in their camper when Mr. Davis awoke with a "suspicious feeling." Looking toward a tree about 12ft away he saw a small man 4.5ft tall, in the tree approximately 6ft off the ground. The being had long blond hair and bright blue eyes and was dressed in a one-piece suit of gray color, including gloves and shoes, and corrugated all over.

He wore a kind of cap with an antenna, from which came a faint glow. Mr. Davis jumped up and the figure, who had been watching the sleeping couple, stared guiltily and floated from the tree, moving across the road 40ft away, and about 2ft off the ground, moving with a slight undulation, "legs swinging, like walking away, only not touching the ground." He was lost to view in the distance. The encounter lasted approximately a minute. Mrs Davis was asleep throughout.

HC addendum.
Source: Dr. D. Herbison-Evans for UFOIC Sydney, Australia.   Type: E

Location: Near Sierra de la Yesa, Valencia, Spain.
Date: August 31, 1968.
Time: 4:00 p.m.

Three hunters from the city of Liria, all around 50 years of age, were resting and getting ready to prepare a "torra" (barbecue) close to a nearby ravine and at about 5km from the small town of La Yesa in this very mountainous region. As they prepared a sudden 'flash' in the sky caught their attention. Seconds later one of the men, Mateo Chover, left his rifle behind and approached the edge of the ravine to urinate. He was then surprised to see on the other side of the ravine where a small arroyo flowed and at about 100 to 150 meters away, a humanoid type figure that had the following characteristics; athletic built, a lizard like head, with two reddish eyes, claw-like hands, one of them holding what appeared to be a transparent helmet with a white visor, and a long cat-like tail that reached the ground.

The parts of the humanoid which were exposed appeared to be gray in color. The rest of its body was covered in a white one piece coverall that covered the humanoid all the way up to its neck, and wrists, it ended in a pair of large white boots. Attached to its back appeared to be some type of metallic 'backpack' or rectangular box aluminum in color, about ½ meter in length and shiny, there was a black antenna-like protrusion on the top. The strange entity was standing under a tree and gave the impression that "it was waiting for somebody or something." Chover was under the impression that the entity extended a large 'beefy tongue' from its mouth every once in a while. The entity appear not to notice Chover as this one hid behind some bushes and called the other two men and told them to approach quietly. The three astounded hunters watched the entity for about three minutes when suddenly they were terrified to see emerge from the top of the tree a dark metallic cylinder-shaped object that reflected the sunlight from each end. They estimated the craft to have been about 30 meters in length and ten meters in width.

The object remained still about ten meters above the top of the tree in a horizontal position, pointing in a northeast-southeast direction. The craft was completely silent. Terrified, the three men crawled on the ground armed with their rifles and hid among some nearby bushes, convinced that "Spain was being invaded by extraterrestrials." All three men waited it out in the bushes until suddenly they heard a very loud sound coming from the direction of the ravine; it sounded to them like numerous "engine motors that were starting and then suddenly stopped." Again they saw a bright flash in the sky. And one of the men, last name of Guillem said out loud, 'Maybe they have gone' while the third man, Rafa Llopis hid in the bush 'shaking like a scared rabbit.'

Finally they left their hiding place and confirmed that both the strange entity and the equally strange object had departed. Now much calmer than before, the men walked down to the edge of the creek/arroyo and filled their canteens with water. They looked around for any signs left by the entity or object and noticed that some of the branches located in the upper sections of the tree appeared to be scorched or burnt. There was also a strong sulfuric smell in the area. They found several footprints on the sandy ground of flat footwear without heels.

They later calculated the height of the entity to have been at least 2.2 meters or more since its head almost touched the lower branches of the tree, and judging from the depth of the footprints its weight at least 150 kilos. Guided by intuition they visited a nearby cave which they knew was located on a nearby hill, thinking that perhaps the entity might have originated from there and maybe "had left something strange behind." But upon arriving at the cave they noticed that it was impossible to enter it due to the very thick and heavy brush surrounding the entrance. Very nervous they decided to leave the "torra" or barbecue for another day.

The three hunters gave up the hunt for the day and returned to where they had parked their motor scooters. While returning home they encountered two Civil Guards (a sort of rural militia) and told them what they had seen. The guards did not write anything down but told the men that "around these parts, it was a normal occurrence" and left. They only told their family and closest friends about the incident.

HC addendum.
Source: http://noticiasovni2013.blogspot.com/2013/04/raimundo-barbado-informa-en-exclusiva.html   Type: C
Comments: Translation by Albert S. Rosales.

* * * * * * *

Location: Point Isabel, Ohio.
Date: Fall 1968.
Time: 10:00 p.m.

Hearing a sound outside the farmhouse Larry Abbott, his father and a relative, Arnold Hubbard, went outdoors to look. Then, from the opposite side of the house, they heard a rustling of weeds. Grabbing a flashlight they saw a "monster" rising from the tall brush about 50ft away. It was walking toward them, and appeared to be about 10ft tall and about 4ft across the shoulders. Its arms were long, like an ape's.

In the flashlight beam the monster's hairy body was a beige color; its eyes glowed over a nose that was beyond Larry's ability to describe. The teeth were prominent and protruding, the ears pointed. But the feature that Larry remembered most was the thickness of the shoulders. "The thing put me into a sort of trance," said Larry. "I couldn't talk. Maybe it was just fright, but I couldn't open my mouth. And nobody else talked either. Maybe we were all in a trance." Larry said when he played the light beam on the monster it dropped down to the ground and was lost from sight.

Then, a few minutes later, they could hear it again, near the garage. Alarmed, Larry's father returned to the house and brought back a .22 rifle and gave it to Hubbard, who wanted to stalk the beast. As the men moved across the open field, the creature suddenly stood up in clear view about 50ft away. When Larry got it in the beam of the light, Hubbard fired. His first shot was a direct hit. The creature screamed hideously, a scream that Larry will never forget. Two more shots were fired.

Unbelievably, before the eyes of all three men, the creature was suddenly enveloped in a white mist. In less than a minute the mist vanished, then darkness. The three men searched the spot where the creature was shot and found no trace of it.

HC addendum.
Source: Leonard H. Stringfield, *'Situation Red: The UFO Siege.'* Type: E

* * * * * * *

Location: Duque De Caxias, Rio de Janeiro, Brazil.
Date: September, 1968.
Time: 1:00 a.m.

Mrs. Kok awoke in the early hours of the morning and got up to make coffee. Seeing a light in her backyard, she looked out her window and was surprised to see three normal looking men standing in the yard, one of who was standing with his back to her. Three bright beams of light shone down on them from above, coming from a Saturn shaped UFO that gave off a shrill sound like "electronic music." The semi-spherical underpart of the object was rotating, and the object appeared metallic. It was slightly higher than the two adjacent buildings.

Mrs Kok could see the men's faces and was surprised by their entirely human appearance since, seeing the object directly above them, assumed they were "spacemen," who she felt must look different than humans. Apparently aware of her presence at the window, the three figures suddenly began rising into the air in the beams of light, disappearing into the underside of the object, which then began rotating more rapidly and, with an increase in sound, took off straight up at a moderate speed.

HC addendum.
Source: Irene Granchi. Type: B

Location: Mendoza, Argentina.
Date: September 1, 1968.
Time: 4:00 a.m.

Two casino workers, Juan Carlos Peccinetti and Fernando Jose Villegas, were driving home after work at 3:30 a.m. when the engine of the car quit and the lights went out. Peccinetti was just getting out of the car when both men found themselves paralyzed and face to face with three strange, 5-foot beings with unusually large heads, with bald pates, and wearing coveralls. Behind them was seen a circular or oval UFO 12ft across and 5ft high, hovering about 4ft above the ground and directing a bright beam of light downward. When the entities came close, the witnesses heard a foreign-sounding voice repeating;
"Do not fear." Then they were told;
"We have just made three journeys around the sun, studying customs and languages of the inhabitants of the system. Mathematics is the universal language."
Meanwhile, another of the entities, using a tool like a soldering iron, was making inscriptions on the doors, windshield, and running boards of the car. Next, the witnesses saw a circular TV-like screen, on which there appeared first a waterfall, then a mushroom-shaped cloud, and then the waterfall again, this time with no water.
Finally the beings took hold of the witness's left hands and pricked their fingers three times, taking blood samples, after which they ascended to their machine along the light beam. There was an "explosive effect" and the object rose and disappeared. The witnesses ran to a nearby military college to report their experience. They later retracted their story, but there are indications that there was coercion; in fact, authorities in Mendoza quickly made the "spreading of UFO rumors" a criminal offense in Mendoza to discourage widespread rumors on this and other cases occurring about the same time.

HC addendum.
Source: Charles Bowen, *FSR* Vol. 14 #6.   Type: C

Location: Point Pleasant, Mason County, West Virginia.
Date: September 15, 1968.
Time: Night.

A teenager driving by the TNT storage area saw a big thing he could not identify. He had turned a curve in his car and on the bank was a creature six feet tall that was white with glowing red eyes. The boy stopped the car but the creature ran off. There were other sightings of the same creature in the area as well.

HC addendum.
Source: George Mitrovic, *'UFOs: An Atlas and History 1800-1977.'*
Type: E

* * * * * * *

Location: Alcala de Guadaira, Sevilla, Spain.
Date: Middle of September, 1968.
Time: 7:30 p.m.

Manuel Lopez Sutil, 52, was returning from work that evening when he noticed right in the middle of the block where he lived with his wife, daughter and son, a tall 'elderly' individual looking around as if searching for something. For some unknown reason, the stranger produced a firm impression on Sutil. Immediately he felt a strong attraction towards the stranger and a bizarre thought came to his mind "This man is an extraterrestrial!" even though there was nothing special on the 'exterior' of the stranger that would make anybody think that, at first glance anyway. Sutil approached the stranger and asked him if he was looking for somebody perhaps.

The stranger answered, *"No, nobody."* Immediately both Sutil and the stranger were engaged in an animated conversation which lasted for about half an hour. When they arrived at the front door of Sutil's home, the stranger then expressed curiosity about the home and Sutil invited him in. Once inside, the tall elderly stranger commented how low were the ceilings and how damaging was this "especially for the heart." He confess to Sutil that he had been in Alcala for several days already and was very happy with its peacefulness, "its bread and its water." This first visit to Sutil's home lasted several hours and the stranger returned two days later at the same time. Apparently none of the neighbors saw the arrival or departure of the grandfatherly stranger. When Sutil's wife first saw the stranger she had the strong impression "that she knew him from somewhere before," and that his face reminded her of someone.

However, the elderly stranger, produced, especially during his last visit, a strange uneasy sensation in Sutil's wife and daughter, however his son did not feel anything. The strange unease felt by the wife became stronger the second night he visited, to the point that she began to wish the stranger did not return again to the house. She commented this to her husband Manuel when the stranger left. But was incapable of explaining to him why she felt such an almost hostile attitude towards the stranger, which apparently had powerful telepathic abilities.

During his visits and while remaining in the house for a long period of time, and as they waited for dinner to be served, the daughter began to intensely want that the stranger leave the house. She was alone in the upstairs part of the house and stills remember in disbelief what occurred. In front of a mirror she mumbled in a low voice, *"Please God see that he leaves already"* or something similar and went down to join the others. The stranger stared at her intently and once he did that he bade goodbye never to return.

The girl knew that somehow the elderly stranger was aware of what she had pleaded for in her upstairs room, and for that reason he had left never to return. According to Sutil, the stranger did not smoke and that one time he grabbed Sutil's package of cigarettes and told him that he was going to demonstrate to him will power and would not smoke for two days. He placed the package of cigarettes on top of the table and told Sutil that he was not going to touch it until he returned. Sutil actually ignored this request and used the cigarettes but took time to place an exact looking pack of cigarettes on the same place that the stranger had left it on. However when the stranger returned and looked at the package of cigarettes and then at Sutil he said, *"I see that you lack willpower."* Somehow he knew that Sutil had switched packages.

One time he told Sutil's son, *"Your father understands me better than you do."* On various occasions he confessed to the family that he held them in high regards and trust. Sutil's wife thought that there was something definitely strange about the man but could not really pinpoint it. The stranger usually evaded airy or windy areas and always sat on corners. One day Sutil accompanied the stranger to the hostel where he was staying and attempted to assist him up the steps by grabbing the stranger's arm, but this one immediately turned around and with great agility climbed up the stairs, telling Sutil that "his assistance wasn't necessary." Sutil noted that not once did the stranger shake hands or touched him. During conversations at times he would mention the words "corn" and "wheat" even though the others had no idea in what context he intended their use.

According to the family the stranger looked "aged and worn" but displayed great agility for his age. He was very tall and robust with scarce hair, almost bald and very pale in skin color. He had 'rare' marked facial features, thick lips, a prominent nose and large protruding eyes. His gaze impressed Sutil's wife who opined that during the stranger's youth his eyes must have been very attractive, and produced in her 'discomfort and mistrust.' He used reading glasses but according to him "he had forgotten them." In one of his ears he had placed a ball of cotton. His hands caught the attention of the family, the fingers were round and thick. They noticed a strange 'defect' on one of his thumbs, it had something that protruded out the size of chick pea. He spoke enough Spanish to get by, but at times used other words in different languages, some unknown to the witnesses. At times he found it difficult to find the correct words in Spanish to communicate with the witnesses. His accent was definitely from another country. He wore extremely shiny shoes, black wool socks, a light-colored straw hat and a small walking stick. His shirt seemed very clean and extremely white in color, and he wore a tie. He also wore what appeared to be very expensive jewelry, according to Sutil's wife. He also wore a very expensive dark colored suit.

According to other locals this strange personage arrived at a local hostel called "La Florita" on August 12, 1968, and stayed there for six to seven months, in a single room which no one else entered, not even the cleaning lady, except for another tenant named Jesus which accompanied the elderly stranger on many occasions. The stranger registered his name as Abraham Talermar with ID #174334, it is not known if this was his passport number of his identity number. No one remembered his nationality even though he claimed he was from Sevilla. He cleaned his own room and was very untrustworthy of everyone else, always locking the room with keys. He bought mostly vegetables in the local market and cooked his own food in the room which many said emanated a foul odor. He left in a taxi claiming he had to go to Sevilla to retrieve some currency and never returned.

Twenty or thirty days after the encounter with the elderly stranger, Manuel Lopez Sutil began to experience strange sensations on the back of his head under the ears. It was a strange feeling which he had never experienced before and whose exact nature he was unable to ascertain. There were strange pulsating feelings different from the regular pulse. The discomfort reach a point that Sutil was forced to visit a local doctor. The doctor prescribed some medication that did not alleviate the situation. One night as he sat on the sofa experiencing the strange pulsating feeling, he suddenly began thinking about his friend Abraham and immediately felt great relief and the strange feeling disappeared.

Soon Sutil began experiencing strange visions in which he would see Abraham apparently floating in space next to an 'object.' He began to see oval-shaped objects and also cigar-shaped objects surrounded in smaller moving objects. In several of the "visions' Abraham would give Manuel Sutil 'tours' onboard the ships. Abraham looked the same as before and according to Sutil he could see everything in "vivid beautiful colors." During this vision, Abraham appeared to be wearing a sort of white tunic and brown colored sandals. Sutil could see different types of birds and pigeons flying around. He would establish dialogues with Abraham and this one would tell him that "God had commanded that he talk to him about something very important."

On one occasion Sutil asked Abraham if he was returning and Abraham only stared at him with an ironic smile. Abraham emphasized that his ships arrived on Earth through a "hole" in space. Sutil imagined this hole as a sort of tunnel to travel from planet to planet. It was sort of a stratified tunnel and according to Abraham to reach Earth they would use special 'pathways' and 'thruways' which somehow were available in deep space and consisted of a spiral structure which surrounded planet Earth.

HC addendum.
Source: Ignacio Darnaude Rojas-Marcos in 'Espacio Compartido.' #22, Barcelona. Type: X

* * * * * * *

Location: Villa Baumer, Joinville, Santa Catarina, Brazil.
Date: September 26-27, 1968.
Time: Dawn.

The witness, Mr. Henry Schneider Jr., an industrial chemist, residing about 5km from the center of Joinville, rose and went to check the fire on the pottery oven in his property, since the oven had to be on constantly at an specific temperature. After ascertaining that everything was in order, he walked a few steps, stopped, urinated and when he was about to light a cigarette he came across a strange object in the courtyard of his pottery building, about five meters away from where he was standing.

Startled but not frightened, he felt paralyzed, unable to move. He described the strange "artifact" as cone-shaped and tapered on top, measuring about four meters high by 2.50m in diameter at its base (it was seated on a tripod, about 80cm or so from the ground). From the bottom a bright light illuminated the ground. There was a rectangular opening on the craft from which a kind of 'conveyor belt' emerged which did not actually touch the ground although it seemed solid. At the lower end of the belt there was a figure which looked like a 'screen' rectangular in shape, measuring about 1.5m high, by 0.5m wide. Behind the first figure, bout 5.5m in a straight line on the same conveyor belt there was another similar 'figure.' The lower end of the conveyor was about 5m from the observer, who thought to ask what 'they' were doing there but could not speak.

However as an answer to his thoughts, without hearing a sound, an answer came to his mind, apparently coming from the figure before him, Schneider heard the following in his mind;

"We are checking the heat and smoke at this site."

At the time Schneider had burnt some tires in his outside oven and it had produced a lot of smoke and heat. For about 10 minutes while the figures were in sight, Schneider asked numerous questions, all mentally, and not all received immediate responses, however brief, that seemed to come from the nearest figure. Among many of the questions the observer remembers the following questions and answers:

Schneider: *"How do you live and eat?"*
Being: *"By impregnation, natural diet, unlike yours."*
Schneider: *"What is your means of propulsion?"*
Being: *"By means of 'attraction' at 36,000 (or 360,000) revolutions per second."*

They came from outer space from a star which Schneider could not remember the name. It was something like the word, *"Mers."* They were governed by a chief and each had a specific function. They traveled a certain route or mission and had come directly to see what was causing the heat. They promised to return to establish new contacts. The whole time that the figure was in sight, Schneider did not seem to be able to take his eyes from it.

As the conveyor was withdrawn without any noise, the observer was able to move forward but always keeping the same distance. He could see three points of bluish light on the object resembling windows. Through one of these points of light he could see another figure that looked like a box. The object was not bright except for the bluish windows and the light emitted from underneath. The ship and the figures appeared to be gray in color, the color of aluminum. Once the conveyor belt was collected inside the object, the door closed with a slight noise. Immediately the object rose rapidly and vertically, emitting a sharp hissing sound. In the center on the bottom the witness could see an intense blue light resembling that of a 'welding torch' and something like concentric rings, also blue, which seemed to turn.

After about 10 meters the object flew towards the south and in a few seconds it was just a point of light in the sky. The departure of the object produced a violent suction of air, which dragged Schneider to where the object had been. There he felt strong heat and noticed a strong odor resembling kerosene which permeated the air (ozone?). The next day at the landing site, Schneider found a circle of about 65cm in diameter, it was burned. Eight or ten tiles of pottery which were close to the landing site were loose or broken. An old truck which was parked nearby had several shortcomings; the battery, dynamo and starter were burned out.

One night about 5 months later Schneider for no apparent reason left his house and felt he should look to the sky, he then saw a bright object crossing the sky at a very high rate of speed. There were other witnesses to this event.

HC addendum.
Source: Carlos Alberto Varasin SBEDV Bulletin no. 94/98 September, 1973 to June, 1974. Type: B

* * * * * * *

Location: Near Kingman, Arizona.
Date: October 15, 1968.
Time: 3:00 a.m.

    Driving through the desert to California at 3:00 a.m. Michael Watts, and a hitch hiking passenger saw a "falling star" that stopped and shot back up again. They got out of the car and walked toward a distant light source at ground level; at the site, they then heard a sound like "digging," and dimly saw two shadowy forms 4ft tall, 15-20ft away. The figures seemed to have large heads and abnormally long arms. Then the hitchhiker suggested they go back for a gun and the figures vanished. Other maneuvering lights were observed.
    The light on the ground proved to be four lights, one of which took off into the air. Then something sounding like a train passed by at a distance; it had a string of lighted windows in which silhouettes of passengers sitting up were visible. After this a dark lens-shaped object having a flat dome on top and a row of pulsating multi-colored lights around the edge approached the witnesses quite closely. As dawn came, the ground light could be seen to be on a pale cigar-shaped object. Cloven footprints were found where the beings had been seen. Watts believed he may have had a memory lapse. The hitchhiker cannot be identified.

HC addendum.
Source: Michael Schutz and Loren Reichert. Type: C & A

Location: Medulla Township, Florida.
Date: October 18, 1968.
Time: 7:30 p.m.

Mr. and Mrs. Buck McMullen had just sat down to eat when their dog, chained outside their modest house south of Lakeland began to whimper and howl. They paid little attention to him although the dog had a reputation for being vicious and usually showed no fear of anything. That night however, the animal was obviously terrified for he tore loose from his chain, ripped a hole in the porch screen and ran into the dining room to cower under the table where they were sitting. Grace McMullen jumped up and ran outside to see what could have frightened the animal.

Fifty yards from the house she saw a transparent spherical object rocking gently about 10 feet off the ground. It gave off a purplish-red light. Inside the object, Mrs. McMullen says she saw two occupants resembling normal men. They were standing, operating a horizontal bar attached to a metallic spindle that ran through the object from top to bottom. They wore dull white, tight fitting clothing, boots, high collars and skull caps. Stunned, Mrs. McMullen turned on the porch light to attract their attention but they didn't appear to be interested. Although she admits she was frightened Mrs. McMullen says she realized that it could be important and tried to remember everything that occurred. Her husband and her son's fiancée Sharon Burgess, who was visiting, came outside and stood dumbfounded, but Mrs. McMullen did verify that they were all seeing the same thing. She had thought that she might be dreaming.

According to the McMullen's description the occupants inside the sphere were operating a horizontal bar with their hands inside some sort of flexible compartment. They stood on opposite sides of the spindle and when one pushed down on his side of the bar, the ship rocked to that side. As they worked the horizontal bar, the ship rocked and as the rocking increased, the ship increased its altitude and speed. Mrs. McMullen thinks it might have been on the ground in a vacant field just in front of their house and was taking off when she got outside. She was able to determine the UFO's size and altitude by its relationship to a tall palm-tree beside the home. Sharon hung back on the porch and suddenly the dog tore another hole in the screen, getting out of the house and ran down the road howling in terror. The object rose slowly, rocking, until it was about a mile from the house, then there was a silent burst of fire and sparks and it sped out of sight. Mrs. McMullen says the UFO was in sight for about 10 minutes.

Mrs. McMullen reports that the object appeared to be made of a substance resembling glass; it made no sound and she saw no source of power aboard. A band of blue light circled its middle and a halo of purplish-red light shone around the top. These lights glowed dully and both beams were aimed upward. The occupants were turned away from her so she could not see their faces. The object was about 30 feet in diameter, a perfectly circular globe, and there appeared to be no place inside for occupants to sit.

HC addendum.
Source: Lee Butcher, *Fate* Magazine, May, 1969.   Type: A

* * * * * * *

Location: Tulacingo, Mexico.
Date: November, 1968.
Time: Early morning.

Engineer Alberto Zecua and other were out camping in an isolated area near the railroad tracks heading towards Cuernavaca, when one morning he woke up feeling a strange attraction to a section of the nearby woods. As he reached a clearing surrounded by tall pines he saw an orange-lighted object hovering just above the ground, seemingly suspended by a column of orange light. The craft was silvery-white in color, disc-shaped with a small turret-like dome on top. Three tall humanoid figures were moving around the object.

Two of the figures were inserting chrome-plated tubes into the ground as if collecting soil samples, the other one stood with its back to the witness. These figures wore tight-fitting coveralls and silvery oval shaped helmets. Apparently sensing the presence of the witness the one standing up suddenly turned around to look at him. The being was described as human-like, very handsome with fine chiseled features and penetrating blue colored slanted eyes. At this point Zecua began feeling nauseated and could not move.

Perhaps sensing his discomfort, the tall figure approached and pressed a button around a wide belt on his waist, a beam of green light emerged, bathing the witness from head to toe. After this took place the witness felt much better. He soon began hearing telepathic communication from the being, telling him to remain calm and not to be afraid. The being was easily over 2 meters tall and as he stood next to the witness, he removed his helmet, showing long blond shoulder length hair. Still using telepathy, the being told Zecua that they recognized him and that they had "collaborated" with him before.

At one point the tall being took Zecua by the hand, pressed another button on his belt and a sort of wispy cloud emerged. On it Alberto saw images of what he was told was his past lives, while all this was taking place, the other two beings continued collecting plant and soil samples. Before leaving Alberto asked the beings for some sort of proof of the encounter, but they refused.

He bid them goodbye and ran towards his tent to obtain his camera and a pair of binoculars, at the same time waking up the disbelieving members of the campsite. As he ran back to the site of the encounter, he saw the craft slowly leaving the area and apparently was able to take several photographs.

HC addendum.
Source: Contacto Ovni. Type: C

* * * * * * *

Location: Near San Juan, Puerto Rico.
Date: November, 1968.
Time: Morning.

Lester Rosas (involved in previous encounters) was on the beach near the University of Puerto Rico when a man with long blond hair approached and gave him the "password" that Rosas had received from his space friend Al-Deena. The man identified himself as 'Vi-Dal' from Venus, and said he was the same spaceman whom George Adamski knew as 'Orthon.' He was here "to help my brothers of other planets in their missions here on your beautiful island."

He added that they were keeping "tabs" on what the Arecibo Observatory was doing regarding space exploration. He wore his hair long so as not to be conspicuous; he added that he will not be spotted because he just looked like a hippie. They went on to talk at great length for two hours and one of the things Vi-Dal told Rosas was that George Adamski was now reincarnated on Venus.

HC addendum.
Source: Janet and Colin Bord, *'Life beyond Planet Earth?'* Type: E

Location: (Undisclosed location) Southern France.
Date: November 1, 1968.
Time: Early morning.

A French doctor was awakened by the sound of his 14-month old son crying. His son was standing in his crib pointing at the window. Behind the shutter a bright light was moving. After the child had gone back to sleep, the doctor went out onto the balcony. He saw two glowing discs in the sky, silvery white on top and bright red underneath. Each had a tall antenna on top and one on either side, and they were directing a narrow beam of white light towards the ground below. The two objects slowly drew closer and merged into a single object, about 200ft in diameter and 50ft thick. It approached the doctor, and then tilted 90 degrees so that the beam of light struck him.

He then heard a loud bang, and the object evaporated into a whitish cloud that dissipated with the wind. A thin thread of flight rose high into the sky before vanishing, as a white dot and exploding like a firework. A few days earlier, the doctor had accidentally cut a vein in his leg while chopping wood, and a decade earlier he had stepped on a landmine in Algeria, leaving his right side partially paralyzed. After the above sighting, he found that the swelling and pain from his leg injury had vanished, and the chronic after-effects of the injuries he had sustained in the Algerian war improved dramatically in the days that followed. A few days after the encounter, the doctor and his child each developed a strange, reddish, triangular mark on the abdomen, and this mark recurred in successive years.

Strange paranormal phenomena began to take place around the doctor and his family, including poltergeist activity and unexplained disturbances in electrical circuits. The doctor began to have mysterious meetings with a strange, nameless man he called 'Mr. Bied.' He would hear a whistling noise inside his head and would feel guided to walk or drive to a certain location where he would meet the man, who would discuss his UFO experience and paranormal matters. Mr. Bied caused him to experience apparent teleportation and time travel, including a distressing episode with alternative landscapes on a road that does not exist. The stranger also once visited the doctor at his home accompanied by a 3ft tall humanoid with mummified skin, which remained motionless while his eyes quickly darted around the room. The doctor experienced uncontrolled levitation on at least one occasion.

HC addendum.
Source: Jacques Vallee. Type: E, G, or F?

Location: Ulfshale, Denmark.
Date: November 2, 1968.
Time: 5:50 p.m.

The witness was in her summer residence, which faces the eastern sea, when she went outside for a walk. Through a hole on the hedge she noticed a bright object floating over a nearby hill. The object resembled a very tall and wide man wearing a long cowl. The figure appeared to be growing in size. As the witness walked into the field to get a closer look, she noticed three more similar glowing figures, one was glowing dark red in color. All three figures floated above the ground and all then disappeared into some bushes and trees. The red glowing figure appeared one more time very briefly and was seen floating up a hill and out of sight.

HC addendum.
Source: Per Anderson, SUFOI. Type: E

* * * * * * *

Location: Lorain, Ohio.
Date: November 9, 1968.
Time: 5:45 a.m.

A couple was awakened by a loud thump on the roof of their trailer. The bump was followed by the sound of something moving near their bedroom window. When they looked out the window, they saw a huge face staring down at them. The creature's two front paws or hands were resting on the windowsill. The husband leaped out of bed and frantically searched for his gun, but by the time he located it the creature was gone from the window.

Running on two legs, it dashed around the east side of the house, weaving from side to side, crossed two streets and disappeared into the woods. The creature stood about six-feet tall. Its front side was grayish brown, the rest of the body a darker shade of the same color. It resembled "a large bipedal lion of around 600 pounds."

HC addendum.
Source: Jerome Clark and Loren Coleman, 'Creatures of the Goblin World.' Type: E

Location: Turnersville, New Jersey.
Date: November 12, 1968.
Time: Night.

The witnesses saw, in area about 30 miles outside Andrews Air Force Base, a glowing ball moving above the tree line. The glowing object was silent and appeared to be 'tracking' them. They ran from the area and all memory of the event appears to end at this point. However 20 years later the main witness had a flashback while watching a UFO show. He remembered that he and his friend Paul ran to the corner of Whitman Drive and Cornwall Terrace and then a blue beam of light came out of the orb and paralyzed them both where they stood.

His next memory was not being able to move and lying on a flat table. He raised his head to see his friend Paul on another table across the room. This was unlike any room he had ever seen before it was filled with a brilliant white light inside. He then saw two beings standing over him, and also two other beings standing over his friend as well. As he became upset the taller being standing over him touched his head and the witness went limp and all his thoughts were calmed. He then asked the tall being who he was, and received the following answer *"We are your friends"* he then asked, *"Why do you look so different?"* All communication was performed telepathically.

At this point he noticed his friend Paul being turned over and he tried to yell at him, and again the tall being touched the witness forehead (he thinks the Pineal Gland) and he became unconscious. His next memory was hearing the tall being tell him never to tell anyone of the incident. Soon both witnesses were back in the street fully clothed, not knowing how they got there. The main witness reported being visited the next night by a man wearing a black rim hat who asked him questions about what had occurred the night before. He warned him that "there was an escaped convict in the area, not to venture outside." He lost track of Paul and believes he was incarcerated.

HC addendum.
Source: http://mufoncms.com Type: G
Comments: Unexplored abduction event.

Location: Parador De Alarcon, Spain.
Date: November 12, 1968.
Time: Unknown.

Businessman Francisco Donis was driving on his way to Malaga when he received a telepathic message instructing him to go a certain isolated location. On his way there his vehicle stopped but was helped by a friendly trucker and managed to re-start his vehicle. Once at the pre-arranged site he was surprised to see a disc-shaped object hovering next to the road. As he watched, an opening became visible on the craft and a retractable ladder descended to the ground, on which a human-like figure descended and approached Donis with arms outstretched in an obvious sign of peace.

Speaking in perfect Spanish, the stranger informed Donis that his named was 'Francisco Atienza' and that he was a descendant of extraterrestrials. The stranger was totally human in appearance and wore a one-piece gray diver's suit. A long conversation ensued between Atienza and Donis, which took place inside the witness car. Atienza told Donis that he came from a planet called 'URIN,' whose original inhabitants were short, large-headed humanoids. However there existed on Urin a human colony, which lived under huge glass domes, since the atmosphere of Urin was toxic to humans. He further explained that life under these conditions had caused a massive sterilization among the human colony, which had more female members than males.

HC addendum.
Source: Sebastian Robiou Lamarche, *Manifesto Ovni en Puerto Rico, Santo Domingo Y Cuba.* Type: B
Comments: Early report describing possible use of humans for colonization purposes on the part of short large-headed humanoids. Interesting if true.

Location: Near Zafra, Extremadura, Spain.
Date: November 14, 1968.
Time: 10:50 p.m.

The witness; Manuel Trejo, was returning home in his car when suddenly the engine of the car began to falter. He was losing speed and the headlights began to dim. Seconds later an invisible "shock wave" struck his Citroen, making the vehicle sway from side to side. There wasn't anybody else on the road and there appeared to be fog on both sides of the road. The witness decided to continue his drive and after rounding a curve at a spot about 300meters away to the left of his car he observed a strange figure which at first he thought was a "Civil Guard."

However, as he approached the figure and the headlights illuminated it, clearly he realized that it was not a guard. He drove slowly by the figure and was able to describe it as man-like and about 1.7-1.8m in height. Its legs remained together and its arms hanging straight down on its sides. The figure was wearing a tight-fitting diver's outfit, completely covered in tiny red, green and blue lights, "like a Christmas tree." As the witness came upon the figure, the intensity of the lights seemed to increase. He could not see any facial details but noticed that it had dark hair, somewhat longer than normal. It wore black gloves and boots and remained completely still as the witness drove by.

A couple of days earlier, a motorist driving on the same road had seen a metallic domed disc hovering above the road.

HC addendum.
Source: Rafael Llamas and Vicente Ballester Olmos. Type: D

Location: Tingo Maria, Peru.
Date: November 20, 1968.
Time: Unknown.

It was reported that in a jungle area a large disc-shaped object descended and came to rest on the ground near three boys that were playing in a nearby field. Curious they approached the object and noticed two short figures standing next to it. One of the boys attempted to get nearer the object but he suddenly went unconscious.

The two short beings signaled the other two boys to approach and to retrieve their fallen friend, which they did. The child was supposedly taken to a local hospital where he died suffering from third degree burns. On the site, an area of scorched brush was found. No other information.

HC addendum.
Source: ONIFE, Argentina.   Type: C
Comments: Another documented case in which the UFO-humanoid encounter resulted fatal to one of the witnesses. There are already several in record, in this instance it appears to have been an accident and not intentional.

* * * * * * *

Location: Macedo, Sao Paolo, Brazil.
Date: November 21, 1968.
Time: 9:30 p.m.

The primary witness was on a bus that stopped for a while at Macedo; there she saw, about 40 yards away, a domed metallic UFO, the size of a small car, hovering only a few feet above the ground. Around the rim a row of changing lights gave the impression of spinning, and beneath it a patch of violet light was cast to the ground.

A door in the object was open, with three steps below it, and standing in front of the UFO were three 6-foot tall figures of human appearance wearing skin-tight shiny black coveralls, and black boots. The suits were one-piece, covering the heads, so that only the face was left exposed. One of the men was carrying a cylindrical implement 2ft long and 3" thick, with a thinner tube of aluminum like material coiled in a spiral around it. Facing the beings was a crowd of about twenty people including three police officers, who had their guns drawn; two police cars were parked nearby.

After a short time, a beam of silver light shot forth from the cylinder and the people closest to the beings were paralyzed; others felt as if in a faint. The men walked calmly back to the object, which they boarded; the craft then took off and rapidly climbed out of sight. The incident had lasted about 15 minutes.

HC addendum.
Source: Dr. Walter Buhler. Type: B

* * * * * * *

Location: Curico, Chile.
Date: November 25, 1968.
Time: 8:30 p.m.

At sunset Alejandro Gonzalez Reyes, 34, went out of his house to seek his wife. Then, 230ft away, he saw a metallic object; descend from the sky to an altitude of 150ft. About 6ft in diameter and 5ft high, it was shaped like two dishes put together, with a Y-shaped antenna on top, and had four legs about 3ft long. The object shone like aluminum. It descended diagonally to the ground or just above it.

Three well-proportioned beings of human appearance about 2-3ft tall got out of it through a door and started to walk about. One held an unlighted flashlight; another scratched at the ground with his hand, and the third some sort of "instrument." On hearing a truck approaching, the three humanoids rapidly returned to the craft; the 3rd seemed to have some difficulty in getting back in; and it began to rock back and forth in "falling leaf" fashion, then took off suddenly at very high speed. The observation had lasted 2 or 3 minutes. No traces were left.

HC addendum.
Source: Elena Marino, LDLN #117. Type: B

* * * * * * *

Location: Lima, Peru.
Date: November 28, 1968.
Time: Night.

Students from the local Recoleta de Montevideo School reported encountering a strange short humanoid with an egg-shaped head, and a blinking light on the chest area and what appeared to be a long antenna like protrusion on his back. It appeared to have duck-like feet, and it was shorter than a 7-year old boy. A priest and a teacher also reported seeing the creature.

HC addendum.
Source: Fabio Picasso. Type: E

Location: Deltox Marsh, Wisconsin.
Date: November 30, 1968.
Time: Night.

Twelve hunters saw a short, dark brown haired, hairless-faced creature that left three toed, webbed tracks in the snow. As it passed in front of them. They were afraid to shoot at it because it looked too human like.

HC addendum.
Source: Loren Coleman. Type: E

* * * * * * *

Location: Constanta, Romania.
Date: Winter 1968.
Time: 10:00 p.m.

The 22-year old witness, S. C., had effectively finished high school early but had failed his first admission attempt at the Institute of Fine Arts. To improve his skills he enrolled at a local art school. He was living alone in a rented room that only had a wooded heat stove and no sanitary facilities. One night before going to bed he had stepped out into the yard to satisfy a small physical necessity. The ground was covered in fresh fallen snow. Suddenly the yard was bathed in a red light. Looking up he saw a red glowing light, the next moment he felt that he was floating over the ground and going higher and higher. He was able to look down and saw the enclosed courtyards of his neighbors which were all separated by high fences.

Suddenly he found himself in a "large hall" illuminated by an indirect light source. The floor reminded him of large chessboard. Soon he began to hear "telepathic voices" coming from at least 3-4 persons which he couldn't see. The language was Romanian but it seems to have been translated mechanically manifested by the fact that every time he heard them "his neck would twinge." He was allowed to ask questions and the first one was; *"What do you want from me and why have you brought me here?"* He heard an answer, *"We want to test you. We heard you failed the entrance exam at the Art Institute, we want you to make a model here on the floor."*

At this point a kind of "robot" with rubber tracks descended on a platform. The trucks were thin flat, square, with sides about half a meter, with the bottom covered in foam grip. The same robot then placed them on the floor apparently in positions for S. C. to arrange or put together (apparently in a sort of test or exam). They were of metallic yellow and green colors. Unfortunately he could not make any combination work successfully. He then tried to suggest two or three models to the unseen entities. "Interesting" said the voices. They then advised him to give up painting and concentrate on the decorative arts.

After this he suddenly found himself lying on the snow. The cold woke him up, and he could not remember how he was returned to the yard. He then returned to his room and realized that several hours had already passed, and the fire in the wooded stove had burnt out. He searched the yard for tracks and only found his, but he gradually remembered most of the experience. He climbed to the top floor of his flat and confirmed the position of objects in his neighbor's enclosed yards. He only told his grandmother about the experience, and she warned him that he had been abducted by "devils." He graduated from the Nicolae Grigorescu Institute of Arts in 1975, specializing in set design.

HC addendum.
Source: Dan Farcas, http://www.asfanufo.ro/index.php/contacte-et/96-cazul-sc   Type: G
Comments: The witness was to have further experiences. Now why would supposed extraterrestrials worry about a young man making into a prestigious institute of Arts?

* * * * * * *

Location: Novosibirsk, Russia.
Date: Winter 1968.
Time: Evening.

A lonely female resident, an ardent Communist Party member who never believed in flying saucers, aliens and other nonsense was found unconscious early one morning, laying on the side of the road by a street cleaner. An ambulance was summoned and doctors at a nearby hospital succeeded in reviving her. When she woke up she said that on the previous evening, while returning home, she noticed a large cigar-shaped object in the sky emanating a violet beam of light. The beam appeared to be searching for something on the ground, scanning over the streets.

Suddenly, the beam shone directly on her, blinding her and she lost consciousness. Details of what occurred after that were apparently erased from her memory. It soon became evident that the woman was pregnant and her relatives were convinced that she had been raped, and thought she invented the bizarre story to avoid shame. However the child she gave birth to later was different from any other. It was a girl, quite small, with an enlarged head, large black eyes, a tiny fragile body, and a very pale skin with a grayish-pinkish tint. (A hybrid?).

The name given to the little girl was Rose. The little girl soon attracted the attention of the KGB because of her uncommon appearance. She began to write and read at a very early age, but even more incredible; she was apparently able to read human thoughts. She never attended kindergarten or any other school. Instead she was been constantly examined and studied at a secret institute in Akademgorodok under close KGB surveillance. One, professor Mysh, PhD, mainly conducted the studies there.

When Rose was 6-years old she told her mother that she was "tired" of being on Earth and added that at the age of 7 she would disappear, and take her mother with her also. Apparently that's exactly what occurred a year later, at age 7 Rose vanished, along with her mother.

HC addendum.
Source: Igor Kolomiets, *the Secret Doctrine*, #21, 2003.   Type: G?
Comments: It appears that the little girl (Rose) was part of an alien hybridization program, one of the first such reported, but apparently not considered such back in then.

* * * * * * *

Location: South Bend, Indiana.
Date: December, 1968.
Time: Afternoon.

Mrs. Mary Block saw a silvery flying object maneuvering over the area, then several days later, answered a knock on her door. Her caller had a deathly-white face, which had absolutely no lines and no expression. The figure wore all-black clothing and wore a black hat.

The stranger got straight to the point. She and her children were not to mention to anybody what they had seen. He left riding in the back seat of a big black car whose windows were heavily tinted. Mrs. Block was so terrified that she did not report this experience until 17 years had gone by.

HC addendum.
Source: Don Worley.   Type: E
Comments: Cars with tinted windows were almost non-existent in the 60's. This appears to be a "classic" MIB encounter.

Location: (Undisclosed location) Idaho.
Date: December, 1968.
Time: Night.

Hearing a commotion in his barn, Lonnie Duggan rushed out and discovered "a strange looking little man, covered with fur-like hair" who was drawing blood samples from his horse's flank with a large syringe like implement. The figure was 4ft tall, had large eyes and a very high, bald forehead, and wore a snug fitting 2-piece suit.

Speaking in a mechanical sounding voice, "like a computer," the being said he was from a planet of Tau Ceti (Cetus constellation), and that his people had been visiting Earth for a hundred years. Suddenly appearing alarmed, he told Duggan to hurry back to the house and stay there for a half hour. Duggan did so, and saw a huge glowing object rose from behind the barn and shot away "like lighting."

HC addendum.
Source: *Saucer News* Vol. 16 #4.   Type: C

* * * * * * *

Location: Near Wairakei, Taupo, New Zealand.
Date: December 18, 1968.
Time: 10:45 p.m.

Miss Gay Harvey, aged 29, a waitress, and Mr. Nino Perego, aged 37, a cocktail barman, both were traveling from Wellington to Auckland and came upon a strange figure on the lonely Taupo-Tokoroa highway about five miles north of Wairakei. Mr. Perego was driving and consequently received a better view of the figure as they passed it on the other side of the road. The "man" was about 5ft 7in. to 6ft. tall, of average build and wearing a shiny, plastic type dark blue suit. It was loose-fitting though, not baggy. There was a belt or division of some kind around the waist, and the trousers appeared to end or be tucked in at the ankles with the feet enclosed in shoes of the same material. The sleeves appeared to be tucked in at the wrists and the hands were also encased in material of substantially the same kind. There appeared to be a collar or division around the neck where the helmet began. The headpiece was more rigid than the body material but was of the same color.

Mr. Perego said this headpiece was cylindrical like a small "kitchen rubbish tin," and it had a flat top. Its size indicated that the figure had a head of apparently normal human size. There was a clear plastic-type window on the front of the helmet. Through this he could not determine any facial features but only a contrasting skin color. The window was square and, on a normal person, would have extended from the eyes to the mouth and from ear to ear. The figure was striding along slowly, like a "zombie" and did not acknowledge the passage of the car. It faced fixedly forward throughout the period it was illuminated. Although Mr. Perego braked after he realized what he had seen, Miss Harvey did not want to return because she was feeling ill and wished to reach Auckland as soon as possible. The night was dry and overcast and the road at the observation point was straight and flat. The surrounding terrain was mainly scrub country. Miss Harvey did not have as good a view as her companion, but was able to confirm the general description of the figure. It was she who used the terms "spaceman" and "diving suit." She had not heard of UFOs before.

HC addendum.
Source: Anthony J. Brunt, the Auckland Univ. UFO Research Group.
Type: E

* * * * * * *

Location: Goulburne, New South Wales, Australia.
Date: December 28, 1968.
Time: Unknown.

The witness had been in the area back in 1950 and at that time had experienced a peculiar incident, which left him with a scar. He returned to the site in December 1968, and saw a craft 40ft in diameter and 10ft high, and met its occupant, who walked around the side of the object.

He was human in appearance with long hair, about 5'6" tall, and wore silver colored shoes. The witness spoke with this humanoid, in English, for about 3 minutes, learning that he was from Saturn; the man seemed to be in a hurry to get away; boarding, the craft rose 15' off the ground and hovered momentarily before moving off and disappearing.

HC addendum.
Source: Dr. N. Lindtner, UFO Investigation Center, Sydney.   Type: B
Comments: Early mention of "scar" left as a result of a close encounter; however there are no details available on the 1950 incident.

Location: Near Vega Baja, Puerto Rico.
Date: December 31, 1968.
Time: 7:30 p.m.

Two men; an uncle and his nephew, were on their way to San Juan from the town of Isabela. Their family awaited for them for the New Year's Eve festivities. As they approached the small locality of Vega Baja and traveling at 40 miles per hour on Route #2, the vehicle headlights illuminated a light colored whitish object that was on the side of the road like a disabled vehicle. The nephew, who was driving, immediately yelled out, pointing the object out to his uncle.

As he looked at the craft attempting to identify what it was, he saw a figure standing next to it. His immediate reaction was to accelerate the vehicle. At this point the uncle looked behind as the vehicle accelerated from the area and saw the object lit up like a light bulb, first bluish-green in color and then turning red. The craft then rose from the ground emitting a soft 'purring' sound and quickly disappeared from sight. The uncle did not see the humanoid but did get a good look at the object.

The nephew described the humanoid, as short, no more than five feet in height, with a mouth that resembled that of an elderly person 'without teeth.' What really caught his attention were the humanoid's eyes which he described as "cat-like" and very shiny. He was under the impression that the humanoid had been caught by surprise outside his craft. The uncle described the object as resembling an "upside down ashtray."

HC addendum.
Source: Sebastian Robiou Lamarche, *APRO Bulletin*. Type: C

* * * * * * *

Location: Midvale, Utah.
Date: Late December, 1968.
Time: Daytime.

During his Christmas vacation, Robert McAllister, a student, was out checking his animal traps when he came upon a circular object hovering 6ft off the ground. About 15' in diameter, the object made no noise and Robert approached to within a few feet. From behind some rocks emerged three figures, their heads encased in helmets; they held a cable at the end of which, floating about 10ft off the ground, was a chair, on which sat a smiling, apparently aged man, with silver hair and a benign smile. He wore a kind of tunic, while the three men on the ground wore uniforms of a hard, shiny blue type of material.

Ignoring the boy, they "escorted" the seated man to the object, in which a door opened; the man and two of his escorts entered the latter by floating up to it. The remaining figure approached the boy and, placing his arm around him, led the child around the craft, pointing out various features and speaking in a strange language the boy did not recognize. Noticing a ball point pen in Robert's pocket, the man took it to write a paper he drew from his pocket. When Robert indicated he could keep the pen, he again reached into his pocket and brought out his own, which he gave gave to the boy, repeating a phrase that sounded like, "*Ab-doon! Ab-doon!*" he floated up to the door and disappeared inside.

The door closed then re-opened, and then man made gestures for Robert to move further away; then the object rose slowly and silently, suddenly shooting off at tremendous speed. After school had resumed, Robert was visited at his home by a stranger who handed him a "deaf mute" card; the man, rather than accepting the offered coins, asked for the pen, (the one given to the witness by the humanoid) which he took and quickly left.

HC addendum.
Source: *Saucer News* Vol. 16 #4.   Type: B

1969

Location: Fatima, Portugal.
Date: 1969.
Time: Afternoon.

17-year old Carlos Cavalho (involved in other encounters) had accompanied his mother to the local shrine, but being an atheist in nature, and concerned about going to war to fight Portuguese colonial wars in Africa (at the time) he stayed behind in the tour bus while everyone else visited the shrine.

Suddenly while sitting there he saw a powerful light in the sky which descended close to his location at very high speed. Within the light he was able to distinguish the figure of a woman totally dressed in white who communicated with him, and told him not to worry that he would not be going to war but to be prepared to what was ahead in the coming years.

HC addendum.
Source: Miguel Pedrero.   Type: E or F?

* * * * * * *

Location: Santa Rosa, Bolivia.
Date: 1969.
Time: Daytime.

A sheep herder and two Indian helpers were watching the flock when a silent disc-shaped object descended from the sky, gliding down gently in a curving approach until it stopped 50 feet above them. As it hovered, it emitted flashes of white light from its underside. This happened about 30 times in quick succession, and the sheep suddenly fell to the ground. Concerned for the flock, the shepherd picked up a stick and ran toward the glowing shiny metallic disc. Suddenly there was a flash of violet light land the shepherd was completely paralyzed. As he watched terror stricken the domed craft descended lower till about six feet from the ground. A trap door with a built in stair opened down from underneath, and two human like feet started down the stair from the center of the ship. Two man-like figures wearing white reflective form fitting suits emerged; both wore transparent dark helmets over the head.

The beings wore matching white gloves and boots, and each carried what looked like a shiny silver fire extinguisher in one hand, and a black nozzle on the end of a white hose connected to the bottle in the other. The two men walked around the flock of sheep putting the "fire extinguisher" nozzle to each of the fallen sheep and completely ignoring the men. After about three minutes the men finished their task and re-entered their craft. The stair retracted as the big, circular object, drifted higher, to about 300 feet. From that position, there was a tremendous noise and the object sped up into the sky at a steep angle and disappeared. The men found all 34 sheep dead and apparently bloodless. Some of the internal organs were also found to be desiccated and spongy.

HC addendum.
Source: Timothy Good, *'Alien Base.'* Type: B

* * * * * * *

Location: Short Hills, Ontario, Canada.
Date: 1969.
Time: Afternoon.

Two 14-year old boys were playing in a conservation area when a huge Bigfoot type creature approached and picked them up, the creature took them onboard a landed disc shaped object. Inside, several short humanoids dressed like doctors, examined them, apparently putting an implant into one of them. The Bigfoot type creature was seen to sit on a large chair inside the object. Several wires were placed on its head, which led to another device nearby.

HC addendum.
Source: Lawrence J. Fenwick, *SBI Report #40*. Type: G

Location: Ciudad Universitaria, Mexico City, Mexico.
Date: 1969.
Time: Afternoon.

Mr. Mercado Orue, involved in a previous encounter, had entered a local bar and had sat down for a drink. As he sat there, a very tall, pale man approached and sat down. Orue noticed that the man wore a metallic-like outfit, soft to the touch.

The stranger told Orue not to eat the ham or drink the whisky since it was damaging to his health. Among other things, the stranger said that he came from a very far place that was not divided into "cities or continents." He then bade goodbye, telling the witness that he would see him again.

HC addendum.
Source: Fabio Picasso. Type: E

* * * * * * *

Location: Yebra, Guadalajara, Spain.
Date: 1969.
Time: Evening.

Juan Barco was inspecting some of the newly plowed fields when he encountered a very tall being estimated to have been over 2 meters in height, wearing a close-fitting metallic gold-colored outfit. The strange being appeared not to have any facial features. Terrified, Barco ran to town and came back with a large group of residents all armed with guns but the strange humanoid had already vanished.

During the encounter, Barco felt "out of place" or confused, and during the same year reported encountering the same or similar being on several other occasions.

HC addendum.
Source:http://www.looculto.260mb.com/ovnisenespana/ovnisenespana.htm Type: E

Location: (Undisclosed location) North Vietnam.
Date: 1969.
Time: Evening.

The main witness reported being on patrol just before dark in the North Two Corp in North Vietnam. They were returning to the hill, when they encountered hostile fire, the squad was caught off guard, so they used what cover was available. The fight had been going on for only a few minutes when movement caught his eye. Through the thick vegetation he saw what he thought was a large man, breaking cover from behind his left side. As the thing ran past him he realized it wasn't a man, and was not really sure of what he was seeing. The figure was about 7 feet tall and had an enormous build, though not completely covered with hair, the figure had reddish brown hair covering a good portion of its body. It had covered about 30 yards very quickly, passing within just yards of his position, when it got hit in the crossfire. The figure stumbled once or twice but never fell. All of a sudden the enemy broke and ran, one even left his weapon behind, they were yelling something, but none of them ever knew what it was they were yelling.

They slowly regrouped and made sure no one was wounded and discussed what they thought they had seen. As it was getting dark and there were hostiles in the area, they decided to get back to the hill. That night they heard several strange howls. Some sounded like they were just outside of the hooch and others sounded more than a mile away. There were all kinds of sounds from whines to growls to sounds that sounded like barks. Needless to say no one slept very well that night. The next morning, all of them that were on the patrol, decided to try to track this creature. It took a lot of talking to get "Tops" (the major) to let them go looking for it, but after hearing the same story from the whole squad he decided to let them have a chance to bring it back.

They returned to the area and found a blood trail, leading into the jungle. They trailed it for quite some time when they found the body of an enemy soldier that had been almost entirely torn apart. They did not know exactly what happened, but he had a good notion to what may have happened. They basically ran out of the area back to their hill. The rest of the time they were in Vietnam, he never head the sounds or saw anything like it again. The talk of what they had seen spread very quickly, and some of the locals called it a name that he could neither pronounce or remember, but the translation if he can recall was "Stench Monkey" or "Foul Monkey," or something similar.

According to the main witness the incident had bothered him so much that he transferred from there to a job on a helicopter so that he wouldn't have to be in the jungle anymore.

HC addendum.
Source: http://www.phantomandmonsters.com/2012/03/solders-stories-rock-ape.html
Type: X

* * * * * * *

Location: Parramatta, New South Wales, Australia.
Date: 1969.
Time: 8:00 p.m.

Mrs. Jo P. reported having been abducted by a spacecraft and being approached in a room full of technical apparatuses by a human-like male with blond hair and blue eyes, dressed in skin-tight green neck to ankle garment. He told her that she had been abducted at random and that she was about to provide genetic material while anaesthetized. He conducted her to a gold-shining 'operation table' like apparatus which rose from the floor. Her clothes were removed as she fell into a deep sleep. Upon awakening she was given her clothes by two female beings (all these human-like people had slightly larger eyes and heads than ours). The male again joined her. All had skin-tight garments and black plastic-like boots.

The male conducted her on an inspection of the spacecraft, but of all the things she saw, it was a room with computer-like machines that was a real sensation to her, for the male told her 'telepathically' that the rows upon rows of oval-shaped black boxes she saw, contained the 'spirit' remains of people gathered from all over the world, and that three other craft like the one she was on employed for the purpose of 'collecting' this material for 're-animation' on another world in a galaxy beyond ours called 'OT.'

Mrs. Jo P. described how she had been abducted as she lay reading one night in bed about 8pm. A fair haired woman in a blue skin-tight garment and boots of the same color, a large head and big eyes, stepped through a wall and at this moment stunned her by the touch of a silver 'wand' about 60cm in length. She was lifted from her bed by her and with no effort, was taken through the wall. It was then that she found herself in the room where the male being appeared to her. How she was returned to her home was another experience in itself. She was 'told' telepathically to walk through a blue haze in the shape of a 10ft square (3.4) 'wall' and found herself in her bedroom standing beside the bed. The clock said 7:45 p.m. "I was gone fifteen minutes but was returned fifteen minutes before I was taken through the wall by the strange woman," (!) she told the late Ufologist Bill Moser.

HC addendum.
Source: Blue Mountains UFO Research Club, August 2008.
Type: G

Location: Near Oristano, Sicily, Italy.
Date: 1969.
Time: Midnight.

A family of four was driving towards Cagliari from Sassari when as they neared the heights around Oristano, they spotted three strange luminous figures standing on the edge of the road. The figures stood to the right side of the road. The wife screamed in terror and told her husband to accelerate and not to stop; meanwhile the three figures appeared to signal to the witness to stop the car, making gestures with their hands. The witness quickly drove away from the area and after arriving at the hotel the wife experienced severe heat flashes while her 14-year old daughter vomited.

Years later the husband died of lung cancer and the son had a cancerous tumor removed from the colon. The wife somehow connected all these ailments with the strange encounter. The beings were described as of average height, glowing white in color and with dark oval-shaped eyes. Days later the woman's 84-year old mother reported seeing three glowing man-like figures outside the window of her house in the same area.

HC addendum.
Source: Giovanni Mameli, CISU Sardinia.   Type: E

* * * * * * *

Location: Near Largo, Maryland.
Date: 1969.
Time: Late evening.

The witness, an undergraduate at the University of Maryland in the late 60's was leaving the campus and heading for his car, when his attention was diverted by one of the many young women dispensing flyers along the path. Not only did he feel unusually compelled to take a flyer from this particular girl, he also felt that "there was a sort of telepathic connection" between them. He says that he knew what the flyer concerned as soon as his eyes met the girl's.

He describes the girl as "short with very fair skin, crystal blue eyes, and straight blond hair; very angelic looking." As the day wore on, the witness felt more compelled to go to the party and to go alone which, he says, was extremely unusual for him. That evening he drove to the rural area indicated on the map and eventually located a large "country/farm type house" which, he was certain upon sighting, was the place he was seeking. Pulling up to the house he noticed two young people on the porch, but no overt signs of a party. He parked his car next to several others that were lined up perpendicular to the side of the house.

As he made his way up to the house he noted that the two people previously on the porch were no longer there. Assuming that they had gone inside, he climbed the steps and peeked in the framed glass door but saw no one, let alone any indication of a party in progress. He knocked on the door and let himself in. At this point he became aware that someone was approaching him, but his "consciousness began to fade or shift and he could not see them."

From this point on he experienced extreme difficulty in perceiving his surroundings, as though he was in a sort of "mental fog," however he could make out a pair of staircases that bordered the back of the entrance hall on each side and led to a second floor mezzanine. On the left staircase he discerned a small figure in black moving up the stairs and on the right several identical figures moving down. The scene was accompanied by an eerie silence. He experienced extreme confusion that gave way to sudden abject terror and an urgent need to leave, which was easier acknowledged than achieved. His next memory was of driving home in his car and feeling numb.

HC addendum.
Source: Paranormal website (exact source missing from files). Type: G?

* * * * * * *

Location: Tres Lagoas, Matto Grosso do Sul, Brazil.
Date: 1969.
Time: Night.

One night Nadia Marzalle was lying on her bed when a bright light and a strange noise invaded the room. She went outside and saw a UFO floating above the ground. Suddenly she felt herself "sucked" inside the object. Once inside, she saw a humanoid similar to a human and next to him two other younger men, with brown hair and taller than the witness.

They wore white coveralls and spoke in an unknown language, which the witness could not understand. They sat her on a metallic and cold chair. Looking out a porthole like opening, she was able to see that they were flying over a world, which had houses that lacked roofs. The craft then floated above some woods under a star-filled sky. The craft never did land and after drinking a sour tasting liquid she was returned to Earth.

HC addendum.
Source: Pablo Villarrubia, and Mario Rangel. Type: G
Comments: Early abduction report from Brazil with human-like aliens.

Location: Sverdlovsk, Lugansk region, Ukraine, USSR.
Date: 1969.
Time: Night.

V. M. Zubaryev, a local resident, reported several alien contacts and abductions that he took at first for "amazingly colorful dreams." He awoke at night, opened his eyes and saw several humanoid entities standing near his bed. The aliens were short in stature, with large eyes and stood near his bed. The aliens then entered into telepathic communication with the witness and then he was transported within a beam of light into their circular spacecraft. There he was subjected to medical examinations. The aliens were using different types of sophisticated instruments that he had never seen before and could not understand what they were.

After that he met an alien female who told him that her name was 'Eziyka' and led him into a large room, resembling a conference hall where he saw a huge circular auditorium filled with extraterrestrials and amazingly also abducted humans, all sitting in rows of seats. Eziyka did not tell him where this large hall was located; it was either onboard of their mothership or inside some alien underground base on Earth or possibly even on the moon. The stunned man was completely befuddled and could not believe his eyes; he had all his life been indoctrinated under the Communist belief and atheistic ideology and did believe neither in God nor in "flying saucers."

The aliens then communicated with the witness and the other abductees for several hours, but details of what was said were not disclosed in the witness's letter. The witness was then transported back home by the same manner he was abducted, inside a beam of light and through the walls of his room. He remained in a state of cultural and mental shock. During the next contact he again entered into telepathic communication with an alien that called himself 'Max.' This humanoid creature was dressed in a uniform, with clearly seen hieroglyphic symbols and letters in an unknown language displayed on its suit. Max did not open his mouth while he spoke to the witness, but the witness understood everything Max said. However, details of the conversation were evidently erased from the witness mind; he could only remember talking with the alien.

He suddenly woke up and realized after looking at the clock that it was 3:00 a.m. Afraid that he was going to forget what occurred, he began writing everything down on a piece of paper, writing down everything he could remember and images of the alien. Later the witness read an article about the alleged UFO shot down in the Kalahari Desert in 1989, and noticed that the symbols on the captured object were similar to those the alien 'Max' had on his uniform.

HC addendum.
Source: *UFOs: Liaisons of the Universe?* Lugansk, Ukraine, #7
December 1994.   Type: G

* * * * * * *

Location: Lake Washington, Washington.
Date: 1969.
Time: Night.

While driving over the Evergreen Floating bridge over Lake Washington a large craft came up over the bridge close to the water. The witness watched the object for a long period of time and experienced a missing time episode. Craft appeared to be gliding and made no sound. However it looked very real.

Later hypnosis revealed that she went onboard the craft where she met small baldheaded beings that took her to a window or computer screen and showed her a galaxy shaped like a man standing. These beings were friendly and she felt comfortable with them.

HC addendum.
Source: http://ufoexperiences.blogspot.com   Type: G
Comments: The witness has been involved in other encounters and contacts.

* * * * * * *

Location: Drumheller, Alberta, Canada.
Date: 1969.
Time: 10:00 p.m.

The main witness, the late Mrs. Turnbull, who in the attic of her farmhouse came on a collection of *Fate* magazines, and in one read how the "space brothers" were seeking honest and fearless contactees on Earth who would brave public opprobrium to spread the truth. As she read on she thought, *"Let them call on me as I would be fearless."*

That night about 22:00 her husband came in and said *"There is something over the pasture,"* so she went out and there was a huge UFO which she watched until 2:30 a.m. during which time a football shaped blue luminous capsule with a humanoid inside, with limbs extended to form an X, emerged from the craft and slowly descended to the ground. On touching the ground a blue flash "like sheet lighting" spread over the meadow, after which the capsule and occupant slowly ascended. This was repeated several times by the same or a similar creature. Her husband described the object as; "big as a boxcar." Her husband had previously threatened her that if she told anyone he would not back her up.

HC addendum.
Source: William K. Allan, *'Canadian UFO Report'* #18 1974.   Type: B

* * * * * * *

Location: Ringarooma, Tasmania, Australia.
Date: 1969.
Time: Various.

The main witness, Gayle, and five other members of her family watched an oval-shaped object land on a paddock only about 100 meters away. The craft emitted a brilliant white light and had a red and a green light. It lit up the paddock like daylight. Soon after the incident the family was visited by a tall gaunt stranger wearing a suit and a tie and driving "a large flashy car." The stranger reportedly said to the witness mother *"nothing exciting ever happens here does it?"* He then drove away leaving the family very confused.

Soon after this, Gayle wandered off to the river alone and crawled onto a log, the river racing under her, suddenly she saw a "bird" only a few feet away on the other side of the river. The strange part is that the bird apparently "spoke" to Gayle, but she does not remember what was said. The bird was a Bowerbird which is not native to Tasmania. Shocked, she left the area and kept looking behind her, thinking someone was following her. Later she saw lights in her bedroom and at times was woken up by somebody calling her name.

HC addendum.
Source: direct from Gayle Leary gle62551@bigpond.net.au Type: E or F?

* * * * * * *

Location: Pirassununga, Brazil.
Date: January, 1969.
Time: Unknown.

A large circular object descended slowly and landed on the grass near some farm animals. Three men wearing white uniforms and helmets emerged from the craft. One carried an object resembling a pair of binoculars, the second a large bright "lantern," and the third carried some type of cartridge. There was a red luminous light source on top of the object. The object later took off at high speed.

HC addendum.
Source: J. Antonio Huneeus, *Fate*, December 1993, Quoting SIOANI
Brazil. Type: B

* * * * * * *

Location: Near Haymarket, Virginia.
Date: January, 1969.
Time: Night.

Four men were on a farm when they heard a peculiar rushing sound coming from near a small lake. Grabbing flashlights they set out to investigate, taking a couple of dogs with them. Suddenly the dogs howled and ran away. The men then noticed standing by a tree, a huge dark man-like figure with wing protrusions and large red orange eyes. The men fled the area in their vehicle.

HC addendum.
Source: John Keel, *Fate*, November 1992. Type: E

* * * * * * *

Location: Los Alisos, Jujuy, Argentina.
Date: January, 1969.
Time: Late night.

A farmer felt a powerful odor apparently emanating from outside. Going out to investigate, he came upon two short green-skinned humanoids with large luminous eyes. The two beings were gesticulating and were walking towards the witness. The frightened witness ran inside and locked the door.
 About the same time hovering balls of fire that ascended rapidly into the sky had been seen by neighbors.

HC addendum.
Source: Hector P. Anganuzzi, *'Historia de Los Platos Voladores en Argentina.'* Type: D

Location: Edina, Missouri.
Date: Early January, 1969.
Time: Night.

Adeline Davis had been asleep when she suddenly found herself sitting up in bed; looking out the window. Outside, about 6 feet away, she saw a curious object, shaped like two deep bowls put together rim-to-rim but separated in the connecting mid-section by a band of windows; the object was resting on three legs, and its color was dark, olive green. The window directly facing her was lit up, and inside was visible an occupant, apparently working on something below the level of the window.

Mrs Davis pinched her arm to be sure she was not dreaming, and went to bathe her face in water. The figure looked up and, apparently seeing the witness, showed surprise; then he reached up for something and the object began backing away slowly from the house, just above the ground. From its bottom projected a "bent" white beam of light. The object then moved out of Mrs Davis's view around the corner of the house. In the morning the electrical clocks were all 20 minutes slow; her neighbors apparently had no such power failure in their homes.

HC addendum.
Source: Ted Phillips for APRO.   Type: A

* * * * * * *

Location: Near Childers, Queensland, Australia.
Date: January 14, 1969.
Time: 4:30 a.m.

George Vas and his wife and two daughters were asleep in their trailer when they were awakened by the barking of their dog, and heard a loud noise like the buzzing of a swarm of wasps. It came from an object shaped like a sombrero, 25-30 yards in diameter, which was brilliantly violet-luminous. From the craft descended three beings "about three times as large as humans" which had "blocky arms and legs and shapeless bodies," and emitted a purple and yellow glow.

For about 10 minutes they gathered sugar cane and other plant specimens, without concern for the observers. Olga Vas said that the beings descended from the larger craft in a small object similar in shape. At one point one of the entities moved close enough to the group for Mr. Vas to call out in alarm. The 'spaceman" showed no concern and, after picking up several rocks, moved away.

They re-entered their craft and the object took off vertically; as it did so, the hair on the witnesses' bodies stood up "as if affected by a form of magnetism." Mr. Vas said it as his third sighting of 'spacemen.' He saw one as a child in Romania in 1918, and another near Belgrade in 1946.

HC addendum.
Source: Keith Basterfield. Type: B

* * * * * * *

Location: Isla Del Altar, El Salvador.
Date: January 15, 1969.
Time: Afternoon.

After feeling a burning sensation from a ring given to him by a presumed extraterrestrial, that was to signify an upcoming contact, Ludwig Pallmann took his motorboat to a local sandy beach. There he noticed that several huge concentric circles ruffled the normally placid waters of the lake. Shortly after that, he encountered the human like humanoid named Satu Ra, who he had met on previous occasions. Satu Ra was sitting motionless on a nearby rock.

Ra was inexpressively sad and was wearing dark green coveralls, a broad instrument belt on which was a much larger device that the one he usually carried. The stunned Pallmann was told that another extraterrestrial, which he knew, Xiti, among others, had been killed. Supposedly a disaster had befallen an expedition on another planet. Shortly after this encounter, locals reported observing a silvery disc shaped object hovering over the capital San Salvador.

HC addendum.
Source: Timothy Good, 'Alien Base.' Type: E or D?

* * * * * * *

Location: Villafranca de los Barros, Badajoz, Spain.
Date: January 15, 1969.
Time: Night.

Several pupils at a local Jesuit college saw a luminous disc descending towards the ground. Sometime later other pupils saw appearing at the window frame located at more than 2 meters off the ground, a gigantic being whose skin or clothing had green reflections and who leaned his enormous face through the window, while being obviously upright. The young people fled in terror but once calmed down the most courageous of the group search the gardens of the school but did not find anything.

However the next day several enormous footprints were discovered of the sports ground. That night and the following nights, the local

Guardia Civil organized a search party in the neighborhood. The events only came to light several years later, since the Jesuit priests swore the students to secrecy and denied the events.

HC addendum.
Source: http://www.ignaciodarnaude.com/avistamientos URECAT-000199 Type: D

* * * * * * *

Location: Alexania, Goias, Brazil.
Date: January 31, 1969.
Time: 8:00 p.m.

A small "astro ship" approached General Moacyr Uchoa and his investigating team, on Wilson P Gusmao's Alexania Fazenda, where UFO phenomena had been frequent for more than a year. It made some maneuvers, and then landed 100 yards away. Gusmao left the group and walked up to within a yard of the vessel, which he found to be only 6.5ft long and 3ft wide, hovering 18" above the ground.

A door opened, and a crewmember stood up in the entrance. He looked at Gusmao while manipulating something on his belt, which Gusmao thought was a camera. Then he turned his back, and "as if obeying an order, a big light arose from the nearby ridge." The man then again faced Gusmao; he put his hand to his belt again, which caused a luminous halo to surround his body. After this the onlookers could see him only as a ball of light. Then, with a little gesture, he slipped down again into the craft, which took off rapidly.

HC addendum.
Source: SBEDV and General Moacyr Uchoa. Type: B

* * * * * * *

Location: Pirassununga, Sao Paolo, Brazil.
Date: February 6, 1969.
Time: Morning.

Barbara Mina Da Silva was weeding rice at a place called "Chacara Do Benedito," when two boys, Joao Batista Da Silva, 9, and Benedito Paulino Ramos, 13, called to her attention to a "shining little tent" 500 meters away. She described it as white, looking like one of the triangular tents used by exterminators of the sauva ant; nearby were three men with helmets, which she took to be the men fighting the ants. The boys told her that the men's clothing was shining, but she described it as gray.

She continued her work, when suddenly the boys cried out, *"Look, the little tent has disappeared."* She saw that both tent and men had indeed gone. Shortly afterward the boys pointed out a "luminous ball the size of the sun" stationary just above the woods. It disappeared after 30 minutes, and at once a Brazilian AF helicopter appeared and descended about 2 km away. The helicopter was seen on several occasions during the next few days.

HC addendum.
Source: SBEVD Members. Type: C

* * * * * * *

Location: Pirassununga, Sao Paolo, Brazil.
Date: February 6, 1969.
Time: 8:15 p.m.

A small silvery disc with a high protruding dome landed on a field. From a small opening, two short humanoids emerged; they seemed to hover just above the ground. The beings were heavy set and human-like, two other being remained inside. The beings spoke among themselves in a hoarse "serious" voice.

HC addendum.
Source: J. Antonio Huneeus, *Fate,* December 1993 and SIOANI Brazil.
Type: B & A

* * * * * * *

Location: Pirassununga, Sao Paolo, Brazil.
Date: February 6, 1969.
Time: Dusk.

The witness name is Mr. Jose Antonio Fioco, 53; the distance of the object and entities is variously given as 20m, and 200m. The object's size 13 x 16 ft. Entities were 1.60 m tall, and they wore "silver shoes," one piece suits with three silver buttons in front. One held a tube or rod 14" long and 2" wide, from which light was emitted at one end, which clearly lit up the hen house 800ft away. Second entity carried a slightly larger rod; the third carried an implement or device like a box camera.

On passing through his gate to get other witnesses, the creaking of the gate apparently alerted the entities to his presence, and they entered the object, which took off immediately. Other members of the family were reported to have seen objects around the same time on several occasions.

Fioco saw four more UFOs subsequently, including two other landings but no more entities.

HC addendum.
Source: Dr. Walter Buhler.   Type: B

* * * * * * *

Location: Pirassununga, Sao Paolo, Brazil.
Date: February 7, 1969.
Time: 7:30 a.m.

People shouting about a mysterious object visible on a hillside awakened Thiago Machado, 19. He got his binoculars and went to see the object, approaching to within 30ft. It was a domed disc, aluminum colored, about 12ft in diameter and 5ft high. A hinged door was open on the top of the dome, and from this two humanoid figures emerged and seemed to float to the ground; two others were visible inside the craft, through windows. The beings, 4.5ft tall, were dressed in tight, silvery garments without buttons, covering them from feet to head.

Their features were seen through transparent helmets. Their skin was yellow, eyes slanting, and the mouth with thin, slit-like lips. They came to within 3-4 meters of the witness. When they laughed at the witness, who was puffing a cigarette. He could see that they had black teeth. He tossed the cigarette pack close to one, who put his hand above it; the pack floated up into his hand. The thumb of his hand was set further back than on a human hand.

The beings spoke in "hoarse, guttural" sounds. When a friend called out to the witness, the entities walked backward and re-entered through the door; the second one, when halfway through, pointed a tube at Machado, which emitted a bluish flame that "floated" toward him. When it hit him, he felt pain and was paralyzed; as the UFO took off, almost horizontally, the witness fainted. A welt remained where the flame had struck him. On the ground were found three landing-leg marks.

HC addendum.
Source: Nigel Rimes, Ned S. Martins and Reginaldo Da Silva.   Type: B

* * * * * * *

Location: Pirassununga, Sao Paolo, Brazil.
Date: February 12, 1969.
Time: 5:40 a.m.

Luis Flozinho De Oliveira, a farm worker, was on his way to work when he was approached and attacked by two aggressive beings 1.5 meters tall, with long hair, beards, and asymmetrical eyes. Both humanoids wore white unbuttoned shirts and long beige-colored pants with what appeared to be colorful inscriptions and drawings on them, they also wore dark shiny medallions around their necks, their skin appeared to be normal in color. Stunned at first, Luis then fought back, knocking both of them to the ground, one on top of the other.

At this point both humanoids rose up and exchanged some words between them in a strange language, and then they told Luis in perfect Portuguese that they were leaving since he was much stronger than them, at which time they both fled into the thick underbrush. The witness dog "rolled up into a ball on the ground for protection" during the attack upon its master. The dog refused to eat anything after the encounter and was found dead a month later, his body completely bloated up. He had refused to return to the place of the encounter.

HC addendum.
Source: Dr. Walter Buhler. Type: D

* * * * * * *

Location: Nuble, Valparaiso, Chile.
Date: February 13, 1969.
Time: 4:00 a.m.

An intense light coming in the window awakened Mr. X and his wife, and their two daughters. They got to see a UFO hovering over the beach, 200ft away. It had the shape of an octahedron, with a cupola on top and with three legs, also two kinds of antennas and several portholes. It was 15-20ft in diameter and almost equally high; it looked metallic and was of an intense sky-blue luminosity.

This object, descending with oscillation and landed on the beach 200ft from the witness house. A luminous ray came from it, and "three beings of humanoid aspect descended by this luminous ray." They were about 6 ½ft tall and dressed in dark blue suits that covered the whole body, including hands and feet; on their chests was a metallic emblem. Each placed 10 tubes in the sand; then they collected all the black stones to be found on the beach; then they picked up their tubes and re-entered the craft, which rose diagonally with oscillations and then went off very fast.

The duration of the observation was 30-40 minutes. Mr. X's watch stopped. As an apparent consequence of the observation, "the skin of the witnesses became covered with a sort of scales, which disappeared after three days." In the sand were found holes 6" in diameter and 10" deep, left by the entities "tubes." Also a circular zone 6ft in diameter, "where the sand seemed to have been absorbed."

HC addendum.
Source: Elena Marino, LDLN #111. Type: B

* * * * * * *

Location: Flinders Park, South Australia.
Date: February 17, 1969.
Time: 2:50 a.m.

Mrs. Leslie Ballestrin was awakened by a whirring noise she took to be her refrigerator; upon checking, she saw an object like an inverted saucer outside some yards distant. There was a horizontal row of white lights encircling the center about three feet apart, and the object was "about three car lengths" in width. A figure then appeared from the right side, walked around the front and bent down, as if examining something, and disappeared into the shadows at the rear of the object; he repeated this action several times.

He appeared normal, of average height (5'8") and medium build, and was wearing white, loose-fitting overalls. Mrs. Ballestrin heard a beeping sound that persisted throughout the 25 minute observation. When the light on the object went out, Mrs. Ballestrin went to her neighbors; they reported having heard a similar whirring sound about the same time, several blocks away.

HC addendum.
Source: Keith Basterfield. Type: C

Location: Pirassununga, Sao Paolo, Brazil.
Date: February 20, 1969.
Time: Night.

Hearing his pigs grunting during the night, the manager of the "Bela Alianca" Fazenda (ranch) went out and saw from a distance of 60ft the landing of a UFO about 12ft wide and 15ft high, which rested on tripod legs. Three crewmembers emerged onto a small catwalk around the machine, each with a different type of implement with which they busied themselves for a period of 2-3 minutes.

HC addendum.
Source: Dr. Walter Buhler. Type: B

* * * * * * *

Location: Near Reno, Nevada.
Date: Spring 1969.
Time: 10:00 a.m.

In a desert area 30 miles east of Reno the 7-year old witness and his father arrived at the location in their Volkswagen Van in order to do some rabbit hunting. The weather was clear with a blue crisp sky. The young witness said his father stayed in the van to drink beer, as he always did while he would go hunting rabbits with his 22 cal. rifle.

A minute or so into the hunt, he shot a rabbit, retrieved it and continued the hunt. According to him, it was just a minute or two later that he saw another rabbit and began to take aim at it when something within his peripheral vision about 8 to 10 feet away off to his right side caught his eye. He was startled and just turned his head slightly to the right and realized he was looking at a "thing" standing there, staring at him.

He described the "thing" as about his height, which was about 4 feet tall, very skinny, with long arms, large head with large dark eyes and was grayish in color. He said he was immediately frightened but had kept his rifle pointed in the direction of the rabbit. He remembers keeping the "thing" within his peripheral vision and noticed that it started turning its head slightly to its right in the direction of the rabbit the witness had intended to shoot. However the creature then turned its head back, looking at him and simultaneously began raising its right arm, held straight out. The young witness became extremely frightened and thought the creature was about to do something to hurt him, so he swung his rifle in the direction of the creature and fired one shot into the upper right side of its chest and it fell to the ground.

As quickly as it happened the witness said he dropped both his rifle and the rabbit he had shot earlier and ran back to the parked Van, crying and screaming for his dad. He said as he got to the Van, his dad, who may have been intoxicated at the time, began scolding him wanting to know why he was crying and not hunting. He tried to explain to his dad that he had shot a "thing" and may have killed it. His dad purportedly responded by telling him he was only supposed to shoot rabbits and began asking what had he done with the rifle. He continued to plead with his dad to go back and see if they could help the "thing" he had shot. However his dad was adamant and 'drunk' and ordered him to go back to get his rifle and the rabbit he had shot and to keep hunting. He did as he was told and went back, found his rifle and the rabbit he had shot earlier, but the creature was gone. He looked in the area where it had been laying after he shot it to see if there was any blood but saw none.

The very next thing he remembers is that as he was standing there where he had shot the creature he suddenly saw a craft hovering just above the ground an estimated 200 feet away. He saw he could only describe it as a cylinder or cigar-shaped object, metallic looking and as long as a football field. The next detail he remembered was being in some type of a "room" with beams like frame work and what appeared to be a lot of dust. He was frightened and crying, and the next he remembers is being in the back seat of the van, alone in the dark, crying for his dad who wasn't there.

His next memory was he and his dad driving home in the dark. He asked his dad why they were going home at night since they usually left in the afternoon but his dad completely ignored the question. He never spoke to his father about the incident again. He believes both were probably abducted and he thinks he has had later experiences in his life.

HC addendum.
Source: MUFON CMS. Type: G?

* * * * * * *

Location: Texarkana, Arkansas.
Date: March, 1969.
Time: Afternoon.

The witness (involved in other encounters) was at the local library researching a school project for her daughter and was sitting at a rectangular long table reading. After reading for more than an hour she heard a gasp in the room and looked up to see one of the most striking, beautiful women she had ever seen in her life. She was very tall, close to six feet. She had on heels and an upswept hairdo that made her look even taller. She was absolutely regal looking; she seemed to have perfect skin and wore a flawless tailored suit.

The strange woman came and sat down on the other end of the rectangular table. The witness was watching her closely, along with most of the other women and a few other men in there. She then noticed that the stranger was gazing at her, she did not stare but calmly watched the witness without let up. The witness felt unkempt and ill at ease under the stranger's stare. After several minutes of the uncomfortable gazing the stranger asked the witness if she would come up and talk to her. Without hesitation the witness got up and went, at the same time wondering why she did, she felt some type of "force" guiding her actions.

The stranger said something to the effect, *"We are going to talk about you"* and then added, *"Your name starts with an R, does it not?"* The witness said, *"Yes, my name is R."* In a matter of fact way the stranger guessed that the witness had four red headed children and that one of her children had been born with black hair which had turn red later, which was an absolute fact. The witness was dumfounded and amazed at the same time.

The stranger predicted that the witness would divorce in 1980 and marry another man (something that did come to pass). Most bizarrely the stranger told the witness that she had a "mission," something to do with "reptilians." To her knowledge it was the first time the witness had heard the word reptilian as in a being or entity. She then asked the witness if she knew what a "coven" was. The witness said no and the strange women explained to her that it was part of the "Wicca" religion, she added, *"It is the study and love of Earth and how to work with Earth energies."* The witness was confused, and was not even vaguely familiar with the terms being used by the stranger.

The woman then told the witness that the number 13 would be "very powerful for her." After additional information regarding other "Wicca" matters the witness was told to go home and draw a pentagram in her den and then make an offering (a cake) and at the same time chant certain words. Later the witness sat on a chair and did exactly what she was told and when she opened her eyes she saw standing before her, in her den, what she was only able to described as an "upright alligator," about 4.5 to 5ft tall, with greenish scaly skin and red glowing eyes with vertical pupils.

At that same time her youngest daughter came down to the den and also saw the strange entity. Terrified they both went to their rooms and had trouble sleeping that night. The witness would see the strange tall woman in the library on other occasions, but was afraid to talk to her.

HC addendum.
Source: Linda Moulton Howe, Earthfiles.com   Type: E or F?

Location: Twinsburg, Ohio.
Date: March, 1969.
Time: Evening.

The curious case of one local UFO sighting began innocuously enough in this city of 7,000 with TV interference at a Glenwood Drive home. It concluded, abruptly, with a bizarre visit to the Twinsburg Police Department from a United States Air Force lieutenant colonel and his mysterious, diminutive sidekick. According to a recently released report from Project Blue Book, the United States Air Force's systematic analysis of UFO reports between 1952 and 1969, a woman, 44, and her son, 19, were watching the news when the color contrast went out on their TV – and then the entire signal. The mother walked outside at dusk to check the antennae, and immediately called Twinsburg police to report an "oval-shaped object that had red and white lights around it."

"Looking up we seen (sic) the strange object, coming over Glenwood Drive," said the woman, whose identity is redacted in the March 6, 1969, report. *"I never seen anything like this before,"* she states. *"It seemed to have stopped near the corner of Glenwood Drive, then proceeded down East Idlewood Drive for about a quarter mile...then just went right up out of sight."* Sgt. Donald Prange, a former Twinsburg officer and Marine Corps veteran who later served as chief of police in Twinsburg in the later 1970s, responded to the woman's call around 6:40 p.m. More than 20 calls referencing the UFO were ultimately fielded by Twinsburg dispatch that evening. In keeping with caution the Twinsburg Police Department did not immediately report the event to the USAF. The USAF was made aware of the event thanks to a Feb. 18 1969, letter from the woman's 19-year old son to Wright-Patterson Air Force Base in Dayton detailing the sighting.

In its April 22, 1969, conclusion to the Glenwood Drive woman, the USAF determined that the object was actually an "aerial advertising aircraft." "A letter was sent to the Twinsburg Police Department requesting information on the sighting, however this office did not receive a reply...the description of the UFO is similar to past reports of aerial advertising aircraft," stated Lt. Col. Hector Quintanilla, chief of the now defunct Aerial Phenomena Branch at Wright-Patterson. Prange said he doesn't buy the USAF's answer in the Twinsburg incident any more than he believes its conclusion from a Portage County case three years earlier.

For the woman and her son, the story ends with the April 1969, correspondence from Quintanilla. For Prange and his fellow officers, the story of the peculiar 'foo fighter' over Twinsburg has one final bizarre chapter.

About a month after the sighting, Prange says his department was visited by a USAF lieutenant Colonel – believed to be Quintanilla – and a "strange little man." *"They brought out a light colonel, another strange little man was with him, to question us individually,"* Prange said. *"The smaller man, perhaps 5 feet tall, was not like us; he had strange features, almost like a child who has aged rapidly. He wore a hat, gloves, and he never spoke to us, never shook our hands, just observed. I don't remember (the colonel) ever even saying thank you. When they left, we never heard from the Air Force again."*

HC addendum.
Source: Andrew Schunk / Editor Twinsburg Bulletin, published February 24, 2015. Type: E?

* * * * * * *

Location: Mexico City, Mexico.
Date: March, 1969.
Time: Night.

Alberto Zecua was sleeping in his bedroom when he suddenly woke up with a feeling of being watched. He opened his eyes and saw three very tall human-like figures wearing tight-fitting gray silvery coveralls looking down on him. They wore some type of metallic bracelets around their wrists and boots and wide belts with a luminous box in the middle around their waists. These were apparently the same beings he had met before in 1968.

Again, using telepathy they told him that they were here to help and not to interfere. They then placed a small square box-like device over his bed that floated over the witness. Then one of the beings walked over to his feet and another to his head. He then felt numb and heard a humming sound, then found himself levitating above the bed. Soon they were done and the witness noticed a strong odor in the air resembling menthol. He was told that they had performed an internal cleansing of his body. The beings then apparently vanished in plain sight.

HC addendum.
Source: Contacto Ovni, Mexico. Type: E

Location: Dillon, South Carolina.
Date: April 4, 1969.
Time: 10:30 p.m.

The two witnesses (apparently enlisted men at the time) were setting out on a hitchhiking expedition from Fort Bragg, North Carolina to Myrtle Beach, South Carolina with vague hopes of scoring with some partying college coeds taking their Spring Break in the popular seaside resort town. They left the base with their backpacks and sleeping bags at about sunset and headed south of Fayetteville on Interstate 95. Soon they were walking through downtown Dillon toward route 25, the old Latta highway cutoff toward Myrtle Beach, still 70 miles away. It wasn't long before two carloads of locals drove by in an apparent attempt to harass the hiking soldiers.

As empty as the town was at this time of night it didn't bother them too much because of the street lights and the occasional traffic on the road. But as they reached the edge of town near the cutoff; with the rowdies going by every few minutes and the chances of a ride looking increasingly doubtful. The two of them began looking for an escape hatch. After the loudmouths passed by them again and drove out of sight they took the opportunity to slip off the road into a dimly lit area behind a vacant, broken-down gas station. Walking by the left side of the deserted building they followed a wheel-rutted dirt path up and over a small crest, by now barely able to see more than a few feet in front of them as they passed by trees on the edge of the gas station lot into almost complete darkness.

But as the two of them picked their way carefully down the car path, the whole area suddenly lit up in an aqua-green glow showing a small field no more than a few acres in size. Now they could see clearly, and what they saw amazed them; there was a three or four-story high, multi-decked UFO standing on what seemed to be metal legs. In addition, there were beings similar to humans; a head with two eyes, two arms and upright on two legs, but colored green, either an effect of the ambient light or the result of their extreme confusion and fear. They were walking in the field and on decks which curved around the ship, with the nearest one about 20 feet away. He/she/it turned their way, and said firmly (the main witness believes telepathically) *"Leave now!"*

In spite of the danger that had caused them to leave the highway in the first place, both men, like the trained soldiers they were, executed a smart about-face and marched right back toward trouble (the highway). They hiked at a pretty quick route step down the road a few miles without saying a word to, or looking at, each other, hoofing just as fast as they could out of Dillon into some farming and pasturage area. Presently the rowdies showed up once more in their cars, making it clear that the witnesses were targets for this night. Once again, as the cars went out of sight they left the highway, into a cow pasture this time. From a spot a few hundred yards off the road they watched as they returned looking for them. Eventually, the night settled down, the cars were gone and they climbed into their sleeping bags. The next morning they continued on to Myrtle Beach.

Only thirty years later the main witness was to recall the whole experience in a flash, when his friend asked him *"Do you remember Dillon?"*

HC addendum.
Source: NUFORC. Type: A & C

* * * * * * *

Location: Orlando, Florida.
Date: May, 1969.
Time: Morning.

The young witness was waiting outside the school for it to open when a strange 1965 black Cadillac pulled up. The occupants sat motionless for a few moments. Finally they got out of the car; both were dressed in old-fashioned black suits, dark tinted glasses, and hats. One stayed by the car, the other walked up to the witness and other students and began asking questions about a fellow student.

The stranger was apparently dressed in drag, (lipstick, and white pancake makeup) and disheveled clothing. Eventually they left. The student that the stranger was inquiring about had experienced several strange incidents and was reported missing soon after the black Cadillac episode.

HC addendum.
Source: CAUS, *'Citizens against UFO secrecy.'* Type: E

* * * * * * *

Location: Mothar Mountain, Queensland, Australia.
Date: May, 1969.
Time: Night.

A couple camped in the mountain scrub one night, afterwards claimed they were approached by a "shimmering yellow" seven-foot tall being with human-like facial features. "He" had long legs and long arms with five fingers much longer than humans, they told two disbelieving policemen afterwards. The being stood looking at them, then moved away to just 'disappear' as if into a nearby vertical rock-face.

HC addendum.
Source: Rex Gilroy, *'The Temple of Nim Newsletter,'* March 2009.
Type: E

* * * * * * *

Location: Bebedouro, Espirito Santo, Brazil.
Date: May 4, 1969.
Time: 3:00 p.m.

Jose Antonio Da Silva, a soldier, was fishing when he heard a cry and felt his legs struck and numbed by a burst of "fire" coming from bushes. He was seized and dragged by two little beings only 4-foot tall, clad in shining, light-colored garments and wearing aluminum masks or helmets. Tubes ran from the masks to small containers on their backs.

They dragged him to a craft that was shaped like a vertical cylinder, terminated by wider saucer shaped top and bottom; rods from the base of the cylinder supported the upper disc. It was only about 6ft high and 9ft wide. Inside was a cubical room, brilliantly lighted from no visible source. Here they fitted on him a helmet like their own, and then tied him down to a seat. He felt a sensation of taking off; during the flight, which lasted for hours, they talked among themselves in an incomprehensible language with many R's.

At one point in the journey the craft seemed to turn on its side for a while. When they landed, he was blindfolded and dragged into a large room, where a little man without a spacesuit confronted him; he had long reddish hair and a beard that flowed to his waist. He was strongly built, and his skin was pale; he had large round, green eyes and a big nose, and his mouth appeared toothless, "like a fish's." To the side of the witness were laid out four human cadavers, one a Negro's. A dozen more little men, all much resembling the leader, were in the room.

They examined his fishing tackle and other possessions. Several carried weapons. The leader then addressed him in his incomprehensible speech, making sketches simultaneously on a light-colored slate beside him. He was given, from a stone cup, a bitter green liquid that restored his energy and made him better able to comprehend what the alien meant to express. The latter was able to convey to Da Silva the idea that he was expected to help them land on Earth, a proposition that the soldier rejected, fingering his rosary. The leader, irritated, snatched the rosary away, and showed it to the others.

At this point a kind of vision appeared to Da Silva of a Christ-like man with long fair hair and beard, dressed like a monk, who spoke to him in Portuguese, giving him a message, which he was sworn to keep secret. After this vision had vanished, Da Silva was again blindfolded, dragged back to the spacecraft, and returned to the earth in the same manner as he had been taken away. Released during the night, when morning came he found that he was near Vitoria, more than 200 miles from Bebedouro, and that four and a half days had passed since his abduction. He suffered various physical ailments later. (Did a different more benign force attempted to help the abductee in this case?)

HC addendum.
Source: Hulvio Aleixo and Dr. Walter Buhler. Type: G

* * * * * * *

Location: Rockville, Virginia.
Date: May 11, 1969.
Time: 1:45 a.m.

20-year old Mike Luczkowich, a student at Manakin, Virginia, was returning home after a date with his girlfriend. Just as he passed the Rockville General Store; Mike noticed something about 50 yards ahead of his car. At first he thought it might be a couple of deer, but he soon realized that he was observing two figures about three and a half to four feet tall. The creatures were wearing spherical helmets that looked as large as basketballs. Circling each helmet was a pale green band that reflected the headlights of the vehicle. The beings were motionless at first, but they soon scurried off and ran up an embankment to the left of the witness.

The first two creatures had barely disappeared when a third small creature appeared from the right side of the road and quickly joined the others by climbing over the embankment. Luczkowich reported that the little men were dressed in light-brown coveralls that were somewhat baggy in the legs but were tight-fitting at the ankles. He did not see any arms, and he could not detect features behind the oversized helmets. The student was shaken by the experience, and he did not tell anyone of the encounter until Sunday.

On Monday Luczkowich and three other men returned to the site. They were able to locate a definite trail through the poison ivy and honeysuckle on the embankment the three beings had scaled. Beyond the embankment they found a barley field with a path through it, such as the three humanoids might have made. After a few feet they noticed two flattened areas, where small entities might have thrown themselves down in the grain field. The crushed barley at one of the impressions, according to Luczkowich showed the imprint of two small bodies, while another impression outlined one small body.

About a half mile west of the area, and about two hours earlier, 18-year old Debbie Payne had reported seeing an oval-shaped luminous object over her house as she arrived home from a date. The object appeared rather bright, then dimmed and became bright twice more before she and her date reached the house.

HC addendum.
Source: Ted Bloecher, 'Occupant Case Detailed,' *Skylook*, November 1974. Type: E or D?

* * * * * * *

Location: Near Gaithersburg, Maryland.
Date: End of May, 1969.
Time: 2:30 am

15-year old Gary Connor, a member of Boy Scout Troop 357, was camping in the fields behind his home with about 22 other scouts and was being accompanied by his best friend John in their own personal 2-man tent. Both were talking outside the tent in their sleeping bags when Gary suddenly noticed a very faint light heading their way in the sky. He told John to look at the "airplane." There used to be a small airplane in the area so Gary assumed that it was a normal aircraft. But as the object got closer and bigger, it was really strange since it didn't make any noise. It didn't seem right and Gary left his sleeping bag and stared at it and then John got up too. As the craft got closer, it got extremely large. The edge of the aerial object was at an altitude of about 250 to 300 feet above them and it was gigantic.

At first as it was approaching, they could not see the under carriage or the upper carriage of the craft because rotating around the outer perimeter of this craft were colored lights. Gary estimated those rotating lights were about the size of searchlights like the ones seen in the malls shining up into the sky. The craft made no noise whatsoever. John was getting into a state of panic, Gary told him to be quiet and to not move. Gary wasn't really that scared, he was nervous but curious. Eventually the lights on the outer rim approached almost right above the top of them. Then Gary could see a reflection of the lights underneath and it looked like two dinner planets and had the front of each facing each other with a slight gap in between. About 30 seconds later, the craft moved off back over to the north side of them. Then the lights on the outer rim that were rotating suddenly went out. At this point they estimated that the craft was about the size of a football field.

The craft then landed extremely slowly. It settled down on its base on the bottom and at first John wanted to wake some of the other scouts, but Gary told him just to be still. All of a sudden on the outside of the craft towards the upper and lower sections, just above the rim and below the rim, the wall of the craft appeared to "turn into liquid." And suddenly an opening appeared with an extremely bright, white light coming from inside. It was a very intense light and bright enough to light up everything around. The beings that approached each side of the door were very tall. They had blond hair. One had extremely long blond hair. One had short blond hair. They were both wearing what appeared to be fighter pilot flight suits, but the color of dark blue topaz. They had sandy blond hair, one was a female the other a male. He could tell the female was the one with the long hair and she was slimmer than the male and not quite as tall.

The male was very tall, with a large chest and very muscular appearing. Their skin was white, slightly tanned. And then a single 'gray being' came out of the craft and approached the witnesses. John moved backwards, terrified. The gray being moved in between the two tall blonds at the door and came down from the craft on a slightly slanted ramp from the liquefied door and approached both witnesses.

The gray being then came up to Gary's face. Gary described the being as about 3.5 feet tall, with grayish-brown, pebbly skin, somewhat like a lizard, with large black eyes pointing towards the nose and larger ovals extending to the sides of the face. Gary remembers that it was as though the gray was telling him something. He was transmitting something into Gary's head. It was apparently an equation. He wrote it down, the original equation is the following;

$M \times -A = -A_2$.

When this took place the gray being seemed to jerk around and panic and headed back towards the craft. He went back pretty swiftly. The blond human looking man and woman in the craft doorway looked around and glanced over to the south. They quickly went back into the craft and that opening appeared to re-liquefy and seal itself and then the craft lifted off the ground. The lights temporarily came back on the rim of the craft. They hovered at about fifty feet above the ground and then went back over their heads and turned due east in the direction they had come from. They were above the field for about 30 seconds.

In the meantime the lights on the craft's rim went out again. And then suddenly a light just appeared on the bottom of the craft, intensely illuminating the bottom of the craft in the shape of a ball about the size of a basketball. The ball of light then slowly radiated to the ground, but when it radiated it radiated into a large cone shape, like an upside down ice cream cone. The light was the purest white light the witnesses had ever seen. There were thousands of little miniature white beams inside coming down to the ground, but they were intensely white. And the light started scanning the field to the left, to the right, forward and back. It did that for maybe fifteen to twenty seconds and then the light slowly rose back into the craft and down to the size of a basketball and then just vanished.

It appeared as though they had been looking for something. Approximately 20 seconds after that, the witnesses heard a tremendous roar coming from the south. It got louder and louder and then they saw an F-4C Phantom aircraft come roaring towards them. The spacecraft above them then dipped at an angle, and then in the blink of an eye, it disappeared into a point of light going straight up.

HC addendum.
Source: *CoasttoCoastAM* with George Noory, November 16, 2002, also in Earthfiles.com   Type: B

* * * * * * *

Location: Near Danang, Vietnam.
Date: Summer 1969.
Time: 1:00 a.m.

Da Nang (Vietnam del Sur - 1969)

PFC Earl Morrison, a private with the United States Marines was sitting atop a bunker with two other men enjoying the warm evening air when suddenly, and for no apparent reason, they were compelled to look up into the sky. There they saw a glowing figure flying downward toward them.

"We couldn't make out what it was at first," Morrison later told an interviewer. "It started coming toward us, really slowly. All of a sudden we saw what looked like wings, like a bat's, only it (the figure) was gigantic compared to what a regular bat would be. After it got close enough so we could see what it was, it looked like a woman. A naked woman. She was black, everything was black. Her skin was black, her body, was black, the wings were black, everything was black. But it glowed, it glowed in the night; kind of a greenish cast to it."

Morrison also got a good look at the creature's wings. "We saw her arms towards the wings," he explained in his report, "and they looked like regular molded arms, each with a hand, and fingers, and everything, but they had skin from the wings, there was no noise at first. It looked like her arms didn't have any bones in them because they were limber just like a bat."

The figure flew directly over the men at about a height of six or seven feet. The three servicemen just stared as it flew by, awestruck. Eventually they heard the flapping of wings as she gradually sailed out of sight.

HC addendum.
Source: Don Worley, *FSR* Case Histories #10.   Type: E

* * * * * * *

Location: Uravan, Montrose County, Colorado.
Date: June, 1969.
Time: Early morning.

The young witness was living in the west end of Montrose County and early one morning he was awakened by the barking of the family dog named 'Tippi,' outside his bedroom. Tippi never really barked unless someone or something was in a yard that wasn't supposed to be. He remembers waking up and hearing Tippi's constant barking and wondering why his older brother sleeping in a bunk bed above him and his parents, were not waking up to tell Tippi to be quiet. Finally he had enough and decided to turn over in his bed and look out the window himself. What he saw he couldn't believe.

He saw a small circular "ship" with its landing gear down and hatch with stairs folded down to the ground. Next to the ship were several green colored lizard-like aliens. Their eyes were bright yellow and they seemed to have webbed hands. Their bodies were thin and scaly and their feet were V-shaped. The witness thought that they 'were searching for something.' Suddenly another alien came out of the ship. 'He' was much bigger than the others and seemed to be giving orders. Tippi again began her barking and the alien closer to the house and appeared to be upset about the barking and began walking towards Tippi, looking her over.

The witness then jumped out of bed and ran into his parent's room to wake them up. He remembered how hard it was to wake his mother up since she acted as if she was drugged or something. Finally she woke up and he told her that something was going on outside and it was going to hurt Tippi. Sluggishly his mother followed him to bed, and she said she couldn't see anything outside; all she wanted to do was sleep. The last thing the witness remembered was seeing a dark figure trying to look into the window and then going to sleep.

HC addendum.
Source: http://mufoncms.com/   Type: B

* * * * * * *

Location: Near Salt Lake City, Utah.
Date: Mid-June, 1969.
Time: After midnight.

Bill McGuire and Nora Johnson, with Nora's 2-year old son Alan, was driving westward from Salt Lake City when they saw a light in the air following them. It came up to within 100 feet of them, and they could see that it was a fish shaped object, with a back "fin" and a flat bottom, with a red light on top. It emitted a strange humming sound, and made them feel "funny vibrations" in their bodies. Nora stepped on the accelerator, but the car slowed down, and would not go above 55 mph. The object continued to follow them until they reached a roadside rest area, where a camper was parked.

Inside the camper, looking out, they saw a "bony, peculiar, not quite human" face. Beside it Bill saw a figure "like a snowman" dressed in a white rubbery suit that walked toward them. Nora could not see it. When the car's headlights were turned on, Bill could not see it either, but when they were switched off, he saw it again, coming closer. They drove away, with the UFO still following them and holding their maximum speed at 55 mph. It left them only with the coming of dawn. After a 2-hour sleep, they again drove westward. They came up with a camper that seemed to be the same one they had seen, and passed it; Nora looked at its drivers and screamed. Wearing black leather suits, they had only "dim outlines" of heads, except for Cheshire-cat-like grins.

Under hypnosis five years later, Nora remembered leaving her body and floating from the car into the UFO, in which she saw a curved instrument panel with gauges and levers. About 20 short humanoids were in it, having oversized heads and large green insect like eyes; they communicated by "buzzing or mumbling." They terrified her. Bill likewise remembered being floated up out of the car and into a white "round room" with a clear dome, where she saw white "little people" with big heads, no hair, minute round mouths, and very big light-green eyes. He felt himself to be in a reclining chair, paralyzed. He felt that the creatures had telepathic knowledge of his thoughts. When they read his thoughts, it made him feel tired. There was some large device in the room around which they clustered. Then he fell asleep, although he was afraid to do so, and remembered nothing more until he found himself back in the car. He thought the experience lasted 20-30 minutes.

HC addendum.
Source: Jerome Clark, *FSR,* Vol.16, #5, p. 21, also Scott Rogo.   Type: G

* * * * * * *

Location: Fort Worth, Texas.
Date: July 11, 1969.
Time: Midnight.

Jack Harris saw a tall white shaggy creature cross the only road going through the area around the Lake Worth Nature Center, and he tried to photograph the creature, but his flash failed. He then took a second hasty picture. The creature ran up and down a bluff as other cars arrived, eventually 30 or 40 people had gathered to watch the creature.

Many of the onlookers were armed with guns, and when it seemed that people were ready to go after the creature, it grabbed a spare tire with a rim on it and threw it at the onlooker's cars, apparently more than 500 feet in distance. The creature walked like a man, was whitish gray and hairy. It was estimated to have been at least 7 feet tall and weighing perhaps 300 pounds. It emitted a "pitiful cry." The creature was seen again, and shots were fired at it, a trail of blood to the edge of the lake was found. Others found dead and mutilated sheep in the area.

HC addendum.
Source: Mark Chorvinsky, *Fate*, October, 1992.   Type: E

Location: Near Denver, Colorado.
Date: July 15, 1969.
Time: Midnight.

A group of four men driving from Denver saw a slow moving 'meteor' and followed it up a road toward a hill. When they got there they saw a UFO land. One man got out of the vehicle and tried to shoot at it but the gun misfired, so he ran off into the dark. The car stalled and two more men got out and went towards the UFO. It was a disk with a dome and two revolving plates going in different directions. It was black and silver with a tail with a red light on it. It had orange and yellow lights that glowed.

They then saw two very large "men" exit the UFO, both about ten feet tall with very long arms that reached to their shins. One entity picked up a rock half the size of a VW Bug and carried it into the UFO. The other entity pulled a giant bush out of the ground and dragged it into the UFO. The UFO hummed like "burnt wiring" but had no smell. The yellow and orange lights then became brighter and the UFO lifted off the ground and went straight up.

They attempted to locate the man who had run off into the dark but decided to go back down the narrow road. Yellow lights followed them and then they were stopped by a road block. They couldn't turn around so they stopped. Five men wearing black shiny helmets that went to their shoulders and wearing one-piece 'braided' uniforms and strange boots with individual toes would not let them pass and came up to the car windows on both sides. It seemed to the witnesses that they were there most of the night.

The next thing they remember was being back in their building with their car parked in the lot. They had no memory how they got home. The man who ran off into the desert showed up in Denver two and a half days later with no memory of how he got home. All four men remember the same thing and thought of reporting the incident at the time, but didn't know to whom.

HC addendum.
Source: Mufon CMS.   Type: G?

Location: West Akron, Ohio.
Date: August 8, 1969.
Time: 2:00 a.m.

Dollie Hansen had been in touch with UFO occupants and had been promised a trip in a spaceship on Thursday, August 7. At 2:00 a.m. on Friday, a knock came at her door, and outside was a superbly built young woman with deep chestnut hair but no features on her face. Nevertheless, Mrs. Hansen had no fear, and went with her to a black car containing, two men, whom, wrapped in a gray mist, conveyed them to the spaceship. She was given the promised ride, but the source gives no details beyond this, except to say that the spaceship was softly lighted and contained no visible seams or welds.

Around the same time a local handicapped boy also reported being taken onboard a UFO and given a ride, his encounter occurred at 2:30 a.m. No other information.

HC addendum.
Source: Brinsley Le Poer Trench, *'Mysterious Visitors.'*   Type: G

* * * * * * *

Location: South Akron, Ohio.
Date: August 22, 1969.
Time: 4:00 a.m.

After Joyce Vellacca and her husband reported seeing a multicolored object maneuvering over the area. Joyce Vellacca decided to lie down on the sofa for a few winks. However she had scarcely stretched out when a big gust of wind swept through the window and blew the curtains out. She jumped up to close the window and froze in her tracks. Mrs. Vellacca stated that she was unable to move literally paralyzed to the spot. And standing on the other side of the window, looking back at her, was a woman, marvelously built, with the most beautiful long dark chestnut, almost black hair she had ever seen. But the woman had no discernible features where her face would be located.

Oddly enough, when Mrs. Vellacca recovered from her frozen immobility, the visitor had gone. She rushed outside and turned on all the floodlights to illuminate the area, but could see nothing unusual. Then there came a high-pitched whine similar to that of a motorcycle, except that when that machine reaches its take-off there is a loud roar. This was not audible. Instead, the noise gained in shrill frequency until it was no longer heard. The dogs in the neighborhood were raising a great ruckus.

HC addendum.
Source: Brinsley LePoer Trench, *'Mysterious Visitors: the UFO Story.'*
Type: E
Comments: Note similarity with the West Akron case, two weeks before.

* * * * * * *

Location: Alum Creek, Columbus, Ohio.
Date: September, 1969.
Time: 9-10:00 p.m.

    The witness; Rick P, remembers that it was a Monday night, back then the area was surrounded by woods and the street was unlit. It was getting cold since it was near the end of September. He turned to put the hay into the rabbit pen and heard a loud clapping noise. He turned and saw a creature. It was walking into the woods. It was dressed in a black uniform with a silver belt. Its arms and legs were long and very small like small pipes. The legs and arms moved in rhythm. Its head glowed with an eerie yellow glow. It was large and the shadows of the tree branches put dark streaks through the head. It had only impressions for eyes but no ears or mouth.
    He stood there shocked. He thought of following it, but did not. He ran to the house as fast as he ever ran before. He swung the door open screaming for his parents. As soon as they found out what had happened the whole family jumped into the car and they went out hunting for it. His parents said that it was probably somebody dressed up. They told him to keep the story to himself. The next morning a neighbor girl, Joyce W. came to the door asking my mother if they had seen strange lights in the field the night before. Both of their parents went to the field and found a large oval place where the grass, weeds, and small trees had been pressed down. Again his parents advised it was best to keep silent about the incident or people would consider him mentally ill.
    Rick added that the figure was too tall and thin to have been somebody in a costume. He was around 70 feet from the figure at the closest. He estimated it was around seven feet high with arms and legs about an inch in diameter. The "head" was large, egg shaped, and illuminated like a neon light. The eyes were impressions or indentations and they glowed also. He couldn't remember anything about a mouth or nose. He said the glowing "head" had streaks through it and he assumed the streaks were the branches of a nearby willow tree viewed against the illumination. Its belt was metallic, like silver, and contained an "instrument panel," but he couldn't remember details. The sound was from its feet hitting the pavement.
    He thought each foot was cubical in form. Although the street was unlit, he thought there had been enough light diffusing from the city for

him to have seen details, because he distinctly remembered seeing its form. He was asked by the source if he thought it was alive or mechanical. He thought alive and seemed to have a pretty definite feeling about this. Curiously he thought, it had no 'brains' because the head seemed transparent. He said its head turned from side to side as it walked, as if were looking around. He thought that it didn't see him. Its walking was stiff instead of flexible and its joints did not appear to bend. He was frozen in fear at the time and couldn't move or scream.

HC addendum.
Source: Dr. Irena Scott, IUR Vol. 12 #1. Type: D

* * * * * * *

Location: Montaña Alta, Gran Canarias, Canary Islands, Spain.
Date: Early September, 1969.
Time: Night.

14-year old Isabel and her aunt were returning home on a clear moonless night. They were walking along a wooded path carrying a small handheld light when at only several meters from their house they saw a powerful light. Looking up, both women were stunned to see a huge transparent sphere resembling a soap bubble with a very tall red-colored humanoid figure standing inside. They could clearly see the tall human-like figure standing inside the transparent sphere. The figure was completely red in color and stood motionless with its legs slightly separated and arms hanging down on its sides. They could not see any eyes or mouth and couldn't tell if it was masculine or feminine. The enigmatic figure did not move or say anything at any time. The witnesses estimated the height of the humanoid at about 2 meters and the sphere in which it stood at about 5 meters in diameter, only five meters separated the witnesses from the translucent sphere and its occupant.

On the base of the transparent sphere they could see what appeared to be a round ring or circle or base on which the red giant stood. It seemed to rotate slowly in a clockwise motion. They could hear a slight sound that seemed to come from the rotating circular base. Everything was illuminated around the sphere, just like daytime, they could see everything around them very clearly; however this strong lighting did not produce any shadows. The two frightened women ran into the house and began to pray immediately while the light from the sphere illuminated the inside of their house as if the light was able to shine right through the walls.

Isabel expressed some bewilderment as no other neighbors were around to see this huge sphere and its occupant. It was so large and luminous that she was convinced that everyone in town must have seen it. But incredibly and inexplicably they had been the only witnesses to this incredible event. They found this very strange. After an unknown amount of time, Isabel stepped out into the patio to see the 'giant soap bubble' slowly rising up along with its singular occupant disappearing from sight towards the northeast towards the village of Moya. The next morning Isabel visited the site where the giant sphere had hovered above and discovered a circular depression on the ground, it seemed large to Isabel but much smaller than the size of the sphere. Isabel remained convinced that what she saw was a "good thing" that it had occurred for a purpose.

HC addition.
Source: Gregorio Gonzalez, La Prensa 3-31-2012. Type: A
Comments: The date might be 1959.

* * * * * * *

Location: Near Dzhambul, Kazakhstan, USSR.
Date: September 11, 1969.
Time: Around 5:00 a.m.

36-year old driver Nikolay Zinov, was on a prospecting expedition in Kazakhstan near the Dzhambul settlement. On that date he was returning by lorry from another settlement together with an engineer, a geologist and a laboratory assistant. They left Karazhal after dark by an unfamiliar road, soon they lost their way and around 5:00 a.m. Zinov stopped his lorry, deciding to wait for dawn. The motor was still idling. Suddenly he noticed a moving luminous point in the sky, when the "point" approached the lorry all saw a flying "man" of normal height dressed in a silvery scaly "space suit."

He flew silently in an almost horizontal position, his arms extended horizontally at only 2 meters above the lorry landing about 25 meters away. Zinov swiftly turned his truck in the direction of the flying man and switched on the headlights. The alien man stood still on the ground and was clearly visible. The geologist told Zinov to go and ask him the right way to the settlement. (!) So Zinov jumped out of his cab and ran towards the man, when he was about 3 or 4 meters from him, the humanoid rose smoothly to an altitude of about 2.5 meters, Zinov took one or two steps more and addressed the stranger, forgetting even to greet him. *"Comrade, we are lost, show us the right way!"* However there was no response, but the man began flying off to the left, gaining altitude as he went.

Zinov quickly returned to his truck and followed the man at a distance of some 20 meters. Soon it grew light and they found themselves on a good dirt road. Looking around the travelers understood that they had missed the settlement by a hundred kilometers. And the man in the silvery "space suit" kept on ascending until he disappeared into the morning sky.

HC addendum.
Source: Vladimir V. Rubtsov, Ph.D, *'Soviet Ufology and its Human Dimensions,'* and *'UFOs 1947-1997, from Arnold to the Abductees, Fifty years of Flying Saucers,'* London, 1997. Type: E
Comments: Another flying humanoid report.

* * * * * * *

Location: Near Bogalusa, West Monroe, Louisiana.
Date: September 26, 1969.
Time: Night.

The main witness was on his way to visit his aunt and uncle, along with a friend who was sleeping in the passenger seat. Both men were enlisted in the Navy at the time. He was driving a split 4 lane highway and it was very dark and calm night and he had his window down. Listening to his radio, which was turned down, he noticed that they were running into some low overhanging fog which was about 20 or 30 feet above the highway and seemed to travel with the car and pulsate like a wave action above the car.

That's when he saw about five bright lights shining at the car from behind. He first thought it was some kind of truck or bus until it passed him off to the left and crossed the low median and positioned itself on the driver's side traveling the same speed the witness was. It was a long cigar-shaped craft with clear windows on its side just above the center of the craft. He could see beings onboard due to the background light inside it. They were not human (not described). He had to keep watching the road ahead while driving but watched the object as much as he could.

The craft was about 60feet long and he could only see about 15 feet of it, protruding below the pulsating fog. His was the only car on the road at the time. There was no sound and his friend never woke up during the incident. The witness does not recall any details. His next memory was of arriving at his uncle's house and having breakfast.

HC addendum.
Source: http://mufoncms.com Type: A or G?

Location: Near Elkader, Iowa.
Date: October, 1969.
Time: Various.

    The first of a series of encounters and contacts by an anonymous young farmer and his pregnant wife, near Elkader, Clayton County. On subsequent occasions, a variety of beings were reported, including very small (most often associated with small objects) 5ft beings and hostile entities of up to 10ft tall (associated with large objects).
    On one occasion a combination of 2ft, 3 ½ft, and 5ft entities were seen in association with a single object. Initially incidents in Clayton and Allamakee Counties were independent, the families later contacted each other and compared notes. The 5ft tall beings wore black belts around their waists that provided protection. A group of these advanced on the farmer on one occasion; he hurled a branch at them and it exploded in mid-air before the marching column. One group had boots or shoes that enabled them to levitate, the 10 footers had a type of boot from which fire was released from the soles.

HC addendum.
Source: Ralph Degraw, Dr. J. Allen Hynek.   Type: C?

* * * * * * *

Location: Makalle, Chaco, Argentina.
Date: October 9, 1969.
Time: Daytime.

    Amaro Lotcket, a well-known farmer in the area, was driving his small truck when he was seized by a sudden sensation of coldness, or of fear. On stopping, he saw 10 meters away, three strange beings occupying an object that was perched in the top of a large tree, weighing it down. The beings were about 80 cm tall, with long blond hair and a single eye. Without any noise, the object ascended into the sky and disappeared. Police later found scorch marks and other traces in the tree.

HC addendum.
Source: Humcat quoting, newspaper source. Type: A

* * * * * * *

Location: Lake Worth, Texas.
Date: November 7, 1969.
Time: 2:00 a.m.

Charles Buchanan had camped out on the shore of Lake Worth and awoke about 2:00 a.m. to find a hairy creature that looked "like a cross between a human being and a gorilla" towering above him. Buchanan had been sleeping in the bed of his pickup truck when the thing suddenly jerked him to the ground, sleeping bag and all. Gagging from the stench of the beast, the camper did the only thing he could think of; He grabbed a bag of leftover fried chicken and shoved it into the long-armed creature's face. It took the sack in its mouth, made some guttural sounds, then loped off through the trees, splashed in the water, and proceeded to swim with powerful strokes toward Greer Island.

HC addendum.
Source: Jerome Clark and Loren Coleman, *'Creatures of the Goblin World.'* Type: E

* * * * * * *

Location: Near Pulaski, Tennessee.
Date: December, 1969.
Time: Unknown.

A respected businessman and his son reported seen a brilliantly lit globe-shaped object hovering overhead. Inside the globe they could plainly see a little man sitting there, he was about 2 ½ft tall to 3ft tall. His head looked too big for his body. No other information.

HC addendum.
Source: http://ufoexperiences.blogspot.com Type: A

Location: Serra do Vulcao, Nova Iguacu, Rio de Janeiro, Brazil.
Date: December, 1969.
Time: 10:00 p.m.

A young couple was parked in an isolated area in a known lover's lane area, when they suddenly noticed a strong luminosity approaching their vehicle from the rear. Horrified they watched three huge beings, estimated to have been at least three meters in height approached their vehicle within the light. The man attempted to start the car but the engine was dead. The luminosity grew stronger as the humanoids approached even closer to the vehicle.

The beings began looking into the window of the car as the terrified couple began to dress frantically. The beings then emitted a sound similar to, *"Kaaan"* and one of them introduced a baton-like object into the opened window of the car, and as it did so the baton released a sort of gas. At this point both witnesses lost consciousness. They woke up in the morning the following day. The man had a strong migraine and had a nosebleed and both noticed that the car was now at a different position from where it was originally parked. Both have refused hypnotic regression.

HC addendum.
Source: G.E.P.U (Grupo Espirita de Pesquisa Ufologica), Brazil.
Comments: This intriguing case has all the signs of an unexplored abduction. Type: E or G?

About the author

Albert S. Rosales, was born in Cuba on January 3, 1958. After living for some time in Spain, in 1967, his family moved to New York City before ultimately settling down in Miami where Albert became a US citizen and attended school. Albert had many strange incidents as a child and developed an interest in UFOs and unusual events from the time he was in high school.

He joined the United States Navy after high school and traveled the world. Later on, after being honorably discharged from the Navy, Albert went into the jewelry business with his father. After his father passed on, Albert joined a local law enforcement agency in Miami and has now been there for over 30 years. Albert is married, with five grown children, one girl and four boys.

For over 40 years, Albert has been studying UFOs, and since 1993, has been regularly updating his Humanoid Encounter catalogue.
You can forward your own humanoid encounters to Albert at:

garuda79@comcast.net

Join us for the world's only 7 day mega conference held every year around late February thru early March. For 2022 we will convene April 17th - 23rd.

* The Laughlin UFO Mega Conference is by design the world's best UFO / Paranormal conference. Every year. Year after year.

* Always respectfully presented one speaker at a time. (We would die and go to hell before we would pit speaker against speaker for your attendance. That is just wrong!)

* Hear the complete story from every speaker; with no extra cost bait and switch "workshops" to be purchased in order to hear it all.

* Always offered at the lowest cost of all major conferences. Way lower cost!

* A "world's best" conference produced for you with our only goal being education and disclosure.

* Bring a student. Free lecture attendance for all full-time students attending with a paying delegate.

* Always the largest number of presentations that you actually get to hear. (The number of presentations vary year to year but 2020 saw 39 presentations offered.)

* Always the largest number of speakers from out of the USA. (For now, foreign speakers travel to the US is COVID dependent.)

* The most speakers. The newest speakers. The best speakers. The most important developments. The biggest revelations. Only at The Laughlin UFO Mega Conference.

* Always the greatest gathering of scientists, researchers, experiencers and contactees to come together at one place and time on the planet.

* Always the only not to be missed conference of the year.

* Magic happens when you gather together for 7 or 8 days with like-minded seekers of truth. NOT KIDDING!

* The Laughlin UFO Mega Conference always "out contacts" that thing in the desert! (Duh... Laughlin IS in the desert! It is the original Contactee Conference in the desert!)

* The Laughlin UFO Mega Conference always "out internationals" the International UFO Congress with 9 scheduled speakers from out of the USA in 2020 alone!

* And we say again, The Laughlin UFO Mega Conference always does it all for way less cost than any other event.

* Early registration discounts lower our low costs even further! Go to Laughlinufomegaconference.com to register now.

* Join us just once. After you experience what a real conference is meant to be you will never again settle for inferior conferences that exist just to get your money. **SEE YOU APRIL 17TH THROUGH 23RD AT THE LAUGHLIN UFO MEGA CONFERENCE!**

Real Disclosure Productions and Saucerian Press

Printed in Great Britain
by Amazon